Creed
without
Chaos

Creed
without
Chaos

Exploring Theology
in the Writings of

Dorothy L. Sayers

Laura K. Simmons

B)
Baker Academic
Grand Rapids, Michigan

Published by Baker Academic
a division of Baker Publishing Group
P.O. Box 6287, Grand Rapids, MI 49516-6287
www.bakeracademic.com

Printed in the United States of America

Library of Congress Cataloging-in-Publication Data
Simmons, Laura K.
    Creed without chaos : exploring theology in the writings of Dorothy L. Sayers / Laura K. Simmons.
        p.   cm.
    Includes bibliographical references and index.
    ISBN 0-8010-2737-3
    1. Sayers, Dorothy L. (Dorothy Leigh), 1893–1957—Religion. 2. Theology. I. Title
    BX5199.S267S56 2005
    230′.092—dc22
                                                        2004026504

Contents

Introduction

What I am going to talk about is theology. . . . I think it only fair to warn you about this, because I so often get letters from people saying that they "don't agree with theology." They don't like it, as some people don't like spiders. If anybody here feels like that, this is the cue for them to rise and make a graceful exit.

Dorothy L. Sayers,
draft of "The Christian Faith and the Theatre"[1]

*I*t's always perilous for laymen to meddle with expounding theology," Dorothy L. Sayers wrote in a 1937 letter.[2] That peril did not deter her. For much of her writing career, Sayers proved as gifted a lay theologian as she was a detective novelist. Her essays, plays, letters, and other writings contain detailed expositions of doctrine and theological reflection on subjects in everyday life. One of her biographers, James Brabazon, referred to her as "the woman who . . . was to attempt, almost single-handed, to put the Church of England back on course."[3] Sayers had a distinct ambivalence about this role, but her

---

1. Wade MS-43. In the final version of this article, this comment was altered to make it a little less provocative.

2. Dorothy L. Sayers to Father Herbert Kelly, October 19, 1937, in *The Letters of Dorothy L. Sayers*, vol. 2, ed. Barbara Reynolds (Cambridge: Dorothy L. Sayers Society, 1997), 51–52.

3. James Brabazon, *Dorothy L. Sayers* (New York: Charles Scribner's Sons, 1981), 30.

11

private letters and and published reviews of her work reveal that her theological acumen was widely respected by everyone from ordinary people to archbishops and professional theologians.

People read and appreciate Sayers through a variety of their own lenses—drama fan, mystery reader, literary critic, feminist theorist, artist, friend. Though her theological contributions have been recognized occasionally,[4] comparatively few approach her work from a theological perspective, which is surprising. Contrast the amount of material others have generated on C. S. Lewis and his theological work. Lewis was a contemporary of Sayers and died nearly six years after she did. Lewis scholar Diana Pavlac Glyer noted in 1998—several years ago now—that fans and scholars had by then written more than one hundred books about him. Nine of these she listed under the heading "The Lay Theologian." When Lewis is mentioned, many people think first of Lewis the apologist. Indeed, a new book on Lewis titled *Mere Theology* was just published in the spring of 2004. When Sayers is mentioned, people usually remember the detective novelist first and foremost.

My goal in this work is to inspire people to read more of Dorothy L. Sayers's writings—and particularly to read beyond her mysteries. Though Sayers died in 1957, her voice is still an important one for us to hear today. She had a unique combination of talents: a keen theological sense coupled with tremendous writing skill and a concern for how ordinary people understand Christianity. In an increasingly complex and fragmented world, we need these gifts more than ever.

Biographical Information

Dorothy L. Sayers was born in 1893 in Oxford to an Anglican clergyman, Henry Sayers, and his wife, Mary. She was an only child who grew up largely in the rectory at Bluntisham in England's fen country. Adults, a few other children, and her imagination were her only playmates. Sayers's father taught her Latin at an early age, and she learned French and German from governesses. Her later gift for interdisciplinary synthesis

4. Carsten Peter Thiede, for example, devotes a small section of *Rekindling the Word: In Search of Gospel Truth* (Valley Forge, PA: Trinity Press, 1995) to "A Critic of the Critics: Dorothy L. Sayers and New Testament Research." Karl Barth recommended Sayers to one of his students, calling her one of the "outstanding British theologians" (see Arnold Ehrhardt to Dorothy L. Sayers, September 1945, Wade document 9/9–10). Barth used Sayers's work to learn English, and he translated three of her essays into German. Claude Welch mentioned Sayers's "extraordinarily interesting" *Mind of the Maker* in his work *In This Name: The Doctrine of the Trinity in Contemporary Theology* (New York: Charles Scribner's Sons, 1952), 85.

was evident even in her youth, when she read about Cyrus the Persian in a children's magazine. In her essay "A Vote of Thanks to Cyrus," she describes how Cyrus "belonged" to classical times in her mental picture of him. She understood that the magazine story was partly historical, but it was partly fairy tale as well:

> Cyrus was pigeonholed in my mind with the Greeks and Romans. So for a long time he remained. And then, one day, I realized, with a shock as of sacrilege, that on that famous expedition he had marched clean out of our Herodotus and slap into the Bible. . . . The palace wall had blazed with the exploits of Cyrus, and Belshazzar's feast had broken up in disorder under the stern and warning eye of the prophet Daniel.
>
> But Daniel and Belshazzar did not live in the classics at all. They lived in the Church, with Adam and Abraham and Elijah, and were dressed like Bible characters, especially Daniel. And here was God—not Zeus or Apollo or any of the Olympian crowd, but the fierce and disheveled old gentleman from Mount Sinai—bursting into Greek history in a most uncharacteristic way and taking an interest in events and people that seemed altogether outside His province. It was disconcerting.[5]

Disconcerting it may have been, but that encounter was to influence Sayers's convictions about the truth of biblical revelation and history for the rest of her life.

Sayers was educated at home initially, then in a boarding school in Salisbury. During her years at the Godolphin School, she was confirmed in the Anglican Church. She had mixed feelings about this experience, later writing to her cousin that being baptized against one's will was not nearly as harmful as being confirmed against one's will, "which is what happened to me and gave me a resentment against religion which lasted a long time."[6] However, Sayers's letters during this period and her later reflections on it also reveal an excitement about certain parts of church life. In 1940, she wrote to some clergymen, "What I should never have mentioned to any grown-up was the secret rapture with which I hailed the all-too-rare appearance in the programme of the *Quicunque Vult*" (the first line [in Latin] of the Athanasian Creed, "Whosoever would be saved . . .").[7] She felt that adults would not approve of this fascination

5. Dorothy L. Sayers, "A Vote of Thanks to Cyrus," in *The Whimsical Christian* (New York: Collier, 1978), 53–54. See the beginning of the book of Ezra and Daniel 5 for more information about Cyrus, Daniel, and Belshazzar.

6. Dorothy L. Sayers to Ivy Shrimpton, April 15, 1930, in *The Letters of Dorothy L. Sayers*, vol. 1, ed. Barbara Reynolds (New York: St. Martin's Press, 1997), 306.

7. Dorothy L. Sayers to Rev. T. A. O'Neil and Rev. A. M. Stack, March 21, 1940, in *Letters of Dorothy L. Sayers*, vol. 2, 154. See appendix B for the full text of the Athanasian Creed, as well as the Nicene and Apostles' creeds.

of Sayers's explicitly religious writings requires that we place them in the historical, theological, and literary context of early to mid-twentieth-century England. Locating Sayers's work in this way illumines her emphasis on the incarnation, her desire to clarify Christianity for her countrypeople, and her particular methods in doing so. This chapter examines nineteenth-century developments and their effect on twentieth-century academic and lay theology and especially the influence of World War II on Sayers's work.

Nineteenth-Century Influences

An important background to Sayers's work was the continuing influence of Darwinism in English intellectual life. Fifty years after the publication of Darwin's *Origin of Species* in 1859, social Darwinism and an evolutionary worldview had permeated the intellectual life of Europe. According to historian Owen Chadwick, this created a new form of religious belief that "makes men stumble up stairs in the dark," a change that affected both theologians and the religious understandings of laypeople.[1] Belief in human potential and progress was especially strong before the First World War. C. S. Lewis critiqued this worship of progress in "The Funeral of a Great Myth," noting that the logical end of the "myth" of popular evolution was that "man has ascended his throne. Man has become God."[2]

Darwinism was joined by what G. K. Chesterton's (and Sayers's) biographer Alzina Stone Dale calls "intellectual winds blowing from Germany," bringing with them biblical criticism that eroded people's faith in the reliability of Scripture and a social gospel that focused more attention on improving this life than on grappling with the role of the transcendent in it.[3] During the first two to three decades of the twentieth century, materialism, modernism, and what C. S. Lewis called "semi-scientific assumptions" were the philosophical order of the day.[4] It was

1. Owen Chadwick, *The Secularization of the European Mind in the Nineteenth Century* (Cambridge: Cambridge University Press, 1975), 184.

2. C. S. Lewis, "The Funeral of a Great Myth," in *Christian Reflections* (Grand Rapids: Eerdmans, 1978), 88.

3. Alzina Stone Dale, *The Outline of Sanity: A Biography of G. K. Chesterton* (Grand Rapids: Eerdmans, 1982), 98.

4. Roger Lancelyn Green and Walter Hooper, *C. S. Lewis: A Biography* (New York: Harcourt Brace Jovanovich, 1974), 113, citing a January 10, 1931, letter from Lewis to Arthur Greeves. In an early manuscript of *Surprised by Joy* now in the possession of Walter Hooper, Lewis discusses the "process by which I came back, like so many of my generation, from materialism to a belief in God."

in the milieu and worldview of these assumptions that Sayers, Lewis, and others were raised and educated.

Scientific, historical, and philosophical trends were not the only nineteenth-century factors contributing to secularization in the early twentieth century, however. Owen Chadwick has identified a variety of other influences, for example, the conflict between increasing nationalism among modern states and Christianity's international ideals, a conflict that "only became open and extreme during the twentieth century."[5] He also mentions the identification of Christianity with the status quo[6] and authority, two elements against which people began to react.[7] Chadwick traces this reaction first and foremost to the emphasis on liberty in the nineteenth century, remarking that people's personal views did not change as much as political and constitutional factors did: "Liberty to attack religion rose less from decline of religion than from love of liberty."[8]

Some late-nineteenth-century Anglican theologians, most noticeably those in the *Lux Mundi* group,[9] attempted to synthesize modern philosophy with traditional Christian doctrines. These theologians, successors of the mid-nineteenth-century Tractarians, focused on the doctrine of the incarnation, which, according to Lewis Smedes in an assessment of modern Anglican thought, has been "the pivot of Anglican theology ever since."[10] Members of the group were still influenced by the prevailing intellectual trends, considering doctrines such as the verbal inspiration of Scripture slightly embarrassing, but the incarnation remained for them "the bedrock of faith and the key to all doctrine," as theologian Colin Brown observes.[11] These scholars were willing to integrate a moderate level of biblical criticism into their work. Their emphasis on the incarna-

---

5. Chadwick, *Secularization of the European Mind in the Nineteenth Century*, 131.

6. Ibid., 134: "Old Christian ideas of an international order, of peace on earth, goodwill to all men, looked like self-interest; like a theoretical justification for not changing a European system which was being changed irresistibly."

7. Owen Chadwick suggests that "among anarchists we see in an extreme form what may be faintly discerned in other more moderate and conservative men—throw off God (not because anyone has disproved him but) because we are against authority and God is part of authority" (ibid., 86).

8. Ibid., 28.

9. Charles Gore, ed., *Lux Mundi: A Series of Studies in the Religion of the Incarnation* (New York: Lovell, 1889) is a collection of essays by theologians such as Charles Gore, Edward S. Talbot, Francis Paget, Arthur Lyttelton, Walter Lock, Robert L. Ottley, R. C. Moberly, Aubrey Moore, Henry Scott Holland, and J. R. Illingworth.

10. Lewis B. Smedes, *The Incarnation: Trends in Modern Anglican Thought* (Kampen: J. H. Kok, 1953), xii.

11. Colin Brown, "Charles Gore," in *Creative Minds in Contemporary Theology*, ed. Philip Edgcumbe Hughes (Grand Rapids: Eerdmans, 1966), 345.

tion was, in part, an attempt to salvage something of the faith from (and to reconcile it with) the intellectual confusion caused by Darwinism and historical criticism. The *Lux Mundi* writers, Smedes notes, argued that the incarnation was the "introduction of perfect moral personality into the world and that error on matters of fact need not in the least impugn Christ's moral perfection." Their approach was to preserve the deity of Christ along with an acceptance of criticism and its "implications as to the consciousness of Christ."[12] Indeed, the synthesis of liberalism and Catholicism that the *Lux Mundi* thinkers embodied set a trend that would dominate Anglican thinking for more than half a century.[13]

In addition to an emphasis on the incarnation, some members of the *Lux Mundi* group also studied the Trinity. J. R. Illingworth published a book on the development of the doctrine of the Trinity titled *The Doctrine of the Trinity Apologetically Considered*, and R. C. Moberly developed an analogy of the Trinity in *Atonement and Personality* not unlike Sayers's "Idea, Energy, and Power" analogy set forth in *The Mind of the Maker*.

When the book *Lux Mundi* was published, many in the theological community (especially older biblical conservatives) were scandalized by the "attempted synthesis of tradition and criticism," wrote (later) Archbishop Arthur Michael Ramsey.[14] The publication dismayed the older theological generation because "the writers put themselves alongside the standpoint of the contemporary inquirer after truth, and were faintly anticipating the method of William Temple: 'I am not asking what Jones will swallow; *I am Jones* asking what there is to eat.'"[15] There was

12. Smedes, *Incarnation*, xv.

13. Cf. Brown, "Charles Gore," 345. John Thurmer, in a conversation with me in December of 1997 in Exeter, suggested that Sayers can rightly be considered one of the inheritors of *Lux Mundi* theology (I would add, an inheritor of the best in *Lux Mundi* theology), though he also concluded that Sayers was probably not influenced by Moberly's understanding of the Trinity, as he had previously believed. Thurmer postulates that a large part of Sayers's own theological education came through sermons heard while she was in Oxford, where she would have been exposed to the preaching of William Temple and others.

14. Arthur Michael Ramsey, *From Gore to Temple: The Development of Anglican Theology between* Lux Mundi *and the Second World War, 1889–1939* (London: Longmans, 1960), viii.

15. Ibid., 7. In the theological current of this time, *Lux Mundi* theologian Charles Gore was one of the most influential figures in Anglican theology until his death in 1932. By that time, Archbishop William Temple was increasing in influence in and beyond Anglicanism, "and in the double fact of his immense debt to Gore and his difference from him we may find a clue to much which was happening in the movement of Anglican thought" (Ramsey, *From Gore to Temple*, vii). Temple and Gore have been considered two of Anglicanism's greatest thinkers and teachers (ibid.). Temple's work, like Gore's, is important in its context: Archbishop Michael Ramsey notes the milieu of the "nineteen-twenties, after which new forces in Biblical theology invade the theological scene with consequences not yet

a strong fear that if a scholar gave any ground at all to biblical criticism, the very foundations of orthodoxy might crumble. However, although members of the *Lux Mundi* group had initially seemed to be rebels, "it was not long before they became the dominant influence in Anglican divinity."[16]

The philosophical currents leading up to the twentieth century gradually affected both popular attitudes toward religion and the trajectory of academic theology. Thomas Langford describes the situation in Britain at the turn of the century: "The church seemed out of step with the time. The situation to which the church must now speak had radically changed; the whole tenor of life was different, and the mind of the age reflected a secular disposition."[17]

One senses from her biographers that, perhaps because of her age, Sayers found the First World War more of an adventure and a novelty than a cause for grave concern.[18] One of her only commentaries on the First World War appears in her poem "Byzantine": "the bitter winds of war lay waste the house of prayer." Building on a growing pessimism from the last decades of the nineteenth century, the First World War dampened some of the enthusiasm for human potential and progress, while the Second World War, with its attendant evils in Italy and Nazi Germany, extinguished it further. With the waxing and waning of modernism and philosophic idealism came a similar movement in the religious attitudes of the British people. As T. S. Eliot biographer Robert Sencourt

---

exhausted. It is against this background of change that the significance of the work of William Temple appears. He gave the greater part of his life to the task of a Christian metaphysic, with the Incarnation as the key to the unity and the rationality of the world" (ibid., viii). Scholars have often noted, as does Ramsey, that "it is almost a commonplace that a theology of the Incarnation prevailed in Anglican divinity" in the early twentieth century (ibid., 16). There were other elements particular to this time though. Describes Ramsey, "This era was one in which Anglican theology had its own marked characteristics. There was the emphasis upon the Incarnation, the striving after synthesis between theology and contemporary culture which the term 'liberal' broadly denotes. . . . But if these were the more dated characteristics, there were also the more permanent ones, seldom absent from Anglican divinity in any age: the appeal to Scripture, and the Fathers, the fondness for Nicene categories" (ibid.). Several of these characteristic elements of Anglican theology were present in Sayers's work, as we will see.

16. Ibid., 11.

17. Thomas A. Langford, *In Search of Foundations: English Theology 1900–1920* (Nashville: Abingdon, 1969), 29.

18. See, for example, Barbara Reynolds, *Dorothy L. Sayers: Her Life and Soul* (New York: St. Martin's Press, 1993), 61 ("Apart from such initial public-spirited activities, Dorothy seems to have resumed her Oxford life relatively unconcerned about the war"), and descriptions of some of her fun activities in wartime (68, 82–84). James Brabazon, *Dorothy L. Sayers* (New York: Charles Scribner's Sons, 1981), 52–53 is also useful in this regard.

wrote, "Everywhere the twentieth century had emptied Christianity's places of worship."[19]

The Fall and Rise of Christian Orthodoxy

The Intelligent Laity

G. K. Chesterton, who scholar Kent Hill called "one of the preeminent 'practical' Christian apologists of modern times," had a tremendous influence on Sayers and Lewis, as well as others.[20] In "The Diabolist," Chesterton traces the effect of his time on him as follows: "I am becoming orthodox because I have come, rightly or wrongly, after stretching my brain till it bursts, to the old belief that heresy is worse even than sin."[21] He concluded that he hated modern doubt because it was dangerous. During Chesterton's time, historian Adrian Hastings notes, Christian intellectuals like him were "now the dissenters, intellectual oddities, objects of veiled sarcasm from the enlightened." What Hastings calls a "confident agnosticism" was the prevailing orthodoxy among most intellectuals as well as being the "message of all the foundational texts of modern culture."[22] While Lewis and Sayers were to benefit from the country's later turn back toward faith, Chesterton was writing for an "inwardly confused people."[23] He noted in 1923 that Christianity was

19. Robert Sencourt, T. S. Eliot: A Memoir (London: Garnstone Press, 1971), 131.

20. Kent Hill, "The Sweet Grace of Reason: The Apologetics of G. K. Chesterton," in G. K. Chesterton and C. S. Lewis: The Riddle of Joy, ed. Michael H. MacDonald and Andrew A. Tadie (Grand Rapids: Eerdmans, 1989), 227. G. K. Chesterton, whom Lewis called "a great Roman Catholic, a great writer, and a great man" (Humphrey Carpenter, The Inklings: C. S. Lewis, J. R. R. Tolkien, Charles Williams, and Their Friends [Boston: Houghton Mifflin, 1979], 217), was active earlier than the Inklings and Sayers, but we know that he influenced many of them. In a letter to Mrs. G. K. Chesterton on the occasion of Chesterton's death, Sayers wrote, "I think, in some ways, G. K.'s books have become more a part of my mental makeup than those of any writer you could name" (Dorothy L. Sayers to Mrs. G. K. Chesterton, June 15, 1936, in The Letters of Dorothy L. Sayers, vol. 1, ed. Barbara Reynolds [New York: St. Martin's Press, 1997], 394). Sayers's words from her introduction to The Surprise about Chesterton's being a "beneficent bomb" and a gust of fresh air for the church are cited in books about both Chesterton and Sayers. We know from Barbara Reynolds's biography (Dorothy L. Sayers, 58) that Sayers read Chesterton beyond Orthodoxy. We know, also, that Lewis was influenced by Chesterton, specifically by reading his Everlasting Man.

21. G. K. Chesterton, "The Diabolist," in Tremendous Trifles (New York: Sheed & Ward, 1955), 181.

22. Adrian Hastings, A History of English Christianity, 1920–1990 (Philadelphia: Trinity Press International, 1991), 225.

23. Ian Boyd notes, "No longer guided by the sources of Christian wisdom, they had not yet abandoned the Christian moral tradition which they had inherited but which they

in 1941, he was interested because he "had long regarded England as part of that vast 'post-Christian' world in need of a special missionary technique—one which must take into account the fact that many people were under the impression that they had rejected Christianity when, in truth, they had never had it."[41] Sayers's work often combats this very tendency to reject Christianity while not really understanding it.

The 1930s and 1940s brought a tremendous surge in lay theology, especially in England.[42] Sayers and Lewis (called "Everyman's Theologian" by his fellow Inkling J. R. R. Tolkien) wrote much of their explicitly religious material during this time, especially during and after the war. T. S. Eliot, whose biographer notes that he was writing for a "world more sharply divided than ever between Christians and non-Christians,"[43] was committed, like Sayers, to rebuilding England on Christian grounds following the war. Robert Sencourt observes, in regard to Eliot's preoccupation with rebuilding the Christian order, "Nobody . . . realized more strongly than he that it was not simply a question of rebuilding the *status quo ante*, but of reformulating the forms, attitudes and outlook of the Christian Church for its mission in the latter half of the twentieth century."[44]

41. Green and Hooper, *C. S. Lewis*, 202.

42. Christopher Derrick, a student of Lewis's, in discussing the "marked success in religious writing for the popular market—success by the popular standards of that market, but also by the different standards of the critical specialist," cautions, "Let us not call them theologians. We debase the currency when we apply that word to people not formally qualified and professional in the field" (Christopher Derrick, "Some Personal Angles on Chesterton and Lewis," in *G. K. Chesterton and C. S. Lewis*, 14). I cannot disagree with Derrick more. Many of the academic theologians of Chesterton and Lewis's time were considered dangerous, misguided, and even silly. Such "currency" perhaps ought to be debased. Furthermore, academic theology is often not immediately accessible to the general public, while lay theologians' theology is. Lewis's biographers even go so far as to suggest, "It is not perhaps too outlandish to claim that what Karl Barth, Paul Tillich and Karl Rahner did for specialists in their works of 'systematic theology' Lewis did for laymen—whatever their creed—in *Mere Christianity*" (Green and Hooper, *C. S. Lewis*, 211).

43. Sencourt, *T. S. Eliot*, 114.

44. Ibid., 143. Eliot has even been called the "lay counterpart to William Temple" (ibid., 143) because of his work in this regard. While Lewis might differ with the characterization of Eliot as "the poet who, more than any other writer in the contemporary world . . . , could be said to speak with the voice of cultural authority and spiritual leadership" (ibid., 158), certainly Eliot deserves to be considered on par with Lewis's Inklings and Sayers. It may be worth mentioning at this point that Lewis, Sayers, and Eliot were rarely credited with saying anything particularly new theologically (apart from Sayers's analogy of the Trinity). For example, Charles Williams once said of Eliot, "The English poets have not waited for Eliot to tell us about the Waste Land, nor English theology to learn from him" (Alice Mary Hadfield, *Charles Williams: An Exploration of His Life and Work* [New York: Oxford University Press, 1983], 128). Christopher Derrick cites one of the strong points

At the same time that these lay thinkers were writing, other authors were also bringing Christianity closer to center stage. Evelyn Waugh was perhaps most like Sayers, writing about the Bright Young People (in *Vile Bodies*), the Emperor Constantine (in *Helena*), and businesses that "are unconcerned about the quality of their product or about maintaining fundamental standards of integrity" (in *Decline and Fall*).[45] Waugh's style was even similar to Sayers's in some ways: He did not view religion or the religious profession as sacrosanct, and he offended many of his more rigid religious readers—and even some lukewarm Christians—with his perceived lack of respect for certain religious notions and practices.

Sayers's Work in Context

In the 1930s and 1940s, the British public began turning back toward Christianity. In part, as many have noted, this was a result of World War II. How did Sayers's work reflect the turning from and then turning back to Christianity on the part of many British people? How were her own writings influenced by the wars? How was she affected by the theological currents of the day?

The Wars

Sayers's biographer Ralph Hone articulates how "the pattern of 'The Long Week-End,'" as British society knew the time between the wars, was drawing to a close.[46] The social revolution impelled by political, psychological, and technological developments caused an identity crisis in many writers and other artists. Hone describes Sayers's own development during the two decades between the end of World War I and the beginning of World War II, suggesting that this time period made a different person of her: "World War I left her in an Oxford tinted with Tristan, romantic and uninvolved. World War II found her informed, pragmatically idealistic, and involved—at least in the ideological front line."[47] We know that Say-

---

of Lewis's and Chesterton's work as being their facility for "restating the gospel and the faith in the language of one's own time" (Derrick, "Some Personal Angles on Chesterton and Lewis," 16), which is also one of Sayers's main contributions.

45. Paul A. Doyle, *Evelyn Waugh: A Critical Essay* (Grand Rapids: Eerdmans, 1969), 6. See Dorothy L. Sayers, *Murder Must Advertise* (New York: Avenel, 1982) for more on the Bright Young People; idem, *The Emperor Constantine* (Grand Rapids: Eerdmans, 1951) for more on Helena and Constantine; and her writings about vocation and work (see chap. 8) for her views on unethical business practices.

46. Ralph E. Hone, *Dorothy L. Sayers: A Literary Biography* (Kent, OH: Kent State University Press, 1979), 82.

47. Ibid., 95.

ers stopped writing Lord Peter Wimsey novels in part because of World War II. She says in *The Mind of the Maker* that she did not want people to be misled into believing that "love and hatred, poverty and unemployment, finance and international politics, are problems capable of being dealt with and solved in the same manner as the Death in the Library."[48]

The bulk of Sayers's explicitly theological work was written around or during World War II. John Thurmer suggests that, without the war, it is doubtful whether Sayers would have written either *The Man Born to Be King* or *The Mind of the Maker*.[49] An underlying assumption of the Bridgeheads series, of which *The Mind of the Maker* was the first (and virtually the only) published volume, was "that no social structure can be satisfactory that is not based upon a satisfactory philosophy of man's true nature and needs."[50] Sayers joined with T. S. Eliot and others to pursue the postwar reconstruction of Britain on Christian grounds, as *Begin Here* and other works explore.[51] A mock sermon "preached" by Theodore Venables and published as part of "Wimsey Papers—II" indicates the role Sayers saw faith playing in postwar reconstruction. Noting that simply clearing the weeds from the ground did not fully remove them, the sermon called for rooting out bad seed and planting good crops in its place. "Just so, it is not enough to overthrow a wicked tyranny; we have to see to it that the seeds of strife and injustice are prevented from sprouting anew in the world, and that in their place we industriously sow the good seed that brings forth the fruits of the Spirit." The sermon points out that in the ongoing struggle between good and evil it is the more diligent side that wins: "Of late years, the evil has been more active and alert in us than the good. . . . If Christian men and women would put as much work and intelligence into being generous and just as others do into being ambitious and covetous and aggressive, the world would be a very much better place."[52]

48. Dorothy L. Sayers, *The Mind of the Maker* (San Francisco: HarperSanFrancisco, 1979), 189.

49. Personal conversation, August 8, 1998, Oxford.

50. Brabazon, *Dorothy L. Sayers*, 184.

51. David Edwards describes the larger context of this movement: "Frequently in the twentieth century Christian thinkers have expressed their hopes for Europe in a language about a recovery of Christendom" (*Religion and Change*, 59). The Christendom movement, associated with the publication by the same name, and Eliot's own publication joined Sayers in pressing for Christian-based postwar reconstruction. Sayers wrote in 1944, "I don't think you would find me very encouraging about the Post-War World, which I view with the darkest forebodings. I think everybody has got the wrong idea about it: they are hastening to fight the dead tyrannies and quite overlooking the imminent appearance of a lively set of new ones" (to Anthony Gilbert, May 4, 1944, in Barbara Reynolds, ed., *The Letters of Dorothy L. Sayers*, vol. 3 [Cambridge: Dorothy L. Sayers Society, 1999], 8).

52. Dorothy L. Sayers, "Wimsey Papers—II," *Spectator* 5813 (November 24, 1939), 737.

During this time, Sayers developed a growing concern about how she and other writers used words. In Hitler's day, it had become clear that they could be used for good or for ill. In her 1939 address to the Modern Language Association Conference of Educational Associations titled "The Dictatorship of Words," Sayers asked the question, "What are we doing, juggling with words at such a time?" Sayers recognized the difference between a more *literate* but not necessarily more *educated* public—people who could read any and all words given to them but did not necessarily possess the tools to understand and properly evaluate what they were reading. For Sayers, "To handle words wisely, and teach the world how to handle them, is the especial privilege and responsibility of people like ourselves, who are trained to the job, and to whom words are our daily tools and proper instruments. If words have been getting rather out of control lately, it is up to us to get control again, and not allow civilisation to be bound under the yoke of a dictatorship of verbiage."[53]

Sayers used as many channels as she could to steward her power as a writer for the greater benefit of her people. (Chapter 8 explores this is more detail.) A weekly newspaper series called "The Wimsey Papers" provided a place for her to communicate information that, in her opinion, the Ministry of Information was not adequately communicating to the British people. In them, she called for the British press to pay more attention to France, the country's wartime ally; asked the media to be more honest with the public (noting that news broadcasts outside England were "much fuller of interesting and detailed information" than those within the country); complained that the opinions of older citizens were not respected by public agencies; called for standardized signs on covered shop windows during blackouts, indicating what goods were inside; suggested that the government implement educational reform on the basis of what it learned from educational conditions during evacuations; and requested that frequent and detailed information be broadcast about how to drive and to be a pedestrian safely during blackout conditions.

World War II inspired in Sayers a particular level of theological reflection. She noted in *Begin Here* how war "gives us a great many things to feel and think about that cannot be grappled with by traditional ways of thinking and feeling. It . . . forces us into close personal contact with elementary realities. It sets us asking whether the things we have always taken for granted ought not to be examined and actively thought about."[54] In addition to inspiring her reflections on work and vocation, wartime living caused Sayers to think and write about people's need for entertainment, their inability to entertain themselves, and their

---

53. Dorothy L. Sayers, "The Dictatorship of Words," Wade MS-67.
54. Sayers, *Begin Here*, 20.

general unwillingness to be creative. The war brought blackouts and fewer books and plays, and people complained that there was nothing to do. Sayers's "How to Enjoy the Dark Nights" challenged this need to be entertained by external stimuli. Sayers even wondered in *Begin Here* whether the war had not "come in the nick of time to destroy a menace to humanity worse than itself."[55]

Theological Currents and the Incarnation

The new emphasis on the incarnation in Anglican theology and the use of Nicene categories and patristic sources—what Adrian Hastings calls a "willingness to listen to the whole past"[56]—provided a background for some of the concerns in Sayers's theology.

Sayers's writings reflect a deeper-than-normal understanding of the early history of the Christian church. It has never been clarified in her biographies or by people who knew her how she might have come by this knowledge, beyond regular attendance at morning and evening prayer, which would have exposed her to one or more creeds on a daily basis. She often recommends G. L. Prestige's *God in Patristic Thought*, published in 1952, but we do not know when she first read it or what level of knowledge preceded her reading of it. Understanding that broader theological developments during this time were steeped in patristic sources and categories and that these were characteristic of Anglo-Catholicism (Sayers's chosen practice) may well explain her understanding of church history.

Within patristic theology, Sayers demonstrated a fondness for things trinitarian and christological. *The Mind of the Maker* was the most obvious example of this preference, as were the particular kinds of heresies mentioned in *Creed or Chaos?* Her attention to the person and life of Christ (including *The Man Born to Be King*, "The Dogma Is the Drama," *He That Should Come*, to some extent "The Triumph of Easter," and "The Greatest Drama Ever Staged") demonstrates her interest in the incarnation. (Chapter 4 addresses this fascination in some detail.)

Equally important, though, given the general philosophical and theological confusion, is her method for exploring the incarnation and other theological themes. Sayers did not shy away from historical-critical methodology—her essays and *The Man Born to Be King* indicate her familiarity with both Old Testament and New Testament criticism.[57]

55. Ibid., 22.

56. Hasting, *History of English Christianity*, 81.

57. Sayers's grasp of biblical criticism was quite extensive for a layperson. "A Vote of Thanks to Cyrus" (in *The Whimsical Christian* [New York: Collier, 1978]) contains some of Sayers's objections to criticism applied to the Gospel of John, for example. Sayers made

She suggested that God was robust enough to withstand questions people had of or about him. In some ways, *The Man Born to Be King* was an embodiment of Sayers's willingness, following the *Lux Mundi* group, to marry doctrinal orthodoxy and a relaxed acceptance of biblical criticism. Her portrayal of Judas went beyond the biblical text; she arranged events in the order that made the most sense in telling the story; and the battles over her use of contemporary language are well documented. John Thurmer points out that for Sayers the incarnate Word was paramount—and the text is not the same as the incarnate Word.[58] She was not cavalier in her use of Scripture, however; she

---

extensive use of this Gospel in *The Man Born to Be King*, which surprised some critics. But the Cyrus essay shows how little credence she gave to some biblical critics' views of the Fourth Gospel. See also her letter to Rev. W. Gill (*Letters of Dorothy L. Sayers*, vol. 3, 137–38) and another to Rev. C. Lattey (ibid., 157–58), in which she wrote of her conviction that if biblical critics examined the work of Dante, "they would have come to the conclusion, not only that there never was a Beatrice . . . but that there never was a Dante either—or else that there were several Dantes." In a letter to the editor of the *Enquirer* in 1950, she protested something written about her that would require too much of her time and energy to refute. She felt it unfair to be put in the position of having to devote a week or more to "summarising the results of New Testament criticism over the last fifty years" instead of referring readers to Sir Edwin Hoskyns and Noel Davey, *Riddle of the New Testament* (London: Faber & Faber, 1931) (see ibid., 496–97). Sayers also participated in the "canon" of Sherlock Holmes criticism (see "The Dates in *The Red-Headed League*," "Holmes' College Career," "Dr. Watson's Christian Name," and "Dr. Watson, Widower," all found in Dorothy L. Sayers, *Unpopular Opinions* [New York: Harcourt, Brace, & Co., 1947]). This particular exercise was begun by Monsignor Ronald Knox, himself a writer. One of its aims was evidently to show that "one could disintegrate a modern classic as speciously as a certain school of critics have endeavoured to disintegrate the Bible" (Sayers, foreword to *Unpopular Opinions*, vi). See also her letter to Ellen Blad on July 9, 1948, in *Letters of Dorothy L. Sayers*, vol. 3, 385–86. In 1941, after Fr. Alec Vidler invited Sayers to join the newly formed Theological Literature Association, she responded, "People want to know the order in which the books of the N.T. were written and what modern scholars think about their dates, authenticity and so on. Most people still imagine that the 'Higher Criticism' has more or less exploded half the Scriptures, and they don't know anything about the results of recent archaeological research or textual criticism. And it's no good giving them bibliographical treatises on the Synopsists, full of tables of comparison and hiccuping references to 'Q' and 'Proto-Matt' and 'M' and 'm' and 'LM' scattered all over" (Reynolds, *Letters of Dorothy L. Sayers*, vol. 2, 330). She mentioned in a 1941 letter that "many . . . of the crude and erroneous ideas about doctrine (especially as regards redemption) are directly derived from the reading of the Bible without sufficient knowledge of its theological and historical background" (to Rev. T. Wigley, September 1, 1941, ibid., 288). She was also familiar with Old Testament criticism. While Sayers's university study of modern languages would have included some material on literary criticism in general, it is perhaps unusual for a layperson to possess and be able to reference so easily such an in-depth knowledge of biblical criticism.

58. Personal conversation, August 8, 1998, Oxford. See also John Thurmer, "Response to Dorothy L. Sayers's 'Worship in the Anglican Church,'" *VII: An Anglo-American Literary Review* 14 (1997): 54.

relied heavily on the Gospel of John, even though some biblical critics would not.

Likewise, Sayers's use of patristic categories is particularly compelling given the context in which she was writing. Biographer Catherine Kenney, in examining Sayers's commitment to rebuilding Britain after the war, identifies an important ingredient in the process: The "vivid image of living in England under siege [what has been described as the "Fortress Britain" mentality[59]] makes it clear why she was driven at this time to speak out on religious and social issues, and why her approach was to go back to the creeds: how could Christianity play a role in remaking Europe, if Christendom itself did not know its own heritage?"[60] Some readers find Sayers difficult to read because she did not always explain the theological concepts she raised, but overall Sayers's work contains a general desire to clarify Christianity for those who misunderstood it or to make it accessible to those who did not know it any longer. (This desire is explored in chapter 3.)

Sayers approached the task of clarifying and restating Christian dogma from a variety of angles. Works such as "The Greatest Drama Ever Staged" and the Nicea scene from *The Emperor Constantine* served primarily to remind people that Christianity is exciting.[61] She was not burdened with Chesterton's challenge to prove that Christianity was a viable intellectual option in a world that suggested it was not, even though she also accomplished this. Essays such as "The Other Six Deadly Sins" and "Creed or Chaos?" challenged readers to examine their moral and theological convictions and whether the basis for those beliefs was sound.

59. Thurmer describes the psychological impact of World War II on Britain: "There was an intense sense of being alone against the powers of evil—you could feel it. There was an extraordinary intensity about it" (personal conversation, August 8, 1998, Oxford).

60. Catherine Kenney, *The Remarkable Case of Dorothy L. Sayers* (Kent, OH: Kent State University Press, 1990), 222. As another scholar notes, "Such an insistence on the importance of dogma was typical of the revived orthodoxy which was arising in the Catholic wing of the Church of England in the early 1940s, in response to the perceived failure of theological liberalism. Sayers clearly aligned herself with such concerns (which were already being voiced in this period by theologians such as E. L. Mascall and J. V. L. Casserly, and by the moral philosopher Donald McKinnon)" (Watson, "Dorothy L. Sayers and the Oecumenical Penguin," 19).

61. "The Greatest Drama Ever Staged" puts it most forcefully: "That is the outline of the official story—the tale of the time when God was the underdog and got beaten, when he submitted to the conditions he had laid down and became a man like the men he had made, and the men he had made broke him and killed him. This is the dogma we find so dull—the terrifying drama of which God is the victim and hero. If this is dull, then what, in Heaven's name, is worthy to be called exciting?" (Dorothy L. Sayers, "The Greatest Drama Ever Staged," in *Creed or Chaos?* [New York: Harcourt, Brace, & Co., 1949], 5).

Concluding Remarks

How does knowing the historical and theological context in which Sayers wrote help us better understand her work? First, the trajectory of faith in the first decades of the twentieth century illuminates the spiritual condition of those for whom Sayers wrote. One writes very differently for an audience with an uncertain spiritual foundation than for those whose belief system has been consistent and secure for decades. Over and over again, Sayers's work reveals and challenges the confusion and uncertainty of her audience. Likewise, the development of academic theology in the same time period clarifies some of the sources for as well as some of the polemic within the work of Sayers, Lewis, and others and suggests why there was such a strong response to it. Academic theology was bowing at the altar of liberalism, modernism, and science, and people were open to more substantial spiritual and intellectual nourishment when the Second World War shook the false foundations on which they were standing.

Without the Second World War, it is unlikely that there would have been such a strong emphasis on the doctrinal and moral verities of the past. Certainly there would not have been the strong emphasis on religiously based postwar reconstruction and the themes that accompanied that discussion. One suspects that the urgency behind some of the apologetic and theological writings of the Inklings, Eliot, and Sayers would have been diminished. Without the emphasis on the incarnation—and perhaps the Trinity—by the *Lux Mundi* group, its inheritors, and the Anglo-Catholic movement in general, some of the themes in Sayers's work might have shifted.

2

The Writer
as Theologian

*It is easy enough for superior persons to scorn the story-teller's
art and patronise his unsophisticated audience. Story-telling
(so they say, and I will not deny it) is a knack often possessed
by very vulgar and illiterate writers; the eagerness to know
"what happened next" is (no doubt) a mark of the eternal
child in all of us. . . . The good story-teller is born, not made,
and this is perhaps the reason why his art is despised by the
learned, for learning can neither bestow it nor account for it.*

Dorothy L. Sayers, "The Eighth Bolgia"

One of Dorothy L. Sayers's most frequent protests was that she
was a writer and a storyteller, not a theologian, an evangelist,
or a preacher.[1] She believed her time and talents were best used in the

---

1. See chapters 3 and 4 of Laura K. Simmons, *Theology Made Interesting: Dorothy L.
Sayers as a Lay Theologian* (Ph.D. diss., Fuller Theological Seminary, 1999), for a more
in-depth assessment of Sayers's protests in this regard. Even though Sayers often protested
that she was not a theologian, others' tributes to her theological acumen and even her
own words indicate how disingenuous this protest was.

service of storytelling, not of expounding theology. However, she was especially effective as a lay theologian in part *because* of her writing gifts. The phrase "lay theologian," when applied to Sayers, refers both to the fact that she was not a member of the clergy or a professional theologian and to how she used her lay vocation, writing, to theologize. How did the different writing opportunities in her career contribute to her theological influence? Sayers wrote in a variety of genres over the course of her life—some for the purposes of earning money, some out of a passion for particular material or creative tasks. A closer look at several of these genres—advertising, detective fiction, translation, and playwriting, in particular—illuminates the specific writing gifts that enhanced Sayers's theology. This chapter also explores the ways in which she believed writers could contribute to the church.

Advertising

One of Sayers's first jobs was in advertising. She is credited with coining the phrase "It pays to advertise," and she participated in well-known campaigns for Colman's mustard and Guinness beer. Advertising requires succinct, clear writing—achieving maximum impact with the minimum number of words. In her article "The Psychology of Advertising," Sayers describes the challenge facing the advertising writer: "In a few hundred words, or perhaps in as few as fifty, he must arrest attention, hold interest, persuade, confute, and stimulate to action. He learns to write in the hardest of all schools, where every word must pull its weight and the smallest error is an expensive disaster."[2] One of the striking elements of all Sayers's writing, religious and otherwise, is how much meaning and energy she conveys with an economy of words. Choosing just the right words to explain something requires a sophisticated grasp of the language, which was not necessarily common among the clergy of Sayers's time. In a March 1940 letter, she protested the efforts of some religious writers to create prayers for national crises, citing their inability to write good English: "I refuse to believe that God is well-served, or a spirit of worship promoted, by knock-kneed, broken-backed phrases that sound as though they were written by a tired journalist in a hurry."[3]

2. Dorothy L. Sayers, "The Psychology of Advertising," *Spectator* 5708 (November 19, 1937): 896.
3. Dorothy L. Sayers to Rev. T. A. O'Neil and Rev. A. M. Stack, March 21, 1940, in *The Letters of Dorothy L. Sayers*, vol. 2, ed. Barbara Reynolds (Cambridge: Dorothy L. Sayers Society, 1997), 155. Evidently, Sayers tried her own hand at composing prayers, although they were never published (see Janice Brown, *The Seven Deadly Sins in the Work of Dorothy L. Sayers* [Kent, OH: Kent State University Press, 1998], 255, referenc-

How did Sayers's precision with words serve her theologically? First, it gave her the ability to identify unclear writing and argumentation, which much of her work then served to clarify. One of her most persistent concerns about the clergymen of her day was their tendency to misuse words, oblivious to the fact that they were misleading their parishioners. They would use words whose meanings had changed and fail to acknowledge the changes. Sometimes members of the clergy simply were not gifted enough with words to communicate their meaning clearly. Sayers complained in a September 1941 letter, "The people who are up-to-date in their theology can't write English, and the people who can write English are either untheological or have only a sketchy impression of nineteenth-century liberal-humanist ethics mixed up with a lot of outmoded 'higher criticism.'"[4] More than once, Sayers wrote that she wished the church would ally more with professional writers so that it could impart an accurate message. In the absence of such an alliance, she and other Christian writers had to bridge the gap—for better or for worse.[5]

Another benefit of Sayers's advertising background was that it inculcated in her an attentiveness to ordinary people's needs, modes of thinking, and tolerances. Her essay "Creed or Chaos?" is perhaps the best example of how Sayers's awareness of the common person served her theological writing. Most of the essay puts the traditional teachings

ing "Prayers for Diverse Occasions," Wade MS-168). When Sayers was asked to write a prayer for a compilation by a Methodist minister, she responded, "I fear the composition of Prayers is not in my line; particularly as my religious training prompts me to use liturgies already provided by the genius of other people" (to Rev. Walter Hull, January 24, 1939, Wade document 326/25).

4. Dorothy L. Sayers to Rev. Neville Gorton (later bishop of Coventry), September 24, 1941, in *Letters of Dorothy L. Sayers*, vol. 2, 300.

5. When she was invited to join the newly forming Theological Literature Association in 1941, Sayers referred to herself and other Christian writers as the "unhappy 'Lay Apostolate'" continually being harrassed by church members, "the hungry sheep who (for various reasons) refuse their official pabulum, baa round . . . insistently, and are fed only with the greatest difficulty from very insufficient material by amateur shepherds. And it's all very well for our bishops and pastors to encourage us with approving shouts—we still have to scratch for the stuff, cook it up and serve it out as best we can to the peril of our souls and tempers, and at imminent risk of handing out a lot of poisonous weeds with it, in our haste and lack of preparation" (to Fr. Alec Vidler, November 28, 1941, in *Letters of Dorothy L. Sayers*, vol. 2, 330). She also mentioned the "Lay Apostolate" in her address "The Church as Teacher," suggesting to her clergy audience, "I should like to see rather more disciplined thought and consideration given to the use made of the 'Apostolate of the Laity,' particularly as regards the work of the Christian artist, with a view to a) protecting the layman from inconsiderate exploitation . . . and b) getting the best results from the stimulus which amateur workers of this kind can give" (date unknown, Wade document 486/95).

of the church in dialogue with the understandings and misunderstandings the average person has about Christianity. Sayers could not clarify Christianity for the laity—or for the unbelieving world—without having a strong sense of what people did and did not believe about the Christian faith.

The skills Sayers learned through her advertising experience also improved the clarity and impact of her own religious writings. Volume 2 of her letters cites theologian Eric Mascall, who, writing in 1965, remembered being impressed by "the extreme trouble which that great Christian apologist . . . Dorothy L. Sayers took in her popular writings on religion to be sure that what she was trying to express in contemporary idiom was the authentic teaching of Christianity and that the technique which she had worked out was neither ambiguous nor misleading."[6]

Sayers also reflected on the ethics of the advertising industry in a variety of contexts. Biographer James Brabazon cites a letter to her parents written early in her advertising career. Evidently, Sayers described her first advertisement as "all lies, from beginning to end."[7] Her novel *Murder Must Advertise* gives readers glimpses into the inner workings of an advertising agency and the ways advertisers manipulate the public. However, her 1937 article "The Psychology of Advertising" also cautions that the public allows itself to be manipulated when it fails to read advertisements carefully. Sayers's advertising background also informed her work on industry and economics, which chides a system that not only produces but actually invents markets for worthless items.

Sayers's facility as a poet should also be noted here, as it gave her writing tools similar to those gained through advertising. Poetry requires one to write in fixed, often severely constraining forms, and it also requires a special precision of language. Barbara Reynolds, in her preface to a volume of Sayers's poetry, states, "In her poems, as in her detective stories, she trained herself to master form. That was the key which unlocked the power of words."[8] T. S. Eliot, whose verse drama *Murder in the Cathedral* preceded Sayers's *Zeal of Thy House* at the Canterbury Festival, suggested that poetry serves to "train the mind in one habit of universal value: that of analysing the meanings of words: those that one employs oneself, as well as the words of others."[9]

6. E. L. Mascall, *The Secularisation of Christianity* (London: Darton, Longman, & Todd, 1965), 107.

7. James Brabazon, *Dorothy L. Sayers* (New York: Charles Scribner's Sons, 1981), 138.

8. Barbara Reynolds, preface to *Poetry of Dorothy L. Sayers*, edited by Ralph E. Hone (Cambridge: Dorothy L. Sayers Society in association with the Marion E. Wade Center, 1996), xi.

9. T. S. Eliot, *The Idea of a Christian Society* (London: Faber & Faber, 1939), 8.

Detective Fiction

The skills Sayers mastered in crafting detective fiction also helped her in clarifying and communicating theology. Lord Peter remarks to Harriet Vane regarding her investigation in *Gaudy Night*, "I'll say one thing for the writing of detective fiction: you know how to put your story together; how to arrange the evidence."[10] Writing detective fiction requires the ability to visualize a complete story and break it down into its constituent parts, composing it so that all relevant clues—and usually some irrelevant ones—are included and can point readers toward the solution. Sayers was committed to what she called the "fair-play rule"—that a detective novelist must lay before his or her readers, however obliquely, the same clues the detective would eventually use to solve a mystery. It was not fair, she believed, to allow one's protagonist to have a sudden brainstorm at the very end of the book and to solve the mystery by means of clues that had not also been presented to readers.

Sayers's ability to map out a story is perhaps most evident in *The Man Born to Be King*.[11] She took information about the life of Christ from the four Gospels and synthesized it in such a way as to make the story coherent. Each of the twelve radio segments stood on its own as an individual play and contributed to the larger story being told over the entire course of the work. Some playlets contained information that was important to subsequent storylines; for example, Judas's character and motivation were developed over the course of several plays. Sayers highlighted certain elements of his behavior and zeal early on so that his betrayal of Jesus was more understandable when it happened.

Sayers's commitment to good storytelling is evident in a March 1942 outburst to a clergy acquaintance:

> The whole notion that the Son of God came in the flesh to the roaring, jostling, . . . joking, quarrelling, fighting, guzzling, intriguing, lobbying, worldly, polemical, political, sophisticated, brutal, Latinised, Hellenised, confused, complicated, careless civilization of first-century Jewry is utterly dissipated and lost. Christ wasn't born into history—He was born into the

10. Dorothy L. Sayers, *Gaudy Night* (New York: Avon Books, 1968), 246.

11. Sayers wrote in 1952 that Christianity "is not primarily an emotional experience, or a set of logical conclusions, or a code of ethics: it is a *story*. It is not constructed out of man's feelings or reason or even his moral imperatives. It is the story of God's act in history" (Dorothy L. Sayers, "Types of Christian Drama, with Some Notes on Production," *VII: An Anglo-American Literary Review* 2 [1981]: 84). Her letters—those published in Reynolds, *Letters of Dorothy L. Sayers*, vol. 2, and the larger quantity archived in the Wade Center—give more detailed descriptions of Sayers's careful process in constructing these plays.

Bible (Authorized Version)—a place where nobody makes love, or gets drunk, or cracks vulgar jokes, or talks slang, or cheats, or despises his neighbours, but only a few selected puppets make ritual gestures symbolical of the sins of humanity. No wonder the story makes so little impression on the common man. It seems to have taken place in a world quite different from our own—a world full of reverent people waiting about in polite attitudes for the fulfillment of prophecies.

Forgive this outburst. Story-telling is my profession, and even if I believed *nothing*, it would offend me to the soul to see that tremendous story so marred and emasculated in the handling.[12]

More than simply telling a story, though, a detective novelist is crafting an argument of sorts. Sayers was not presenting a random jumble of information; each clue had to help readers understand the conclusion.[13] In her theological writing, Sayers was similarly persuasive. In "Creed or Chaos?" for example, she anticipated the responses of the uninstructed person to the various doctrinal assertions in the Christian faith. The essay proceeds in a very methodical fashion through an explanation of the importance of various aspects of Christian doctrine.

In addition to providing skill in crafting a tale or an argument, writing detective fiction also gave Sayers vital experience in researching background material. She spent two years learning campanology in preparing to write *The Nine Tailors*, studied the properties of muscarine while composing *The Documents in the Case*, and familiarized herself with the effects of prolonged consumption of arsenic for the purposes of writing *Strong Poison*. Sayers's research capabilities obviously helped her synthesize the diverse Gospel accounts in *The Man Born to Be King*. One of the greatest examples of her extensive research is *The Emperor Constantine*.[14] Research notebooks archived at the Marion E. Wade Center at Wheaton College contain exhaustive lists of Eastern and Western

12. Dorothy L. Sayers to Father Taylor (possibly Charles Taylor of Chichester, who had written to her in January of that year), March 1942, in *Letters of Dorothy L. Sayers*, vol. 2, 354.

13. Robert S. Paul, in writing on theology and detective fiction, made an interesting observation about the relationship between the genre and the details of everyday life: "In modern detective fiction the things we use and which surround us are significant in explaining the truth about us. Things matter. And this refers not simply to the things which are large or which immediately hold our attention, but to everything, however small and apparently insignificant" (Robert S. Paul, "Theology and Detective Fiction," *Hartford Quarterly* 6, no. 3 [Spring 1966]: 23).

14. Janice Brown concurs that "this play involved more research than any of her others have done, for she was determined to develop as accurately as possible three different lines of historical material . . . [including] the life of Constantine himself; and . . . the whole religious controversy that led to the formulation of the Nicene Creed" (Brown, *Seven Deadly Sins in the Work of Dorothy L. Sayers*, 301).

bishops, biblical quotations used by Arius and Athanasius (the major players in this story of early Christian theological conflict) in crafting their arguments, and extensive timelines detailing events and person-alities affecting the church from A.D. 274 to 326. Sayers even contacted someone from the Eastern Orthodox Church to learn how baptism was done in their communion so she could have Constantine baptized ap-propriately in her play. As a playwright, she was gratified to learn that her Eusebius of Nicomedia could baptize Constantine by pouring water over his head. She wrote that she was "most thankful that we will not have to provide a . . . tank and haul him into it from his bed. It is always agony having to lift large actors about, and they are always afraid of being dropped, or that their legs will look funny!"[15]

Sayers's research skills also came into play when she embarked on translating Dante's *Divine Comedy*. The introduction, notes, and essays accompanying her translation indicate how far-reaching and complex her research was, encompassing history, theology, literature, language study, and more.

Sayers's background in detective fiction, as in advertising, also contrib-uted to her ability to examine situations from the viewpoint of the average citizen. In *Begin Here*, Sayers notes that "the writer of any kind of fiction is . . . the specialised representative, as it were, of amateur opinion. He can speak for the man-in-the-street, because he is himself the man-in-the-street, with perhaps a little more imagination than the average and with a better training in the art of putting ideas on paper."[16] For Sayers, the best detective story ever written was Wilkie Collin's *Moonstone*, a novel written from the points of view of several characters. Sayers employed this technique in *The Documents in the Case*. Training oneself to view a story from several angles allows a depth and a richness both in telling a story and in understanding it.[17] Sayers, in clarifying theology, did not just look at what orthodox doctrine *taught*; she also acknowledged what the pagan or the person in the pew *heard*. Her ability to explain theology "from the inside out" benefited from her ability to understand both heav-enly and earthly mysteries from a variety of points of view.[18]

15. Dorothy L. Sayers to Miss Hella Georgiadis of St. Basil's House in London, Febru-ary 26, 1951, Wade document 525/46.

16. Dorothy L. Sayers, *Begin Here: A Statement of Faith* (London: Victor Gollancz, 1940), 132.

17. A technique frequently used in inductive Bible study is to examine a scene from the Bible from the point of view of those experiencing it. What would it feel like, for example, to be the older son in the parable of the lost son, the wedding host at Cana, the woman at the well, or the centurion at the cross?

18. C. S. Lewis hints at another aspect of Sayers's history that may have influenced her theological capabilities: her literary background in general. His critique of biblical criti-cism begins with a condemnation of those scholars as critics: "They seem to me to lack

Along with looking at life from many points of view came something slightly less tangible: imagination. One of Sayers's most frequent grounds for criticizing others' thought, be it in the church or in the government, was its lack of imagination. This emerged with particular force in the "Wimsey Papers," where she bemoaned the fact that what she considered England's greatest assets—the poetic imagination and the talent for practical statesmanship—had "suffered a public divorce." She critiqued the government for its lack of imagination in educational reform and its failure to understand what it was like to be a pedestrian or a bus rider in wartime. One of her comments was particularly scathing. In the words of Miss Climpson, "They do rather feel that the Government has been a little UNIMAGINATIVE about some things—*dislocation* of *commerce*, and *evacuation* and that kind of thing. They seem (the Government I mean) to have thought out the *beginning* of everything very well, and then to have rather *stopped thinking*."[19] In "Wimsey Papers—XI," Peter wrote to Harriet, "You have the imagination which the politicians so singularly lack. You must write, you must speak, you must besiege the Press and the wireless. . . . You must rouse the people. You must make them understand that their salvation is in themselves. . . . They must not look to the State for guidance—they must learn to guide the State."[20]

---

literary judgment, to be imperceptive about the very quality of the texts they are reading" (C. S. Lewis, "Modern Theology and Biblical Criticism," in *Christian Reflections* [Grand Rapids: Eerdmans, 1978], 154). Citing biblical critics' questions about the authenticity of the Fourth Gospel, Lewis says, "I have been reading poems, romances, vision-literature, legends, myths all my life. I know what they are like. I know that not one of them is like this. Of this text there are only two possible views. Either this is reportage—though it may no doubt contain errors—pretty close up to the facts. . . . Or else, some unknown writer in the second century, without known predecessors or successors, suddenly anticipated the whole technique of modern, novelistic, realistic narrative" (ibid., 155). Sayers, like Lewis, had extensive literary training and experience in literary criticism (she wrote weekly book reviews in the London *Times* for over a year). This may well have enabled her to navigate the waters of biblical criticism more skillfully than the average layperson, as well as to mine Scripture for elements someone with less literary background would not find. Likewise, Lewis notes how he understands biblical "deconstruction" or "reconstruction" differently because of how critics treated his own work, by creating "imaginary histories of the process by which [the author] wrote it. . . . What public events had directed the author's mind to this or that, what other authors had influenced him, what his over-all intention was, what sort of audience he principally addressed, why—and when—he did everything" (ibid., 159). Sayers had similar experiences. In Lewis's memory, his reviewers and critics had been wrong in their guesses 100 percent of the time, but they wrote with such authority as to sound convincing. Might it therefore not be the same with biblical critics? (ibid., 160).

19. Dorothy L. Sayers, "Wimsey Papers—III," *Spectator* 5814 (December 1, 1939): 770.

20. Dorothy L. Sayers, "Wimsey Papers—XI," *Spectator* 5822 (January 26, 1940): 105.

Translation

One gift that helped Sayers communicate how theology applies to one's everyday experience was her ability to translate. Sayers was a translator before she was a novelist, crafting "Tristan in Brittany" and a preliminary version of the "Song of Roland" just after her Oxford years. The ability to substitute new words for those that are foreign or perhaps simply dead is an important skill; telling a story in a new language brings it to life for people in a way that the original language may not be able to. As Sayers remarked about translating Dante, "The slight shock of hearing a familiar statement rephrased quickens one to the implications of the original: that is why *The Man Born to Be King* startled quite a lot of people into realizing what the Gospels were actually saying."[21]

Christians concerned about Sayers's use of contemporary language initially protested *The Man Born to Be King*. She had translated directly from the Greek New Testament in writing the plays[22] and chose occasionally to include words her contemporaries regarded as slang. Once the plays were broadcast, however, many listeners applauded her presentation of a message for the twentieth century in twentieth-century language. Another reader likened her use of the vernacular to modern Bible translations that, in contrast with older versions, cause people to "take notice because they are hearing the Word in their own language."[23]

In addressing a group of clergy, Sayers wondered aloud how to make Christian doctrine comprehensible to and accepted by those for whom traditional language and imagery had lost their meaning. Observing that to many contemporary Christians the technical vocabulary of theology was as obscure as the technical vocabulary of nuclear physics, she added, "Indeed, it is worse than obscure—it is misleading."[24] Part of her task as she understood it, then, was to clarify the technical vocabulary, translating it into terms understandable to the common person so that it was

21. Quoted in Barbara Reynolds, *The Passionate Intellect* (Kent, OH: Kent State University Press, 1989), 123.

22. John Thurmer's description of the hegemony of the Authorized Version in England at the time of the broadcast illuminates how radical it was for Sayers to have made her own translation (see John Thurmer, "The Greatest Story," in *Reluctant Evangelist: Papers on the Christian Thought of Dorothy L. Sayers* [W. Sussex: Dorothy L. Sayers Society, 1996], 10, 15).

23. S. L. Meggesson, letter to the editor, *Daily Telegraph*, January 2, 1942, page unknown. See, too, an anonymous review of *The Man Born to Be King* in the *Listener* (London), May 20, 1943, in which the reviewer says that Sayers's use of modern language "makes Christ uncomfortably real, but brings a new understanding of the Gospel" (Ruth Tanis Youngberg, *Dorothy L. Sayers: A Reference Guide* [Boston: G. K. Hall & Co., 1982], 54–55).

24. Sayers, "Church as Teacher," Wade document 486/70–71.

no longer misleading. She suggested that if old-fashioned statements were translated into modern terms, what seemed to be incomprehensible dogmas would be perfectly understandable. In *Begin Here*, for example, she wrote, "Take, for instance, those dark pronouncements in the Athanasian Creed that God is uncreate, incomprehensible, and eternal, and restate them like this: 'The standard of Absolute Value is not limited by matter, not limited by space, not limited by time.' It may seem more acceptable that way."[25]

In "Wimsey Papers—IV," Sayers also suggested that translation forces one to think of other viewpoints, to "alter one's mental attitude." This, in turn, leads to an expansiveness of thought: "The mere knowledge that other attitudes are possible is a safeguard against insularity of thought."[26]

Plays

Sayers's first play was about Lord Peter Wimsey, but she moved quickly into writing plays with religious themes. One recurring compliment paid to Sayers's plays and other theological work is that she brought history and theology to life. She found the medium of the play, which she preferred to more didactic modes of communication, ideal for "incarnating" truth and ideas. *The Emperor Constantine* is one of the more vivid examples of this incarnation, given how the audience responded to its most theologically complex scene. As Sayers explained to a clergyman in July of 1951, "The unsophisticated audience simply lapped up the big scene of the Council of Nicaea! It was probably the first time they had ever really heard a theological question argued with heat and passion, and they listened spell-bound while texts and Greek words and expressions like 'substance,' 'consubstantial,' 'uncreate,' 'sole-begotten,' 'anathema,' 'Subellian' [sic], and 'Apocalypse' hurtled like brickbats across the stage."[27] People even wrote to say they had expected Nicea to be boring but that the scene had exactly the opposite effect on them; some even returned to see the play again because of it. Sayers's theological research, background in the creeds, and writing skill had managed to convey dense and complex theology in a way that made it accessible even to laypeople.

For Sayers, a play was literally an incarnation. She felt a playwright could understand God the Creator better than any other type of artist

25. Sayers, *Begin Here*, 155.

26. Dorothy L. Sayers, "Wimsey Papers—IV," *Spectator* 5815 (December 8, 1939): 809.

27. Dorothy L. Sayers to Rev. Ralph Russell, July 30, 1951, Wade document 406/36.

or author because these writers hand over their work to fallible human beings with free wills to carry it out. "Speaking only for myself," she wrote, "I can only say that this miracle never fails to move me. It is experienced at its freshest [and] most astonishing at the first rehearsal of each new play, [and] I think that if I were to write a hundred new plays, it would never lose its power to startle [and] move me."[28] The play provided a medium for material that could not successfully be communicated via other media. For example, Sayers considered the incarnation the most dramatic thing about Christianity, but she observed that for most people it was simply bewildering. The solution she proposed was "to put it on the stage . . . and let it speak for itself."[29] One might suggest that much of what she wrote served to put dogma on the stage so it could speak for itself.

Sayers's radio play cycle on the life of Christ, *The Man Born to Be King*, shocked some British people almost as much as Martin Scorsese's *Last Temptation of Christ* threatened American Christians—albeit for different reasons. She portrayed the disciples not as "sacred personages" but as human beings—Matthew had a Cockney accent, and John had a stammer (in part to distinguish their voices for a radio audience but also in part to accent their ordinariness). They also occasionally used slang words such as *sucker*. Since Sayers made her own translation from the Greek, much of the language of the story was different from people's familiar Scripture versions. Being reminded of the company Jesus kept and of the reason he was called "a glutton and a winebibber" did not always sit well with the British public. Upon hearing small snippets of one of her radio plays, the Lord's Day Observance Society and the Protestant Truth Society immediately protested them, asking the BBC not to air the controversial material.

For Sayers, though, it was imperative that people be jolted out of their religious complacency. As she wrote in "The Dogma Is the Drama":

Let us, in heaven's name, drag out the divine drama from under the dreadful accumulation of slipshod thinking and trashy sentiment heaped upon it, and set it on an open stage to startle the world into some sort of vigorous reaction. If the pious are the first to be shocked, so much worse for the pious—others will pass into the kingdom of heaven before them. If all men are offended because of Christ, let them be offended; but where is the sense of their being offended at something that is not Christ and is nothing like him? We do him singularly little honor by watering down his

28. Dorothy L. Sayers, "The Christian Faith and the Theatre," Wade MS-43, 10.
29. Dorothy L. Sayers to Father Herbert Kelly, October 4, 1937, in *Letters of Dorothy L. Sayers*, vol. 2, 43.

personality till it could not offend a fly. Surely it is not the business of the Church to adapt Christ to men, but to adapt men to Christ.[30]

Sayers noted in "Playwrights Are Not Evangelists" that a story incarnated in play form could often make a more lasting impression than volumes of technical theology. In this way, playwriting served a function similar to that of translation: It provided people with a different way of viewing or understanding an otherwise complex concept.

Writers and the Church

Throughout her writing career, Sayers complained that the church was not successfully teaching its people the things of God. She identified woefully inadequate theology—for example, mistaken views of God and sin—and a tremendous ignorance in general on the part of the "sheep." In her November 1941 correspondence in the role of the "Lay Apostolate" (those intelligent lay Christians who were writing at the time), Sayers wished that "having . . . attracted the sheep to the church-door, we could then hand them over, saying: 'Go in—you'll find all the stuff there.' But they won't go in, and half the time the stuff isn't there, but something that looks quite different."[31] Therefore, she and other Christian writers had to contribute more to feeding the people of God than she was comfortable doing.[32] Sayers sought a partnership between the church and the Christian writer: "A drama (or any other work of art) will not by itself make anybody a Christian. It can provoke attention and stir the heart, but unless its 'message' is taken up and integrated into the pattern of the Church's life, it will probably do no more than arouse that 'interest in religion' which offers itself as so plausible a substitute for the real thing."[33]

30. Dorothy L. Sayers, "The Dogma Is the Drama," in *Creed or Chaos?* (New York: Harcourt, Brace, & Co., 1947), 24.

31. Dorothy L. Sayers to Alec Vidler, November 28, 1941, in *Letters of Dorothy L. Sayers*, vol. 2 (without Vidler's name), 329.

32. In part, this was due to the fact that theologians did not write well: "Some of them are so clumsy and obscure that one can hardly shake the good ideas out of the mist of enveloping verbiage" (Dorothy L. Sayers to Mrs. Robert Darby, May 31, 1948, in *The Letters of Dorothy L. Sayers*, vol. 3, ed. Barbara Reynolds [Cambridge: Dorothy L. Sayers Society, 1999], 376). Sayers had complained earlier that year that so many people took for granted that "difficulty of thought *ought* to be accompanied by obscurity of style" and that anybody who wrote clearly was assumed to be shallow (Dorothy L. Sayers to T. S. Eliot, January 12, 1948, in *Letters of Dorothy L. Sayers*, vol. 3, 350).

33. Dorothy L. Sayers, "Playwrights Are Not Evangelists," *World Theatre* 5, no. 1 (Winter 1955–56): 64.

What contributions did Sayers feel she could and should make as a writer within the Christian fold? Her specific writing experiences and her understanding of her task as a writer illuminate a 1954 letter to John Wren-Lewis about the role of Christian authors. She identifies five contributions writers could make to the church and the reading public.

1. "We can write a book, play, or other work which genuinely and directly derives from fragments of religious or human experience as we ourselves have (*The Zeal of Thy House . . . The Just Vengeance . . .*). But you must leave it to us to choose what we shall write about, because only we know what experience of ours is genuine."[34] This identifies perhaps the strongest difference between a lay theologian and a professional one. Someone who does theology for a living may be expected to write in any given area, even while concentrating on particular topics of interest. For Sayers, who was concerned about not having "proper training" as a theologian, it was important to write only about subjects with which she had some acquaintance. This explains why her explicitly theological work tends to cluster around certain doctrines, themes, or sources (the creeds, the incarnation and the Trinity, the ecumenical church councils, Augustine and Aquinas, the seven deadly sins, vocation and work) and not around others.

The evolution of subjects on which she was comfortable writing also illuminates her remark about how only the writer knows what experience is genuine. For example, early in her career Sayers did not write much about ecumenism. After she was asked to review J. S. Whale's *Christian Doctrine*, however, she became more interested in articulating the doctrines that a variety of church traditions could agree on. This, in turn, brought her more exposure to representatives from the Free Church (Whale's tradition) and other denominations, which contributed to her work on the "Oecumenical Penguin" project. Sayers had long desired a guide to doctrine that would be accessible to nontheologians,[35] but the

34. Dorothy L. Sayers to John Wren-Lewis, March 1954, in *The Letters of Dorothy L. Sayers*, vol. 4, ed. Barbara Reynolds (Cambridge: Dorothy L. Sayers Society, 2000), 141.

35. See her correspondence with Father D'Arcy, with whom she had at one point hoped to partner in creating such a guide. As to the ecumenical focus of the "Penguin" project, according to Giles Watson ("Dorothy L. Sayers and the Oecumenical Penguin," *VII: An Anglo-American Literary Review* 14 [1997]: 17–32), Sayers had insisted that the project involve an Eastern Orthodox theologian as well as Anglicans, Roman Catholics, and other Protestants. The project was unsuccessful due to a variety of circumstances detailed in Watson's excellent article and in the original documents between Sayers and other participants recently acquired by the Wade Center. Interestingly enough, the World Council of Churches in 1982 published a document, *Baptism, Eucharist, and Ministry*, endeavoring to articulate the common ground it could find among churches on particular items of doctrine. No evidence has yet surfaced as to a direct line of influence from Sayers's "Oecumenical Penguin" to the World Council of Churches document, but the latter is quite similar to what Sayers had envisioned.

interdenominational thrust of this project was new for her. This is one area in which initially Sayers may not have had enough personal experience to write, but she developed that experience over her lifetime.

Another example of how her writing and knowledge evolved relates to her understanding of early Christian creeds. In the manuscript for a 1941 broadcast on "God the Son," Sayers suggests that the Nicene Creed was drawn up in Nice, France, a howler of a mistake, since it came out of the Council of Nicea, which met in Bithynia.[36] By the time of her play *The Emperor Constantine*, in which an entire scene is set at the Council of Nicea, Sayers had done extensive research on the background of the council. Likewise, we witness an evolution in her confidence in utilizing medieval theology, as she learned more of it in preparing notes for her Dante translation.

2. "We can (if we feel like it) write a direct statement about our own experience (*The Mind of the Maker*)."[37] Here Sayers referred to her work about the creative process, her thoughts on which had evolved from her novel *Gaudy Night* through her play *The Zeal of Thy House* before being fully articulated in *The Mind of the Maker*. Not just any Christian writer could create a work of such theological profundity, a fact Sayers did not acknowledge. It took exposure to, indeed, some mastery of, trinitarian doctrine to write *The Mind of the Maker*. The chapter titled "Scalene Trinities" reveals the depth of Sayers's knowledge about early church heresies relating to the Trinity. While the book was a direct statement about Sayers's own experience, her unique combination of exposure, training, thought patterns, and writing experiences coalesced to make *The Mind of the Maker* an important volume of lay theology.

3. "We can show you in images experiences which we ourselves do not know, or know only imaginatively (*The Man Born to Be King*). Because in this, we do not need to pretend anything about ourselves. . . . Even so, it is devilishly easy to falsify the imagination. And you must never think that we are the things we show."[38]

The relationship between showing an image and being true to oneself is an intriguing one. We know, for example, that Sayers made Lord Peter Wimsey the wealthy gentleman he was in part because she was living in near poverty at the time she began writing novels. Thus, she was imaging forth something she did not know—although readers subsequently speculated that either Lord Peter or Harriet Vane was Sayers

36. The manuscripts for these broadcasts can be found in lot 292, iii of the material recently acquired at a Sotheby's auction by the Wade Center from Sayers's estate. The material had not yet been accessioned as of the time of this writing.

37. Sayers to Wren-Lewis, March 1954, in *Letters of Dorothy L. Sayers*, vol. 4, 141.

38. Ibid.

in disguise. However, the question of being true to oneself came into play much more once she utilized her imagination in regard to religious themes. Suddenly, Sayers's motives for incarnating particular ideas carried eternal weight. The temptation to "falsify the imagination," and the cost of doing so, was much greater.

4. "We can interpret another man, who has what we have not (we can translate and edit Dante). Our intellect can assess him, and our imagination feel what he feels. This, too, is not lying, because what we offer is not ourselves but him. Even so, we can only truly interpret a thinker with whom we have something really in common. (My contact with Dante is the 'passionate intellect.'"[39]

Mary Ellen Ashcroft suggests that translators shift meaning "from one incarnation into another. The artist who wrote the original did the work of creation, making something bigger than real-life. . . . The job of the translator is to offer the original creation to new readers."[40] It is certainly true that Sayers saw herself filling this role in translating Dante, and one could argue that it is true of her religious and theological "translations" as well.

5. "We can, so far as our competence goes, help to disentangle the language-trouble by translating from one jargon to another. For this, we need to know both jargons thoroughly."[41] One of Sayers's great contributions as a lay theologian was that she knew both jargons thoroughly. Few other professional writers had the same degree of theological acumen, the ability to interpret, clarify, and embody theology for people. As Sayers frequently complained, few theologians had an understanding of the jargon, or language competence, of the common person, which is why they could not reach that person with theology. Sayers's combination of competencies made her work an ideal meeting point between theology and the layperson.

Sayers also encouraged training laypeople in the technical vocabulary of theology. They needed to know, for example, that certain words such as *reason*, *substance*, and *person* had different meanings in theological discussion than in everyday conversation. Sayers advocated education for the layperson and alertness on the part of the clergy and professional theologians. The common person needs, she wrote in March of 1942:

> a) to be told that certain terms *are* technical; b) to have the technical use of the terms explained to him; c) to be warned about confusing the technical use with the current use (a thing in which he finds no difficulty

39. Ibid. No closing parenthesis given.
40. Mary Ellen Ashcroft, "Exorcising the Angel by Craft: Writing as Incantation/Incarnation in the Work of Dorothy L. Sayers" (Ph.D. diss., University of Minnesota, 1992), 196.
41. Sayers to Wren-Lewis, March 1954, in *Letters of Dorothy L. Sayers*, vol. 4, 142.

when dealing with, e.g., engineering or electrical science). Theologians and ecclesiastics should learn to keep an eye on this matter themselves, and watch for the moments when their technical terms are liable to be misconstrued by the common man.[42]

Laypeople "trained in the current and poetic use of words" would be a good resource for helping the clergy and theologians understand how other laypeople might misunderstand terminology, but it should not be the responsibility of those writers to clarify the misconceptions.

Sayers showed herself willing to provide clarification where it was needed, even as she objected to Christians who portrayed Christianity inaccurately and clergy who failed to communicate the faith understandably to their parishioners. This clarification is one of Sayers's greatest gifts to her readers, both in her day and in a new century.

42. Dorothy L. Sayers to J. H. Oldham of the *Christian News-Letter*, March 4, 1942, Wade document 341/21. He published her letter in the April 1 edition that year.

3

Rescuing Christianity
from "Slip-Slop and Fiddle-Faddle"

A great many religious difficulties arise out of entirely mis-conceived and mistaken notions of what Christian doctrine actually is.

Dorothy L. Sayers to Rev. T. Wigley, September 1, 1941

Despite her conviction that lay Christian writers should not be responsible for clarifying theology, Dorothy L. Sayers invested a lot of time and paper in doing exactly that. In a 1941 letter to a clergy acquaintance, Sayers wrote that she found herself often required to defend Christianity against not only atheists and others outside the church but also what she called "slip-slop and fiddle-faddle."[1] One of her most consistent frustrations was that people rejected or critiqued Christianity without ever understanding it. Not only did those outside the church misunderstand the Christian faith, but those inside the church possessed, at best, an inadequate understanding. Sayers observed as early as March of 1939 that "nine people out of ten in this country are

1. Dorothy L. Sayers to Rev. Father D'Arcy of Oxford, July 19, 1941, Wade document 205/18.

61

ignorant heathens. I do not so much mind the heathendom, but the ignorance is really alarming."[2] One of the most important gifts Sayers gave to her readers was a consistent clarification of what Christians really believe. She taught the essentials of Christianity as clearly as she could, challenged people's theological ignorance, and called the church to a stronger articulation of its faith.

In studying Sayers's letters, both published and unpublished, one thing becomes immediately clear: Sayers cared passionately about helping people understand Christianity better. Some of her longest letters are to those who wrote to her with questions (or misunderstandings) about Christianity. In July of 1948, for example, Sayers received a letter from a woman in Essex who was confused about Christianity's teachings. This woman, not a Christian, had discussed cinema going with a Christian acquaintance. She was writing to Sayers to gain a better understanding of why seeing movies might be prohibited for Christians and of the larger question of Christian "morality" claims. Sayers's response was immediate and detailed, and she even put her phone number on the letter should the woman have additional questions. One of the first things Sayers wrote in response was, "I wonder how many people, after having their young lives made dreary, have been alienated from Christ by the rigid and repressive doctrines of these well-meaning and sincere Puritan Christians. . . . Let us be quite clear about what our Lord himself actually said and did."[3] Much of her work served to distinguish "what our Lord himself actually said" from what God's people, through their words and actions, suggested he may have said.

In her response, Sayers indicts her fellow Christians as much for their laziness as for anything else:

> The trouble is, you know, that it is easier to dismiss things in one sweeping condemnation than to use right judgment about them. It is easier to say that all films are wicked than to select them with care, and learn to tell good art from bad, and control one's own reactions and teach one's children obedience. There is always a laziness in generalisations; they save one from innumerable difficult decisions.[4]

This unwillingness to explore the nuances of the faith is, if anything, more prevalent today in the United States than it was in Sayers's context.

2. Dorothy L. Sayers to Rev. A. R. James, a vicar from Shanklin, March 10, 1939, in *The Letters of Dorothy L. Sayers*, vol. 2, ed. Barbara Reynolds (Cambridge: Dorothy L. Sayers Society, 1997), 119.
3. Dorothy L. Sayers to S. Bates, July 22, 1948, Wade document 28/3.
4. Ibid.

The Nature of the Problem

In her essay "Creed or Chaos?" Sayers identifies ignorance both inside the church and outside it and cautions her fellow Christian thinkers not to assume an understanding of Christianity on the part of others: "It is fatal to imagine that everybody knows quite well what Christianity is and needs only a little encouragement to practise it. The brutal fact is that in this Christian country not one person in a hundred has the faintest notion what the Church teaches about God or man or society or the person of Jesus Christ."[5] She believed that only roughly 1 percent of the British population really understood Christianity. She divided the rest of the population into three groups:

> There are the frank and open heathen, whose notions of Christianity are a dreadful jumble of rags and tags of Bible anecdote and clotted mythological nonsense. There are the ignorant Christians, who combine a mild gentle-Jesus sentimentality with vaguely humanistic ethics. . . . Finally, there are the more or less instructed church-goers, who know all the arguments about divorce and auricular confession and communion in two kinds, but are about as well equipped to do battle on fundamentals against a Marxian atheist . . . as a boy with a pea-shooter facing a fan-fire of machine-guns. Theologically, this country is at present in a state of utter chaos, established in the name of religious toleration, and rapidly degenerating into the flight from reason and the death of hope.[6]

Much of Sayers's drive toward clarification was directed at correcting the heathens' misconceptions about Christianity. In a 1941 letter to the editor of the *New Catholic Herald*, she complained about these misconceptions, "ranging consistently from Baby-worship to savage blood-sacrifices." She suggested that she did not have "a pastoral mind or a passion to convert people; but I hate having my intellect outraged by imbecile ignorance and by the monstrous distortions of *fact* which the average heathen accepts as being 'Christianity' (and from which he naturally revolts)."[7]

5. Dorothy L. Sayers, "Creed or Chaos?" in *The Whimsical Christian* (New York: Collier, 1978), 35.

6. Ibid. Consider this description from James Welch, head of religious broadcasting at the BBC, of the climate causing him to commission *The Man Born to Be King:* "Everywhere there was great ignorance of the Christian Faith: of, for example, a group of men entering the Army only 23 per cent knew the meaning of Easter, and one bright youth attributed the second Gospel to the author of *Das Kapital*" (Dorothy L. Sayers, *The Man Born to Be King* [London: Victor Gollancz, 1944], 11).

7. Dorothy L. Sayers to Count Michael de la Bedoyere, October 7, 1941, in *Letters of Dorothy L. Sayers*, vol. 2, 310.

Some of this misunderstanding came from nonbelievers' failing to ask questions about Christianity; some of it came from believers' failing to live and communicate their beliefs appropriately. In some cases, believers simply did not have a good enough grasp of their own doctrine to communicate it clearly. This picture of Christianity is familiar even today:

> No language, however strong, violent, or emphatic will expunge from the mind of the average anti-Christian the picture he has formed of Christian Soteriology, viz: that Jehovah (the old man with the beard) made the world and made it so badly that it all went wrong and he wanted to burn it up in a rage; whereat the Son (who was younger and nicer, and not implicated in his Father's irresponsible experiment) said: "Oh, don't do that! If you must torment somebody, take it out of me." So Jehovah vented his sadistic spite on a victim who had nothing to do with it all, and thereafter grudgingly allowed people to go to heaven if they provided themselves with a ticket of admission signed by the Son. . . . This grotesque mythology is not in the least exaggerated: *it is what they think we mean.*[8]

Sayers placed part of the blame for people's poor understanding of theology on the schools and their failure to teach Scripture as anything but literature or even fairy tale. She believed teachers shied away from teaching theology (or were encouraged not to) out of a fear of offending parents. "But Scripture without theology," wrote Sayers, "is Hamlet without the Prince of Denmark, and children who have been taught 'the Bible' along these lines are hardly to be blamed if they grow up believing the whole thing to be meaningless nonsense. . . . We make a great mistake if we try to make the whole subject seem too easy. We ought not to smooth away all the mysteries."[9]

When Sayers wrote *The Man Born to Be King*, a radio play about the life of Christ, she received some fairly strong criticism from those in the Christian community who preferred not to have their concept of Jesus (ingrained by centuries of exclusive use of the Authorized Version, or the King James translation, of the Bible) challenged. To one particularly scathing letter, Sayers responded with both sarcasm for the writer and compassion for the lost. Concerned that Jesus Christ was more of a cardboard character than a "living reality" for many in her country, she wrote:

8. Dorothy L. Sayers to Rev. Dom Ralph Russell, October 28, 1941, in *Letters of Dorothy L. Sayers*, vol. 2, 316.
9. Dorothy L. Sayers, "Introducing Children to the Bible," Wade document 486/125ff.

The common people . . . do not and *will not* read the Gospels; and their children are growing up in a stark and pagan ignorance. They will read only if, by some means, their interest is first awakened. . . . The over-scrupulous reverence of the pious has shut the Lord Christ up between the pages of a Book from which the hearts of the ignorant turn in apathy and distaste.[10]

It was this aversion to Christianity that disturbed Sayers. If people truly understood the faith, she believed, they would be less averse to it.

Sayers had many opportunities to converse with clergy about her concerns. The bishop of Nottingham in January 1939 asked her to address a clergy gathering, and she almost rejected the request, feeling unqualified to speak to such an esteemed group. She reconsidered, however, on the grounds that perhaps the clergy needed to hear from laypeople once in a while. She decided to speak to them about the "extraordinary ideas which anti-Christians, un-Christians, and semi-Christians have contrived to get into their heads, and possibly suggestions of a few ways of countering the prevalent impression that the Christian religion is unreal, depressing, and fit only for very stupid people."[11] One of her solutions is addressed later in this chapter.

Sayers's essay "The Dogma Is the Drama" contains a parody of an exam on what Christians believe, with all the wrong answers:

Q.: What does the Church think of God the Father?
A.: He is omnipotent and holy. He created the world and imposed on man conditions impossible of fulfillment; He is very angry if these are not carried out. He sometimes interferes by means of arbitrary judgments and miracles, distributed with a good deal of favoritism. He . . . is always ready to pounce on anybody who trips up over a difficulty in the Law, or is having a bit of fun. He is rather like a dictator, only larger and more arbitrary.
Q.: What does the Church think of God the Son?
A.: He is in some way to be identified with Jesus of Nazareth. It is not His fault that the world was made like this, and, unlike God the Father, he is friendly to man and did His best to reconcile man to God (see *Atonement*). He has a good deal of influence with God, and if you want anything done, it is best to apply to Him.
Q.: What does the Church think about God the Holy Ghost?

10. Dorothy L. Sayers to Miss C. W. Mackintosh, January 16, 1942, lot 290, ivc, folder 2/3, Wade Center.
11. Dorothy L. Sayers to Talbot, bishop of Nottingham, January 25, 1939, in *Letters of Dorothy L. Sayers*, vol. 2, 116–17.

A.: I don't know exactly. He was never seen or heard of till Pentecost. There is a sin against Him which damns you forever, but nobody knows what it is.

Q.: What is the doctrine of the Trinity?

A.: "The Father incomprehensible, the Son incomprehensible, and the whole thing incomprehensible." It's something put in by theologians to make it more difficult—it's got nothing to do with daily life or ethics.

Q.: What was Jesus Christ like in real life?

A.: He was a good man—so good as to be called the Son of God. He is to be identified in some way with God the Son (see above). He was meek and mild and preached a simple religion of love and pacifism. He has no sense of humor. Anything in the Bible that suggests another side to His character must be an interpolation, or a paradox invented by G. K. Chesterton. If we try to live like Him, God the Father will let us off being damned hereafter and only have us tortured in this life instead.

Q.: What is meant by the Atonement?

A.: God wanted to damn everybody, but His vindictive sadism was sated by the crucifixion of His own Son, who was quite innocent, and, therefore, a particularly attractive victim. He now only damns people who don't follow Christ or who never heard of Him.

Q.: What does the Church think of sex?

A.: God made it necessary to the machinery of the world, and tolerates it, provided the parties (a) are married, and (b) get no pleasure out of it.

Q.: What does the Church call Sin?

A.: Sex (otherwise than as excepted above); getting drunk; saying "damn"; murder, and cruelty to dumb animals; not going to church; most kinds of amusements. "Original sin" means that anything we enjoy doing is wrong.

Q.: What is faith?

A.: Resolutely shutting your eyes to scientific fact.

Q.: What is the human intellect?

A.: A barrier to faith.

Q.: What are the seven Christian virtues?

A.: Respectability; childishness; mental timidity; dullness; sentimentality; censoriousness; and depression of spirits.

Q.: Wilt thou be baptized in this faith?

A.: No fear![12]

Sayers acknowledged that the answers were "inadequate, if not misleading" if taken as statements of Christian orthodoxy. But she believed

---

12. Dorothy L. Sayers, "The Dogma Is the Drama," in *Creed or Chaos?* (New York: Harcourt, Brace, & Co., 1949), 21–23.

they were true representations of people's understanding of the Christian faith, "and for this state of affairs I am inclined to blame the orthodox. Whenever an average Christian is represented in a novel or a play, he is pretty sure to be shown practising one or all of the Seven Deadly Virtues enumerated above."[13] She indicted Christian believers for their timidity, their failure to understand their own faith and to continue learning about it, the difference between their beliefs and their lives, and their lack of grace toward sinners. Perhaps the worst condemnation, though, is that "somehow or other, and with the best intentions, we have shown the world the typical Christian in the likeness of a crashing and rather ill-natured bore—and this in the Name of One who assuredly never bored a soul in those thirty-three years during which He passed through the world like a flame."[14]

The Importance of Right Thinking

Why was it so important to Sayers that people understand Christianity and think rightly about it? She found that many (if not most) people who reject the Christian faith do so not because of what Christians believe but because of misconceptions about Christianity. She felt intellectual integrity required that "if we are going to disbelieve a thing, it seems on the whole to be desirable that we should first find out what, exactly, we are disbelieving."[15] As early as 1919, soon after college, she wrote to a friend, "I do honestly believe that clear thinking is necessary to the right kind of faith."[16] Thirty-six years later, in June of 1955, she wrote to a fellow Dante scholar that she did not care too much *what* people believed "provided that they clearly understand what it is that they are disbelieving."[17]

What incensed Sayers was that people were willing to condemn Christianity without exploring its true significance, but they would never do so in other areas of life. Eric Fenn, who worked at the BBC while Sayers was involved there, wrote to her in 1946, asking for a letter "setting forth the Christian Faith and the Christian Way of Life"[18] for the

13. Ibid., 23.

14. Ibid., 23–24.

15. Dorothy L. Sayers, "The Greatest Drama Ever Staged," in *Creed or Chaos?* 7.

16. Dorothy L. Sayers to Muriel Jaeger, January 11, 1919, Wade document 22/108.

17. Dorothy L. Sayers to Professor Paolo Milano, June 24, 1955, in *The Letters of Dorothy L. Sayers*, vol. 4, ed. Barbara Reynolds (Cambridge: Dorothy L. Sayers Society, 2000), 243.

18. Eric Fenn to Dorothy L. Sayers, date unknown, maybe March 1946, Wade document 28/51.

average person to read. She wrote back to him in frustration, probably not knowing that he would forward her response and that it would be published in a newsletter:

> The only letter I ever want to address to "average people" is one that says—
>
> I do not care whether you believe in Christianity or not, but I do resent your being so ignorant, lazy, and unintelligent. Why don't you take the trouble to find out what is Christianity and what isn't? Why, when you can bestir yourselves to mug up technical terms about electricity, won't you do as much for theology before you begin to argue about it? Why do you never read either the ancient or the modern authorities in the subject, but take your information for the most part from biologists and physicists, who have picked it up as inaccurately as yourselves? (You wouldn't take the Bishop of Rum-ti-foo's opinion on biology, or be content with the Rev. Mr. Pulpit's exposition of atomic physics). . . . Why, when you insist on the importance of being modern and progressive, do you never read any textual criticism of the Bible that is not fifty years out of date . . . ? . . . You would be ashamed to know as little about internal combustion as you do about the Nicene Creed.[19]

Sayers identified a habit among some unbelievers of resting their unbelief on simplified impressions of Christianity formed when they were young. A woman wrote to Sayers in November 1941, confused about her essay "The Greatest Drama Ever Staged." Sayers's reply was quite extensive (four pages or more) and her conclusion firm:

> I think you would find things clearer if you were to read a little real theology, because, if I may say so, you give me the impression of never having been grounded properly in the subject. I get the impression that you have acquired a sort of "child's-eye view" of Christian doctrine in early youth, and have never done any stiff reading on the subject, so that you are now judging with an adult mind doctrines which have only been presented to you in very simplified form.[20]

Sayers was influenced in this comparison by Michael Roberts's *Recovery of the West*, a book she often recommended others read. She notes that when people "find themselves comparing their adult knowledge and science and politics with the simple notions of Christianity they acquired at their mother's knee, . . . [they] naturally conclude that the

19. Dorothy L. Sayers to Eric Fenn, date unknown (March or April 1946), Wade document 28/45–46.

20. Dorothy L. Sayers to Amy Davies, November 26, 1941, in *Letters of Dorothy L. Sayers*, vol. 2, 324.

Christian religion is only fit to be put away with the other childish things."[21] Part of her desire to clarify doctrine for people, then, was that they might be able to make a legitimate choice in favor of or against Christianity rather than a knee-jerk response based on unorthodoxy (wrong belief).

Sayers was also concerned that people not be exposed to incorrect thinking or doctrine because of how easily they might be influenced by it. In 1953, she was involved with a collaborative project titled "The Pantheon Papers," which was serialized in *Punch*. In a moment of frustration with Malcom Muggeridge, one of the editors, she wrote to one of her collaborators about how much she despised journalists. "Nine years' advertising experience rubbed it into me that it is wiser never to put a wrong idea into a reader's mind, even negatively. He is apt to remember simply the phrase, in the connotation familiar to him, and to forget what was said about it."[22]

Clergy and Language

We know that Sayers was frustrated with Christians in general for failing to study what they believed and for presenting an inaccurate picture of Christ and the Christian faith. In what ways did she hold the clergy responsible for these misunderstandings? Sayers condemned the clergy chiefly for using language to obfuscate instead of clarify theology. She believed people would be interested in Christianity if they were taught true dogma, but they usually were offered not dogma but "a set of technical theological terms which nobody has taken the trouble to

21. Dorothy L. Sayers to J. B. Upcott of Windsor, September 1, 1941, in *Letters of Dorothy L. Sayers*, vol. 2, 291. J. B. Upcott had written to Sayers of his students that "Christian principles without Christian dogma leaves most of them stone cold. But they'll take dogma with both hands and ask for more" (date unknown, Wade document 347/17). In her "Memorandum for the possible formation of a statement of oecumenical doctrine based on the highest common factor of consent among the Christian Churches" (this document would come to be referred to as the "Oecumenical Penguin"), Sayers quotes Roberts directly: "To-day the average university graduate does not know that an intelligent Christian philosophy exists. He rejects the doctrine of religion because he is comparing his childish knowledge of religion with his adult understanding of science, anthropology and politics; he contrasts the simple doctrines that he learned from his mother with the sophisticated polish of statistical mechanics or psycho-analysis, and firmly believes that he is 'thinking for himself.' And what the university graduate does on one level the ordinary schoolboy does on another" (Michael Roberts, *The Recovery of the West* [London: Faber & Faber, 1941], 100).

22. Dorothy L. Sayers to Uvedale Lambert, January 1, 1953, lot 292, v, folder 2/5, Wade Center.

translate into language relevant to everyday life."[23] Because technical theological language was no longer understood in an unchurched age, Sayers argued, theological fundamentals needed to be translated to be understood by laypeople. How could the ordinary person ever understand theological doctrines, she wrote in 1955, "unless they can be brought home to him in terms of 'ships and sealing-wax'?"[24]

The chief obstacle to translating theology for the common person was that many clergymen were not particularly fluent with language. This is one of the reasons Sayers was willing to speak and write as much as she did about religion, despite her lack of formal theological training. She found that the clergy and theologians either were not trained in English[25] or had no idea how the words they spoke came across to the average listener. Her anguish about being a Christian schooled in letters among people who were not is apparent in a 1941 letter to a clergyman:

> One of the lay-apologist's great difficulties is the difference between the technical and every-day meaning of the words in the theological vocabulary. . . . Over and over again one hears preachers preaching merrily away, and one wants to call out, "Stop! stop! The words you are using don't mean to the people what they mean to you. . . ." And after a time, the people get to imagine that theological statements mean nothing, never did mean anything, and were never intended to mean anything; because, if the words are understood in their current colloquial sense the statements make nothing but nonsense.
>
> That's why it does seem to me that it may be useful for some common or garden person like myself to come along and say, "Look here! This isn't just verbiage and mumbo-jumbo. It means something quite concrete and relevant. It applies in the most matter-of-fact way to my everyday experience. In current speech it means this."[26]

23. Sayers, "Creed or Chaos?" 39. Her concern about technical terminology may have been influenced by her reading of G. L. Prestige, *God in Patristic Thought* (London: SPCK, 1952), another book she recommended frequently. Prestige writes in his introduction, "Some knowledge of the precise meaning of terms in general use is desirable before a serious study is made of doctrinal history" (xii). Regarding the origins of his book, he notes, "Before attempting to estimate the value of what the Fathers taught, I have tried to ascertain as exactly as possible the meaning of what they said, interpreting their language not so much by speculative reconstruction of their supposed intellectual systems, as by examination of the facts of linguistic usage" (x).

24. Dorothy L. Sayers to Miss Alice Curtayne of Dublin, March 30, 1955, Wade document 25/53.

25. Fragments of a letter from Dorothy L. Sayers to Fr. Alec Vidler, undated, Wade document 398/48.

26. Dorothy L. Sayers to Rev. Dom Ralph Russell, October 28, 1941, Wade document 406/78. Portions of this letter, but not this section, are published in Barbara Reynolds, ed., *The Letters of Dorothy L. Sayers*, vol. 2 (Cambridge: Dorothy L. Sayers Society, 1997), 315–17.

This last statement is actually quite significant. Throughout her correspondence, Sayers repeatedly protests being asked to speak and write on religious themes. She considered herself first and foremost a storyteller, not a preacher. She eventually wrote a form letter, which she referred to as NMR (No More Religion), which was sent to those who invited her to speak about Christianity. She was concerned that her lack of theological training might eventually cause her to mislead someone:

> One of the obvious dangers is, of course, that in trying to translate theological language into a language understood by the people, one tends to over-simplify, and so encourage in other people—even if one avoids them oneself—whole crops of bright and attractive-looking little heresies. I agree, on the other hand, that if the professional theologians cannot translate their language at all, their good seed falls on completely stony ground.[27]

Sayers's willingness to use her writing gifts for the benefit of the church, in spite of her misgivings about her theological training, is remarkable. She recognized that few people were gifted both with words and with an understanding of theology. T. S. Eliot and C. S. Lewis, two of her contemporaries, were among these. Lewis, especially, lacked the theological exposure Sayers had as the child of a clergyman, and she had a lively correspondence with him about writing beyond one's range.[28]

Her task, then, was not only clarification of doctrine but also translation of technical terminology. For this Sayers was uniquely qualified. She had been involved in translation since college, when she made her first translation of *Chanson de Roland*, a later translation of which is still in print. Sayers's labor of love in translating Dante for the common reader is instructive for her theological translation as well, as Barbara Reynolds writes in introducing volume 3 of *The Letters of Dorothy L. Sayers*: "What made her devote the greater part of the remainder of her life to expounding Dante and making him newly accessible was the fact that she found him *buried*—buried, she believed, under misinterpretation, misleading translation, locked in a cupboard to which only scholars were allowed the key. 'Yet Dante,' she said, 'wrote to be read by the common man.'"[29] This observation informs Sayers's theological

27. Dorothy L. Sayers to the bishop of Dover, February 17, 1948, Wade document 198/57, after he wrote on behalf of the archbishop of Canterbury to invite her to speak on "The Atonement and the Modern World."

28. See Diana Pavlac Glyer and Laura K. Simmons, "Dorothy L. Sayers and C. S. Lewis: Two Approaches to Creativity and Calling," *VII: An Anglo-American Literary Review* 21 (2004): 31–46.

29. Barbara Reynolds, ed., *The Letters of Dorothy L. Sayers*, vol. 3 (Cambridge: Dorothy L. Sayers Society, 1999), xvii.

work as well as her translation. Sayers's writings served to "un-bury" doctrine, as well as Dante, for the common person.

In 1945, someone wrote to Sayers thanking her because an agnostic friend of his had converted upon reading *The Mind of the Maker*. The book had resolved the difficulties this friend had with understanding the Trinity, which had been a block to faith for him. Sayers responded:

> All this confirms me in thinking that many intellectual difficulties about Christian doctrine are due to the conventional and abstract language in which the doctrine [*sic*] are customarily presented to people's attention. If they can be related to some truth with which, in daily life, the inquirer is familiar (in this case, the make-up of the creative mind as we know it) a great deal of what appears to be obscure theological ratiocination resolves itself into something quite reasonable and acceptable.[30]

Sayers's upbringing in the church and her experience as a professional writer made it possible for her to draw analogies, clarify technical terminology, and otherwise provide a bridge between the language of common people and the language of the church and theology.

The Blessings of Clarification

Sayers, although eschewing the label "evangelist," cared deeply about the relationship between understanding and belief. She recognized that permitting inaccurate pictures of Christ and Christianity had real consequences. To one of her critics of *The Man Born to Be King*, Sayers wrote that believers who were offended by her "preaching by dramatic presentation" were not required to listen, but she challenged them not to "stand in the way of those to whom it offers a unique chance of breaking down the barriers between the Gospel and the people."[31]

Clear doctrine not only eased the path to faith but also prevented what Sayers saw as one of the worst historical consequences of religious misunderstanding:

> You see, it is such a mistake to think that these Bible characters were a special sort of far-away, unreal, old-fashioned people quite different from ourselves, always speaking in stately, dignified, poetical speech, and thinking about nothing but religion and prophecies. They were just as

30. Dorothy L. Sayers to E. M. Royds Jones, October 3, 1945, Wade document 151/47.

31. Dorothy L. Sayers to Miss C. W. Mackintosh, January 16, 1942, lot 290, ivc, folder 2/3, Wade Center.

"modern" to themselves as we are now to ourselves. They chattered and joked and used slang, drove hard bargains, talked politics, followed the latest fashions and so on, just as we do. The men who killed God were exactly like you and me and the people we read of in the papers—Timid politicians; respectable religious officials; rough, careless soldiers; silly, thoughtless, gossiping folk; noisy mobs led away by paid agitators; weak, well-meaning souls who hadn't the strength of their own convictions; stupid, short-sighted, parochially-minded people—just ordinary people. That is what makes the story so terrifying, because one feels that the very same thing might easily happen to-day.[32]

32. Dorothy L. Sayers to H. J. Lord, Esq., August 28, 1942, lot 290, ivc, folder 1b/3, Wade Center.

PART 2

Theological
Reflections

4

The Incarnation
and the Nature of Christ

*I met a Jew . . . the other week-end who had been converted
by "The Man Born to be King."* . . . *His difficulty had been
the Incarnation—it is always the Jewish difficulty. After hearing the plays, he felt that so good and great a man must have
been God. Before, he hadn't been able to see how so great and
good a God could have become man.*

Robert Speaight, who spoke the character of Jesus
in the radio broadcasts of *The Man Born to Be King*,
to Dorothy L. Sayers, July 28, 1943

"The dogma of the Incarnation is the most dramatic thing about
Christianity," Dorothy L. Sayers wrote in October 1937, "and
indeed, the most dramatic thing that ever entered into the mind of man;
but if you tell people so, they stare at you in bewilderment."[1] One of the
doctrines on which Sayers reflected perhaps more than any other was
the incarnation. A proper understanding of Christ's essence, character,

---

1. Dorothy L. Sayers to Father Herbert Kelly, October 4, 1937, in *The Letters of Dorothy L. Sayers*, vol. 2, ed. Barbara Reynolds (Cambridge: Dorothy L. Sayers Society, 1997), 43.

and mission on earth was "the difference between pseudo-Christianity and Christianity," she wrote in June of 1945.[2] The relationship between the God who created the world and God's Son, Jesus, who walked in it, was a crucial part of her theology.

Why Understand the Incarnation?

Sayers's passion for clarifying doctrine had at its heart a concern that people who do not understand the Christian message will be susceptible to repeating their forebearers' mistakes. This becomes clear when she addresses people's misconceptions about Christ's incarnation, as she does in introducing *The Man Born to Be King*:

> The writer of realistic Gospel plays . . . has to display the words and actions of actual people engaged in living through a piece of recorded history. He cannot, like the writer of purely liturgical or symbolic religious drama, confine himself to the abstract and universal aspect of the life of Christ. He is brought up face to face with the "scandal of particularity." *Ecce homo*—not only Man-in-general and God-in-His-thusness, but also God-in-His-thisness, and *this* Man, *this* person, of a reasonable soul and human flesh subsisting, who walked and talked *then* and *there*, surrounded, not by human types, but by *those* individual people. The story of the life and murder and resurrection of God-in-Man is not only the symbol and epitome of the relations of God and man throughout time; it is also a series of events that took place at a particular point *in* time. *And the people of that time had not the faintest idea that it was happening.*[3]

Sayers's work insists repeatedly that the incarnation is the most central Christian doctrine, essential to understanding all others. She suggested in a November 1940 letter that "the average Englishman has no idea whatever what is really meant by the term, so that a great deal of Christian doctrine is completely incomprehensible to him."[4] In a 1942 review of J. S. Whale's *Christian Doctrine*, she noted that Christians' understanding of both sacrifice and sacrament is dependent on their understanding of the incarnation.[5] But even Christians, she believes,

2. Dorothy L. Sayers to Irene Amesbury of Bristol, June 1, 1945, in *The Letters of Dorothy L. Sayers*, vol. 3, ed. Barbara Reynolds (Cambridge: Dorothy L. Sayers Society, 1999), 150.
3. Dorothy L. Sayers, *The Man Born to Be King* (Grand Rapids: Eerdmans, 1943), 5.
4. Dorothy L. Sayers to Lady Boileau at Wymondham, November 22, 1940, in *Letters of Dorothy L. Sayers*, vol. 2, 199.
5. Dorothy L. Sayers, review of *Christian Doctrine*, by J. S. Whale, *International Review of Missions* 31 (January 1942): 119.

have an immature or inadequate understanding of this doctrine. After the broadcast of her Advent radio play "He That Should Come," Sayers replied to a critique from a listener: "If you mixed as much as I do with people to whom the Gospel story seems to be nothing but a pretty fairy-tale, you would know how much of their contemptuous indifference is due to one fact: that never for one moment have they seen it as a real thing, happening to living people. Nor, indeed, are they fully convinced that Christians believe in its reality."[6]

The unreality of the incarnation is reinforced when Christians formalize and institutionalize their religion, making the vitality of Jesus unrecognizable to those outside. Part of the controversy surrounding Sayers's radio play *The Man Born to Be King* related to its reality. Her characters stammered, spoke in local accents, used slang (even American slang, which was highly offensive to some in the British public), and seemed human. The Christians who protested the play's broadcasts preferred their Christ slightly separate from humanity, more stylized, speaking in the formal tones of the King James translation of the Bible (the Authorized Version, as they understood it) to people who were just as formal and nice. The BBC's director of religious broadcasting, James Welch, wrote to Sayers after the first broadcast in the series that "we are prepared for our Lord to be born into the language of the A.V., or into stained-glass or into paint; what we are not prepared to accept is that He was incarnate. Incarnatus est is a phrase; we bow when we say it; but how many of us are prepared really to believe it. . . . What has always thrilled me about your plays has been this combination of Christology with a full belief in the Incarnation."[7] In a letter to a listener, Sayers wrote that one cannot understand Christ truly

unless one realizes that he was born, not into an allegory, or a devotional tableau, or a Christmas card, with everybody behaving beautifully; but into this confused, coarse, and indifferent world, where people quarrel and swear, and make vulgar jokes and spit on the floor. He was a real person, born in blood and pain like any other child, and dying in blood and pain, like the commonest thief that was ever strung up on the gallows.[8]

The church's understanding of Jesus Christ as fully human and fully divine requires that people believe human flesh can be a suitable vehicle for divine incarnation. Any philosophy or religion that despises the flesh

---

6. Dorothy L. Sayers to Mrs. E. Day, January 20, 1939, lot 290, iie, Wade Center.

7. Rev. J. W. Welch to Dorothy L. Sayers, December 24, 1941, Wade document 434/145. *Incarnatus est* is a phrase from the Nicene Creed as recited in the Latin Mass. Often translated into English as "was born," it literally means "was made incarnate."

8. Sayers to Mrs. E. Day, January 20, 1939.

for any reason is incompatible with Christian theology, as Sayers made clear in a 1940 broadcast titled "The Sacrament of Matter":

> Now we must say, straight away, and without possibility of misunderstanding, that any doctrine which maintains that matter is evil in itself is entirely heretical and entirely un-Christian. The Church does *not* say that matter is evil, nor that the body is evil. For her very life, she dare not. For her whole life is bound up in the doctrine that God Himself took human nature upon Him and went about this material world as a living man, with a human body and a human brain, and that he was perfect and sinless in the body as out of the body, in time as in eternity, in earth as in heaven. That is her creed; that is her dogma; that is the opinion to which she stands committed. If she were for one moment to admit that matter and body were in themselves evil things, she would blast away the very foundations of her existence and utterly destroy herself. For her, matter is so good that God could make Himself a part of it, and take no hurt to His perfection, nor to His holiness.[9]

Early Christians struggled against Gnostic and Manichaean thought, which elevated spirit over matter. Nonetheless, even some interpreters of Christianity have tried in various ways to reject the body or matter in favor of the spirit. Sayers acknowledges how such a rejection could come about: "We know very well that material things are apt to be a snare and a delusion. Preachers are, indeed, continually warning us against putting our trust in the body and in material things, and sometimes the struggle between the spirit and the body is so hard that we are inclined to think that there must be something evil about the material universe as such."[10] Sayers also saw some of this happening in the political climate of her day. In April of 1941, the *Church Times* made reference to a "repressive and reactionary brand of Puritanism which adopts, though for vastly different reasons, the characteristic Nazi attitude of mingled fear and contempt towards the thinker and the artist."[11] On May 16, Sayers wrote in response:

> With what you say about the Puritan temper, which has helped to "drive the living imagination" out of the Church, and thus ultimately "out of the world," I heartily agree, and should only like to emphasize that here, as usual, a perverse temper has its root in a perverse theology; viz. in that unsacramental and, indeed, Manichaean, denial of the intimate unison between spirit and matter which is in fact a denial of the Incarnation.

9. Dorothy L. Sayers, "The Sacrament of Matter," BBC radio addresses delivered in 1940, lot 292, iii of the Sotheby's collection, Wade Center.
10. Ibid.
11. *Church Times*, April 25, 1941, Wade document 347/50.

Similarly, a "humanist" brand of Christology which has largely succeeded (as far as the ordinary man is concerned) in setting up a distinction between the man Jesus and the Divine Logos, has helped to drive the controlling intellect out of religion and thus out of the world of practical affairs. Both these heresies have played straight into the hands of those whose vested interest it is to flatter the "average man" into uncritical acceptance of a debased and commercial valuation of life. Once acquiescent, the average man is an equally easy prey for Totalitarian barbarism, which cannot afford the criticism of the free intellect and the uncorrupt artist, but could not so readily have silenced it if intellect and imagination had not already been discredited in the eye of the people.[12]

In this case, a wrong understanding of the doctrine of the incarnation drives or permits a dualism between body and spirit, which breeds, in Sayers's view, fear and a rejection of critical thinking. When Sayers calls for a renewed understanding of doctrine, she is not merely valuing ideas for the sake of valuing ideas; she sees them as having real consequences in public life.

Avoiding Heresy in Theological Reflection

The early Christian church spent several centuries honing its doctrine about the dual nature of Christ. Sayers likens the process of clarifying theology to that of refining a medieval recipe, adding over time more and more specificity in quantities, ingredients, cooking time, and temperature so that people are not made ill by eating it. There were many tempting traps on either side of the orthodox theological path, and the church rejected those who taught these various beliefs. When Sayers embarked on communicating theology, she did so with fear and trembling, well aware of the pitfalls lying in wait for her. In 1943, she wrote to a colleague after a theological misunderstanding:

Forgive the unconscionable length of this letter. I don't want anybody to think I'm indulging in random heresies . . . but it is extraordinarily difficult to explain one's self briefly without giving people to understand far more or less than one means. If one distinguishes too abruptly between the divine and human knowledge, somebody leaps up crying, "Nestorian!" and if one correlates them too much, a hideous voice hisses "Monophysite!"; and whenever one tries to make anything intelligible in common speech there rises up before one an awful array of the Men Who Made Things Too Simple—Arius, Apollinarius, Eutychus, Sabellius, Ebionites,

---

12. Dorothy L. Sayers to the editor of the *Church Times*, May 6, 1941, Wade document 347/39.

Adoptionists, Patripassians, Theopaschites, Monothelites, Marcionites, Manichees, and the enthusiastic but misguided people who offered cakes to Our Lady and whose name escapes me for the moment, all saying in warning accents: "Here, my girl—you leave it alone—we started trying to explain things and LOOK WHAT HAPPENED TO US!"[13]

The fact that she took the trouble to reflect on the nature of Christ in spite of all those theological traps is indicative of how important she found the incarnation to be. She encountered the same challenges when she embarked on her translation of Dante's *Divine Comedy*. In 1949, she wrote to a fellow Dante scholar:

I have just been working my cautious way through Paradiso xiii, where his extreme care to avoid anything "emanationist," or anything that would divide the Trinity, or subordinate the Second Person, or divide, diminish, or distribute the Godhead, or make Christ anything but true God and true Man, keeps the translator in a perpetual sweat lest he should accidentally disturb this delicate doctrinal balance for the sake of an elegant phrase or a tempting rhyme![14]

Christology

The doctrine of the nature of Christ is known in theological circles as Christology. Sayers made several radio broadcasts to British troops during wartime, and in one of these she articulated the central questions of Christology in a simple, accessible way:

The people who think about Christ nearly always tend to sway in one direction or the other. Some of them emphasise the "human Jesus" at the expense of the divine Jesus; they incline to think that He was just a man with a very special awareness of the divine spark that is in all men—a great teacher and prophet, but no more. All those who do not believe in Christ of course take that view—but so do quite a number of those who profess and call themselves Christians. . . . And there are also quite a number of pious people who (without always knowing it) emphasise the divinity of Christ at the expense of His humanity; out of an exaggerated sense of reverence they shrink from the idea that he talked about, behaved, and was treated by other people like an ordinary human being. They rather give the impression that he never lived in this rough-and-tumble world at all, but always went about in stiff attitudes, like a

13. Dorothy L. Sayers to Fr. J. P. Valentin, June 11, 1943, Wade document 510/138–39. See the glossary for more information about these heresies.
14. Dorothy L. Sayers to Colin Hardie, June 12, 1957, Wade document 370/13.

figure in a stained-glass window, never smiling or joking, and speaking in a special sort of voice, as though He lived permanently in church. I think it is these people who, with the best intentions, antagonise the ordinary man. They make him feel that Christianity is a kind of prim tea-party, reserved for a very respectable and spiritually-minded upper class—quite regardless of the fact that Jesus Himself was notorious for the vulgar and shocking company He kept.[15]

In the introduction to *The Man Born to Be King*, Sayers observes that religious art historically alternates back and forth between emphasizing Christ's humanity—his closeness to our state—and his divinity and distinction from us. At the time she was writing, the country's theaters operated under a "law forbidding the representation on the stage of any Person of the Holy Trinity," which had "helped to foster the notion that all such representations were intrinsically wicked, and had encouraged a tendency, already sufficiently widespread, towards that Docetic and totally heretical Christology which denies the full Humanity of our Lord."[16] Docetism was an early church heresy that suggested that Jesus only seemed to be human. Playwrights had tried to include Christ in their plays without actually representing him on stage by having a voice call in from the wings, but this made Jesus seem unreal to theatergoers. When Sayers wrote *The Man Born to Be King*, she insisted on as much realism as possible, arguing that the radio medium did not present the same confusions and temptations to idolatry as a visual medium might. In negotiating in August 1941 with James Welch, the director of religious broadcasting at the BBC, she argued:

> I have taken the line that nobody, not even Jesus, must be allowed to "talk Bible." I expect we shall get a good many complaints that I have not preserved the beauty and eloquence of the authorised version, and that Jesus has been made to say things which don't appear in the sacred original. It seems to me frightfully important that the thing should be made to appear as real as possible, and above all, that Jesus should be presented as a human being and not like a sort of symbolic figure doing nothing but preach in elegant periods, when all the people around him are talking in everyday style. We must avoid, I think, a Docetist Christ, whatever happens—even at the risk of a little loss of formal dignity.[17]

Critics of *The Man Born to Be King* attacked it for a variety of imbalances in its presentation of Christ. Sayers found that various critics

15. Dorothy L. Sayers, "Creed or Chaos: 1. The Christ of the Creeds," BBC Home Service, August 11, 1940, lot 292, iii, Wade Center.

16. Sayers, *Man Born to Be King*, 1–2.

17. Dorothy L. Sayers to James Welch, August 1, 1941, Wade document 433/37.

canceled one another out. She responded to an April 1945 correspondent who leaned on the divinity side of the equation, "Many thanks for your interesting letter about *The Man Born to Be King*. Laying it alongside the numerous letters and articles which say that I have overstressed the Humanity (or even, gleefully, that I have debunked the Divinity) it gives me a comforting assurance that I have probably kept the two Natures in fairly level balance."[18]

Why is it so important for Christians to understand that Christ is both fully divine and fully human? For Sayers, it is crucial to understand the divinity of Christ for a variety of reasons. In a 1940 broadcast on the BBC, she articulated:

> It is important that we should know, because, if Christ was only a man, however noble or amiable, then there is no more reason for believing what he said or trying to do as he did, than for believing or imitating Diogenes the Stoic, or Good Queen Bess, or, for that matter, the Emperor Nero or Adolf Hitler. . . . But if Jesus Christ is God of God, and made the world to His own pattern, then the situation is very different; for in that case, by disregarding Christ we shall come into collision with the very nature of the universe.[19]

Christian history teaches that if Jesus were not fully divine, he could not have fully represented humanity before God the Father. As Sayers sees it, one of the pitfalls of ignoring or denying the divinity of Christ is that "God the Father appears as the villain of the piece."[20] Understanding how Christ could atone for the sins of humankind requires accepting that Jesus is fully divine.

What about Christ's humanity? Why is this important to Christians and thus worth Sayers's time, ink, and reputation? In that same 1940 BBC broadcast, she explained:

> It is important, then, that Jesus should be truly God, but if he is so exclusively God that he was never in any real sense an ordinary human being with human limitations like our own, then it is clearly meaningless for us to try and follow in his steps. The conditions that influence us would simply not apply to Him in any way. The whole story of his suffering and death, for instance, would become completely unreal. His body would not be a genuine body, but only a sort of pretend body, like that of a mythical divinity, incapable of death or pain.[21]

18. Dorothy L. Sayers to Rev. W. Gill of Manchester, April 17, 1945, in *Letters of Dorothy L. Sayers*, vol. 3, 137.

19. Sayers, "Creed or Chaos: 1. The Christ of the Creeds."

20. Dorothy L. Sayers to Father Herbert Kelly, no date given (but after October 1, 1937, letter from him), Wade document 261/78–89.

21. Sayers, "Creed or Chaos: 1. The Christ of the Creeds."

Jesus' full divinity and full humanity assure Christians that God the Son understands their lot: "Against these heresies, and the innumerable variations of them, stands up the Catholic Church, affirming in the teeth of the world that that which died upon the cross was true God and true Man—that every agony that man can undergo—grief, pain, fear, shame and defeat and death, passed through the consciousness of God and are for ever part of God's experience."[22]

How else do Christ's full divinity and full humanity affect Christian belief and practice? In one of her BBC addresses, Sayers clarified:

> The Church's own belief—that Christ was both God and man—has certain important consequences for human life. For one thing, it implies that religion is concerned, not merely with what happens in the spiritual world, or what becomes of us after death, but also, with what happens here and now in this world; it is concerned with society, as well as with the individual soul. It is active, positive, and creative; a Christian's business is not just to *sit* about *being* good, but to *go* about *doing* good.[23]

Sayers recognized that her insistence on orthodoxy in portraying Christ made even Christian believers uncomfortable. This drove many of the protests against *The Man Born to Be King*, which C. S Lewis said "has edified us in this country more than anything for a long time."[24] But Sayers was happy to shock people because she believed the gospel *should* be shocking. In her introduction to *The Man Born to Be King*, Sayers complained that Christians and nonbelievers alike were far too ready to view biblical characters as

> sacred personages, living in a far-off land and time, using dignified rhythms of speech, making from time to time restrained gestures symbolic of brutality. They mocked and railed on Him and smote Him, they scourged and crucified Him. Well, they were people very remote from ourselves, and no doubt it was all done in the noblest and most beautiful manner. We should not like to think otherwise.
>
> Unhappily, if we think about it at all, we must think otherwise. God was executed by people painfully like us, in a society very similar to our own. . . . He was executed by a corrupt church, a timid politician, and a fickle proletariat led by professional agitators. His executioners made vulgar jokes about Him, called Him filthy names, taunted Him, smacked Him

22. Dorothy L. Sayers, "God the Son: 4. The Death of God," BBC Forces Programme, June 29, 1941, lot 292, iii, Wade Center.

23. Sayers, "Creed or Chaos: 1. The Christ of the Creeds."

24. Humphrey Carpenter, *The Inklings: C. S. Lewis, J. R. R. Tolkien, Charles Williams, and Their Friends* (Boston: Houghton Mifflin, 1979), 189.

in the face, flogged Him with the cart, and hanged Him on the common gibbet—a bloody, dusty, sweaty, and sordid business.

If you show people that, they are shocked. So they should be. If that does not shock them, nothing can.[25]

While Sayers did not design her radio plays with evangelism in mind, both listeners and church officials experienced them as powerfully evangelistic. According to a biography of Sayers, even the archbishop of Canterbury, William Temple, "agreed with Dr. Welch [director of religious broadcasting for the BBC] that the plays were 'one of the most powerful instruments in evangelism which the Church had had put into its hands for a long time past.'"[26] Sayers would suggest that their power came from the incarnational medium of the play. As she wrote, "A thing shown in action affects the imagination and sticks in the mind more insistently than any amount of verbal instruction or argument."[27]

25. Sayers, *Man Born to Be King*, 7.

26. Barbara Reynolds, *Dorothy L. Sayers: Her Life and Soul* (New York: St. Martin's Press, 1993), 329.

27. Dorothy L. Sayers, "Sacred Plays: II," *Episcopal Churchnews*, January 25, 1955, 25.

5

The Trinity

You feel this is the way theology should be written—and that is particularly gratifying, because my literary friends don't look upon it as theology at all, but as an experiment in literary criticism. This encourages me to hope that I've so far succeeded as to get theology and letters where I want them—as two expressions of a single experience.

Dorothy L. Sayers to V. A. Demant, April 10, 1941, about *The Mind of the Maker*

"Christian doctrine belongs . . . to the common man, and not only to the scholar," John Thurmer wrote in *A Detection of the Trinity*. "Religious doctrines which can be understood only by experts are not worth much."[1] The Trinity is one doctrine many Christians and even theologians avoid discussing, preferring to defer to mystery (in part because the Trinity is admittedly difficult to explain). Sayers herself said that the doctrine of the Trinity "enjoys the greatest reputation for obscurity and remoteness from common experience" of all Christian doctrines.[2] In fact, as she relates in a set of notes related to the "Oecumenical Penguin" project, "About two years ago I was asked by a publisher whether the Holy Ghost was still

1. John Thurmer, *A Detection of the Trinity* (Devon, U.K.: Paternoster, 1984), 7.
2. Dorothy L. Sayers, *The Mind of the Maker* (San Francisco: HarperSanFrancisco, 1979), 35.

considered to form part of the Trinity, since nothing seemed to have been said about Him lately. . . . The episode suggests that a certain obscurity veils the whole position in the mind of the common man."[3]

The Mind of the Maker is the source of most of Sayers's reflection on the Trinity, although trinitarian doctrine is also central to *The Emperor Constantine*. Thurmer has committed several decades of his life to studying Sayers's work on the Trinity, and his conviction is that "whether she intended it or not, Dorothy L. Sayers provided the most developed and usable analogy of God the Holy Trinity in the English language."[4] He correctly wonders why this facet of Sayers's work has not received more theological attention. In pondering why *The Mind of the Maker* did not have a stronger reception at the time of its writing, Thurmer suggests that "maybe the middle of the second world war was not a very receptive time for theological ideas. Moreover, academics generally dislike theses which cross the usual disciplinary boundaries, and the prominence of literary criticism in *The Mind* may have discouraged theologians from taking it seriously."[5] Thurmer calls *The Mind of the Maker* "a remarkable *tour de force*, a theology waiting to be discovered, a time-bomb which has not yet exploded."[6] He is quick to caution readers of his book *Reluctant Evangelist* that any secondary analysis of *The Mind of the Maker* will necessarily be limited, encouraging them to peruse the entire volume themselves: "To experience its range and *panache* you must go to the book itself. You may or may not like it; but you will certainly find it unlike any other theological book. It is combative, uproariously funny, and owes little to anyone or anything else except the New Testament and the creeds."[7]

What do we know of Sayers's intentions in composing *The Mind of the Maker*? In August of 1941, soon after its publication, she wrote to a clergy friend:

3. "Notes 2" from "Oecumenical Penguin" documents, lot 292, i, Wade Center.

4. John Thurmer, "Sayers on the Trinity," in *Reluctant Evangelist: Papers on the Christian Thought of Dorothy L. Sayers* (W. Sussex: Dorothy L. Sayers Society, 1996), 38. His research assesses Sayers's analogy in the light of other theologians' attempts to understand the Trinity, including those of John Macquarrie, Karl Barth, St. Augustine, R. C. Moberly, Karl Rahner, and others. We know that Sayers consulted Augustine in writing *The Mind of the Maker*: "Of course one couldn't write about the Trinity without seeing what he [Augustine] had to say" (Dorothy L. Sayers to Father Herbert Kelly, May 7, 1941, Wade document 260/71). See Thurmer's *Detection of the Trinity* and the essays in *Reluctant Evangelist* (particularly "Sayers on the Trinity") for more information.

5. John Thurmer, "Re-Review: *The Mind of the Maker*," *Modern Churchman* 30, no. 3 (1941): 38. Two of his essays in *Reluctant Evangelist* also suggest reasons why it was not well received (see pp. 3, 47–48).

6. Ibid., 39.

7. John Thurmer, "Dorothy L. Sayers and *The Mind of the Maker*," in *Reluctant Evangelist*, 3.

I wanted to get formulated a dim feeling I had that the Trinity-doctrine did mean something quite closely related to what one was doing; so I plonked it all down, in the hope that if there was anything in it, the qualified people would be able to sort it out and turn it into something more correct. I mean, I thought the artist's way of making might be useful material for the Trinitarian theologian.[8]

There has been some confusion over whether Sayers really intended to write a theological treatise, and her own writings do little to clear up the confusion. Sayers refers to *The Mind of the Maker* both as a book on the creative mind and, in other references, as a book on the Trinity. To one friend she described it as a "dull book about the Trinity," and her friend responded, "If it is, my goodness what would you call an exciting one! I think it's just thrilling."[9] Sayers wrote to one reader, "The book has been read by professional theologians (for I have had no scholarly training in the subject) and pronounced quite orthodox so far as it goes. I mention this because amateur explanations are often rightly suspect of achieving lucidity at the expense of orthodoxy, thus leaving the matter in a worse confusion than ever."[10] In fact, a clergyman wrote to say that he was using her work to teach dogmatic theology to priests under his tutelage: "The book was splendid—such a treat to find someone contructing [sic] orthodox Trinitarian thought which would reach the poor modern mind. I see your difficulties very well and am so glad the theologians have been sensible. I realised that you were not out to save the souls of theologians (God help them), but providing good food for the far more important hungry sheep."[11]

Idea, Energy, and Power

Sayers's clearest and most forceful exposition of her understanding of the Trinity has its roots in the speech by the archangel Michael at the conclusion of her play *The Zeal of Thy House*. She quotes this speech, with minor clarifications, in *The Mind of the Maker*:

8. Dorothy L. Sayers to Monsignor Ronald Knox, August 26, 1941, Wade document 249/27. Evidently, Knox had written to her suggesting that someone wanted to write a very lengthy (fourteen-volume) analysis of the Trinity after reading Sayers's book.
9. Sayers mentions this interchange in a letter to E. V. Rieu, April 6, 1941, Wade document 19/59.
10. Dorothy L. Sayers to Mrs. R. E. Large, April 6, 1948, lot 291, v, Wade Center.
11. Rev. Ralph Russell to Dorothy L. Sayers, November 8, 1941, Wade document 406/75.

For every work (*or act*) of creation is threefold, an earthly trinity to match the heavenly.

First (*not in time, but merely in order of enumeration*) there is the Creative Idea, passionless, timeless, beholding the whole work complete at once, the end in the beginning: and this is the image of the Father.

Second, there is the Creative Energy (*or Activity*) begotten of that idea, working in time from the beginning to the end, with sweat and passion, being incarnate in the bonds of matter: and this is the image of the Word.

Third, there is the Creative Power, the meaning of the work and its response in the lively soul: and this is the image of the indwelling Spirit.

And these three are one, each equally in itself the whole work, whereof none can exist without the other: and this is the image of the Trinity.[12]

Sayers thus uses the analogy of a trinity of Idea, Energy/Activity, and Power—as experienced in the creative process—to help her readers understand the Trinity of Father, Son, and Holy Spirit.

Her analogy is perhaps easier to understand when applied to a specific creative work. As Sayers was an author, she could explain things most clearly using the image of a book or a play. The chapter titled "Pentecost" in *The Mind of the Maker* offers the examples of book-as-thought (Idea), book-as-written (Energy/Activity), and book-as-read (Power). Writing a book enfleshes or incarnates the Idea into visible form, thus the correspondence of the Energy/Activity to God the Son in the Holy Trinity. When a writer says, "I have an idea for a book," that Idea is as much the book as the finished product. Likewise, the Activity/Energy and the Power are complete examples of the book. This is evidenced most obviously by the language an author uses during the writing process and the language of the reader or audience.

To apply this language to Sayers's play *The Emperor Constantine*, for example, when she first had the idea for the play, she could say, "I am very excited about *The Emperor Constantine*." Even though it was not yet manifest on paper, the Idea was still a complete entity in her mind. Likewise, while she was in the process of writing it, she could say, "*The Emperor Constantine* is coming along well." Again, it was a complete entity; she would not speak about it as the *section* or *portion* of the play that was already "incarnate" but as the entire play itself. We know that members of the audience liked a particular scene in this play so much that they often returned to see the play again. For many of them, though, they would tell their friends, "You must see *The Emperor Constantine*; it's amazing," as opposed to saying, "Part of it is amazing" or "You must see this one scene." They experienced the Power as the whole play.

12. Sayers, *Mind of the Maker*, 37–38.

In this way, Sayers uses her analogy of the creative process to help readers understand what the creeds mean when they say the Father, Son, and Holy Spirit are one God. Just as Idea, Energy/Activity, and Power are three discernible facets of one creative work, the Father, Son, and Holy Spirit are three *personas* (to use the Latin) or *hypostases* (the Greek equivalent) sharing one *substantia* (Latin) or *ousia* (Greek). Because Idea, Energy/Activity, and Power are "essentially inseparable," Sayers argues, a writer cannot say which one is the "real" book or play or composition: "Each of them is the complete book separately; yet in the complete book all of them exist together."[13] She points out that an artist (and a reader or audience, for that matter) can "distinguish the persons" of her Trinity, but they cannot "divide the substance"—phrases straight out of the Athanasian Creed.

Sayers's analogy assists in explaining a variety of other elements of the Holy Trinity as well. For example, the creeds use the language of "begetting" to refer to the relationship of the Son to the Father, and "proceeding" to articulate the relationship of the Holy Spirit to the other two Persons of the Trinity. One feature of the Arian heresy in the early church was the suggestion that God the Father preceded God the Son in time, that there was a time when the Son was not. Sayers's play *The Emperor Constantine* depicts a very real and common event during the time of this controversy: followers of Arius taunting their opponents by chanting, "There was when he was not," sometimes to the tune of popular ditties. In *The Mind of the Maker*, Sayers explains how "the Idea . . . cannot be said to precede the Energy in time, because (so far as that act of creation is concerned) it is the Energy that creates the time-process. This is the analogy of the theological expressions that 'the Word was in the beginning with God' and was 'eternally begotten of the Father.'" Similarly, in Sayers's trinity, the Power "proceeds from the Idea and the Energy together," just as the creeds articulate that the Holy Spirit proceeds from the Father and the Son.[14]

This is one area in which Sayers's analogy may be either particularly useful to understanding the Holy Trinity or particularly challenging, depending on one's tradition. The Eastern Church split from the Western Church over the issue of whether the Holy Spirit proceeds from the Father directly or from the Father *and* the Son. The Latin phrase for "and the Son" is *filioque*. The Eastern Church split over the *filioque* clause, or the section of the Nicene Creed about the procession of the Holy Spirit. Eastern articulations of this creed lack this phrase.

13. Ibid., 41.
14. Ibid., 38–39, 40.

Because her understanding of the creative process informs how she sees the Holy Trinity, and because her creative trinity requires that the Power proceed from the Idea and the Energy, Sayers would likely insist on retaining the *filioque* clause in the creed. She suggests that creative artists, if required to give evidence of the *filioque* clause, "must come down heavily on the Western side of the controversy, since their experience leaves them in no doubt about the procession of the ghost from the son."[15]

The incarnation is also clarified by Sayers's trinitarian analogy. She writes of how the Energy is the only way the Idea is made known to itself and to others, similar to Jesus' revelation of God the Father. She calls this the "expression in temporal form of the eternal and immutable Idea." At the same time, it is "essentially identical with the Idea—'consubstantial with the Father.'"[16] This is a phrase from the Nicene Creed, the phrase over which the early church battled most. The Arians preferred to say that the Son was of *similar* substance with the Father, not of one substance or consubstantial. Athanasius and others argued that unless the Son was consubstantial, he could not represent God's forgiveness to humanity.[17] In Sayers's trinity, the Idea is not dependent for its existence on a material manifestation, although the creative mind has an "urgent desire" for expression in material form.

Scalene Trinities

One of the boldest and most striking sections of *The Mind of the Maker* is the chapter titled "Scalene Trinities." This chapter discusses works of art (mostly books) that are "father-ridden" (heavy on the Idea but weak on the Energy and the Power), "Son-ridden" (detailed activity bolstering an insufficiently developed Idea), and "ghost-ridden" (full of emotional Power but lacking in Energy and Idea development). Interestingly, a recent column by an American movie critic addressed this very idea. Lisa Schwartzbaum, one of the film critics for *Entertainment Weekly*, was asked the difference between a bad movie and a truly offensive one. Schwartzbaum's response suggests that she defines a bad movie by how weak it is in concept (which parallels the Idea in Sayers's model), execution (similar to the Energy),

15. Ibid., 171.
16. Ibid., 40.
17. See Athanasius, *"De Incarnatione Verbi Dei"* (On the Incarnation of the Word of God) and Anselm's *Cur Deus Homo?* (Why the God-Man?) for more in-depth arguments on this point.

or what she calls a "whammo combination of both" (which would affect the Power).[18]

Sayers adds that to be father-centered, Son-centered, or ghost-centered "is not a major heresy or a mortal sin. . . . The image of God is a little out of drawing; if it were not, we should not merely become 'as gods'—we should *be* gods. What is really damaging to a writer's creation is a serious and settled weakness in any side of his Trinity."[19] Although she suggests that all human (and therefore fallen) makers will "have their trinities permanently a little out of true—slightly scalene," she also believes that there will be moments when the writing is more or less balanced, "when, for once, Idea, Energy and Power are consubstantial and co-equal."[20] (Chapter 11 gives an example of how Sayers's idea of a balanced trinity of Idea, Energy, and Power still rings true when applied to artistic creation.)

Sayers goes on in "Scalene Trinities" to discuss dramatic Gnosticism, artistic Arians, Manichaean writers, and Patripassian authors—only once explaining one of these movements in a footnote. (Manichaeans, like Gnostics, practiced an extreme dualism. Patripassianism proposed that the Father, not the Son, suffered.) This betrays Sayers's more elitist side: The assumption of her readers' extensive knowledge of church history and of foreign languages suggests that she wrote for a fairly educated audience and expected the uneducated somehow to keep up.[21] However, this chapter also serves to introduce the uneducated to these elements of doctrine. Sayers's play *The Emperor Constantine*, itself a reflection on the Trinity, is an example of her using a medium of "incarnation" to show people the importance of resolving a complicated trinitarian heresy.

If we return momentarily to the guidelines for lay theology found in the introduction, we find that Sayers's work on the Trinity is among her most pure lay theology. *The Mind of the Maker* involves Sayers's thinking theologically about her vocation and bringing the information of her work experience into dialogue with Christian tradition. *The Emperor Constantine* gives Sayers the opportunity to use the medium

18. Lisa Schwartzbaum, "Offensive Play," *Entertainment Weekly*, July 23, 2004, http://www.ew.com/ew/article/latest/0,11892,7451,00.html (accessed July 30, 2004).

19. Sayers, *Mind of the Maker*, 157.

20. Ibid., 155–56. *Consubstantial* was the (hotly contested) word from the Nicene Creed referring to the fact that the Father, Son, and Holy Spirit share one substance (*substantia*).

21. Sayers's work exhibits her fondness for sprinkling quotations throughout—with or without quotation marks. Sayers wrote about this habit in an obituary for her friend Helen Simpson: "She was adept at the game of conversation by quotation. It is, of course, a game that only civilised people can play, but they play it with remarkable relish. The flavour of this kind of talk, like that of all high spirits, is apt to evaporate if left standing" (Wade document 15/16).

of her vocation to present or to "show" theology and doctrine to people. Who is the audience for her exploration of the Trinity? It is not merely the church, especially as she did not set out necessarily to make a theological statement. For *The Emperor Constantine*, her audience is the general public, many of whom even expected to be bored by the play's theological content before they discovered how exciting it could be. In part, her audience for *The Mind of the Maker* is creative artists. While we are not aware of her "Scalene Trinities" chapter having specifically improved anyone's scalene art, we do know that various artists contacted her in response to her work. In one letter she gratefully noted that a musician had told her that her trinitarian model fit as well in music as in writing or visual art. Many of her clergy acquaintances read and appreciated *The Mind of the Maker* as a theological volume, although few if any advocated in a published venue its study as such. C. S. Lewis reviewed and recommended it as indispensable, although Thurmer suggests that Lewis's opinion did not carry credence among academic theologians any more than Sayers's did.

Harold Child, a critic from the *Times Literary Supplement*, wrote to Sayers about *The Mind of the Maker*: "It ought to go on year after year being read by people who will find it clearing up their bewilderment and giving them new guts. . . . The creative has never been so clearly and logically explained before, nor has its practical importance been made so plain. . . . I dare say it will suggest to you that the working out of your Analogy seems to me not only a masterly piece of thinking but also a revelation of truth."[22] His testament to her articulation of trinitarian doctrine as both art and revelation nicely encapsulates the gifts Sayers brought to her work. For every person who found her analogy helpful in understanding creativity, others expressed gratitude that it helped them understand their faith better. The Trinity may always be a mystery, but it is slightly more accessible because of Sayers's interpretation.

22. Harold Child to Dorothy L. Sayers, no date, Wade document 19/66–67.

6

Sin and Evil, Redemption
and Atonement

Constantine: Mother, tell me, whose blood is on my hands?
The blood of Maximian, the blood of Maxentius, of Crassus,
Lucinius, Marcia, Bassianus, Fausta—the blood of Crispus?

Helena: The blood of God, which makes intercession for us

Dorothy L. Sayers, *The Emperor Constantine*

Sin and Evil

Barbara Reynolds remembers Sayers lecturing on "The Faust Legend and the Idea of the Devil" at Oxford in 1944: "In the course of her lecture she said, 'We do not take evil seriously enough.' Thereupon a bomb fell nearby shaking the building. D.L.S. continued, calmly: 'What did I tell you?'"[1]

What theologians call the problem of evil plays a central role in Sayers's oeuvre, not merely in her mysteries but also in her essays, plays, and

1. Barbara Reynolds, *The Letters of Dorothy L. Sayers*, vol. 3 (Cambridge: Dorothy L. Sayers Society, 1999), 120.

some poetry. Sayers's thoughts on evil are closely tied to her understanding of sin, which will also be addressed here. Sayers was driven to
write about evil in part by the milieu in which she lived and wrote. Her
mysteries occupied her time between the wars, but when World War II
arrived, she felt it inappropriate to continue writing detective fiction. In
The Mind of the Maker, she writes about the difference between fictional
evil and real evil. Someone had written to her with a question about
her novel *Gaudy Night*:

> He said: "Why do you allow the academic woman to have any doubts that
> she pursued the right course with Annie's husband? She seems to think
> she may have been wrong. Doesn't that conflict with your whole thesis?"
> What is obvious here is the firmly implanted notion that all human situa-
> tions are "problems" like detective problems, capable of a single, necessary,
> and categorical solution, which must be wholly right, while all others are
> wholly wrong. But this they cannot be, since human situations are subject
> to the law of human nature, whose evil is at all times rooted in its good,
> and whose good can only redeem, but not abolish, its evil. The good that
> emerges from a conflict of values cannot arise from the total condemnation
> or destruction of one set of values, but only from the building of a new
> value, sustained, like an arch, by the tension of the original two.[2]

Sayers stopped writing mysteries in part because of this human tendency
to see all problems as easily solved; in wartime, this was too simplistic
a worldview to encourage.

The complexity of sin and evil requires a nuanced response, whether
on the world scene or between individuals. Unlike C. S. Lewis, Sayers
does not automatically consider what might be called the "pastoral"
implications of every situation and relationship, but in her discussion
of *Gaudy Night*, she raises the possibility that there may have been
more pastoral ways of addressing Arthur Robinson's academic indis-
cretions. Miss De Vine admits to Lord Peter that even though actions
have natural consequences, "One ought to take some thought for other
people. Miss Lydgate would have done what I did in the first place;
but she would have made it her business to see what became of that
unhappy man and his wife."[3] Miss De Vine's was a sin of omission but
sin nonetheless—interpersonal "evil" rooted in the good of academic
integrity, as it were. Janice Brown, in *The Seven Deadly Sins in the
Work of Dorothy L. Sayers*, identifies Miss De Vine's sin as "a deficiency
of love" and a form of pride: "It led to a narrowness of vision, which

2. Dorothy L. Sayers, *The Mind of the Maker* (San Francisco: HarperSanFrancisco,
1979), 191.
3. Dorothy L. Sayers, *Gaudy Night* (New York: Avon Books, 1968), 375.

caused her to be insensitive to the human suffering that was bound to result from her ruthless, but just, action in exposing Robinson's dishonesty."[4]

In exploring the real brokenness of humans, Sayers articulates an orthodox Christian understanding of the relationship between evil and free will. In a 1953 essay on evil, she muses:

> How could anything evil get into the universe? How could the creation, or any part of it, "go wrong"? That is the great and puzzling question. For the *fact* that something is very wrong with this planet on which we live is only too obvious. Man in particular is very far from being altogether united and loving, and much that he is and does is destructive rather than creative, and is false rather than real or true.[5]

She observes that other elements in nature (plants, rain, etc.) operate without rebellious tendencies:

> But some other of His creatures were made by God with the power of choice; and Man is one of these. Man was made with a free will, so that his obedience to God's will might be, not an automatic necessity, but a spontaneous act. He was made so that he might do the harmonious, creative, loving, real and *good* thing—not because he was unable to do otherwise, but because he *wanted* to do it, and this was to be his happiness.[6]

How does that free will lead to evil? God refuses to coerce humans into behaving well, and sometimes the free choices they make have negative consequences:

> From the very beginning, man abused his power of free will by refusing to accept his own limitations. . . . Man rebelled against the limits set on him by his created nature; he wanted to have and do what it was not possible for a limited creature to be or do; he wanted to be "as God." He was persuaded that there was something that God knew and he did not (which indeed was perfectly true), and he was determined to know it, although he was warned that it was something which Man could not know and live. But he insisted on knowing; and the thing that he chose to know was Evil.[7]

4. Janice Brown, *The Seven Deadly Sins in the Work of Dorothy L. Sayers* (Kent, OH: Kent State University Press, 1998), 156.

5. Dorothy L. Sayers, "Is There a Definite Evil Power That Attacks People in the Same Way as There Is a Good Power That Influences People?" in *Asking Them Questions*, ed. Ronald Selby Wright (London: Oxford University Press, 1953), 44.

6. Ibid., 44–45.

7. Ibid., 47.

Sayers's first mystery, *Whose Body*, contains extensive reflection on human evil in the person of Julian Freke, one of Sayers's more sinister villains. But Sayers also had many real models of evil in the world governments of her time. Unfortunately, she found Britain lacking in an understanding of sin and evil, which may explain why she wrote as much as she did on these topics. In "They Tried to Be Good," she indicts the British people and government for becoming "too enlightened to believe in sin," which affected England's willingness to enter World War II against its old ally, Germany.[8] She also writes pleadingly in March 1942 to the bishop of Winchester (later archbishop of York), the chair of the BBC's Central Religious Advisory Committee, about why it is important for her to write realistically about Jesus' suffering:

> My Lord, the people have forgotten so much. The thing has become to them like a tale that is told. They cannot believe it ever happened. They look at the atrocities of wicked men today, and wonder that God does not interfere. They forget that those same atrocities were once perpetrated upon God. Priests and elders and Roman dictators no longer seem to them to be "wicked men," as we understand wickedness, for the old familiar obsolete phrases have been sterilized by pious associations and hurt nobody anymore. In trying to avoid the hurt, we draw a veil between man and his own sin, and in trying to avoid irreverence we protect the wicked from the world's judgment. But how can it honor God to make His enemies seem less cruel, less callous, less evil than they were?[9]

It was important for Sayers to portray evil realistically in her plays and other writings as part of her ministry to a country at war with evil itself.

Did Sayers see evil simply as the result of human free will, or did she believe in a personal devil who interfered in human activity? While she commended Winston Churchill for being "Christian enough to allow for sin and the devil,"[10] she was hesitant to give the devil more than his due, so to speak. In a 1953 essay, she suggests:

8. She goes on to say, briskly, "I have no use whatever for Enlightened Opinion, whose science is obsolete, its psychology superficial, its theology beneath contempt and its history nowhere; besides, it is a craven thing. . . . I hope we shall pay no attention to it" (Dorothy L. Sayers, "They Tried to Be Good," in *Unpopular Opinions* [New York: Harcourt, Brace, & Co., 1947], 127).

9. Dorothy L. Sayers to the bishop of Winchester, March 17, 1942, in *The Letters of Dorothy L. Sayers*, vol. 2, ed. Barbara Reynolds (Cambridge: Dorothy L. Sayers Society, 1997), 357.

10. Sayers, "They Tried to Be Good," 126.

Satan's pride revolted against being a mere dependent creature; he wanted to assert himself and show that he was as great as God. But what could he do? He could not create anything, for all creation belongs to God. The only thing the proud, perverted will can do to assert itself is to destroy. Just as God is one, creative, loving, and real, so the evil power can exercise itself only in division, destruction, hatred, and unreality. God is a Person; but it is scarcely accurate to say that there is a "personal" Devil, for evil breaks up the personality. Of that proud spirit, there is now nothing left but a ravenous, chaotic will, a motiveless and unmeaning malice, at once cunning and witless, like that of a maniac; an empty rage of destructiveness, without hope or purpose save to rend and divide, and reduce all creation to the same hell of futility as itself. It was to this spirit of strife and destruction that man opened the doors of his mind when he learned to see God's good creation as an evil thing.[11]

Sayers is quick to remind her readers that evil cannot create; it can only distort what is already created, "seizing upon some good thing and giving it an ugly and destructive twist."[12] This face of evil disguised in a thinly distorted good confuses people who do not have a theology that includes evil.

In "Creed or Chaos?" Sayers writes about the relationship between the Christian understanding of human depravity and the obvious evil in the world of her day. Ordinary humanity, believing in progress and the essential goodness of people, would rightly be shocked by human sin:

To them, the appalling outbursts of bestial ferocity in the totalitarian states, and the obstinate selfishness and stupid greed of capitalist society, are not merely shocking and alarming. For them, these things are the utter negation of everything in which they have believed. It is as though the bottom had dropped out of their universe. The whole thing looks like a denial of all reason, and they feel as if they and the world had gone mad.[13]

For the Christian, on the other hand, while these kinds of sins are also grievous, "he is not astonished. He has never thought very highly of human nature left to itself. He has been accustomed to the idea that there is a deep interior dislocation in the very center of human personality." Sayers argues that the "Christian dogma of the double nature in man—which asserts that man is disintegrated and necessarily imperfect in himself and in all his works, yet closely related by a real unity of substance with an eternal perfection within and beyond

11. Sayers, "Is There a Definite Evil Power?" 48–49.
12. Ibid., 49.
13. Dorothy L. Sayers, "Creed or Chaos?" in *The Whimsical Christian* (New York: Collier, 1978), 45.

him—makes the present . . . state of humanity seem both less hopeless and less irrational."[14]

Just as the doctrine of human depravity helped Christians weather the evil of their day, so did a general Christian understanding of evil. For the secular person, evil is presented as an external force, "something imposed on him from without, not made by him within." Sayers notes that, historically, any number of external forces have been "invoked to assure man that he is not responsible for his misfortunes and therefore not to be held guilty." However, such a belief leads to a "dreadful conclusion . . . , that as he is not responsible for evil, he cannot alter it. . . . Today, if we could really be persuaded that . . . the trouble is not outside us but inside us, and that therefore, by the grace of God, we can do something to put it right—we should receive that message as the most hopeful and heartening thing that one could imagine."[15]

Sayers's comment about being able to "do something to put it right" raises the question of her theology about human depravity. Strong Calvinists would suggest that humans have no ability to influence their world for good. Anglo-Catholics would disagree with this stance, according to Sayers. This difference in viewpoint led some Calvinists to accuse Sayers of Pelagianism, the view that people "can achieve salvation by cooperation with the divine will" through their own efforts, as scholar Earle Cairns describes it.[16] In a 1955 letter responding to a charge of Pelagianism, Sayers states:

> I am a Catholic of the Anglican Communion. And Catholics are not Pelagians, though it sometimes pleased Dr. Barth to call them so.
>
> St. Paul, St. Augustine, St. Thomas Aquinas, and every Catholic theologian would cordially agree with Tertullian, Calvin, and Karl Barth that our nature is in some sense "depraved" and "very far gone from original righteousness." Where the two parties would disagree is about the sense in which the depravity can be called "total."
>
> It is quite Catholic to maintain that the whole of nature (body, mind, and spirit) is maimed (vulnerata), and all its operations defective, by reason of original sin; it is Calvinist to maintain that, by reason of original sin, natural goodness is wholly extinguished.
>
> The latter doctrine (the only one of which the terms [sic] "total depravity" is technically and correctly used), tends in effect, to exclude God from the nature which He created.[17]

14. Ibid.

15. Ibid., 47.

16. Earle E. Cairns, *Christianity through the Centuries: A History of the Christian Church* (Grand Rapids: Zondervan, 1981), 138.

17. Dorothy L. Sayers to the editor of the *Church of England Newspaper*, May 2, 1955, Wade document 328/27, in response to a reader who had misinterpreted her previous letter.

Sayers was able to be good-natured about her theological differences with Calvinist thinkers, saying in May 1941 of Karl Barth, "He is a Calvinist, and accuses me of being a Pelagian—but what is a little total depravity between friends?"[18] She also recognized that "those who take Hell and the devil seriously are always those who have felt the abyss of the consent to evil opening up within themselves."[19] She was well aware of this "consent to evil" in her own life but refused to limit God's activity by her own sinfulness.

Many have written about Sayers's illegitimate child and the unfortunate and painful choices she made in some of her relationships with men and how those choices gave her a humility about her own sinfulness. She was also able to joke about sin, paradoxically. On being reminded that she had confused Asher and Dan in one of her writings, she responded in a letter to Ronald Knox:

> Dear Monsignor Knox,
> I should have written earlier to apologize for having deprived Asher of his breaches and given them to Dan. I confess the fault, which I find in analysis involves a) vainglory (in supposing that one knows one's Bible by heart); b) sloth (in neglecting to verify one's references); c) blasphemy (in perverting the words of Scripture); d) failure to honor one's parents (in that it might lead people to imagine that my father had not instructed me properly, he having been a parson); e) schism (in separating myself from the body of Anglican believers, who hold perfectly sound views about Asher and Dan); f) theft (in misappropriating Asher's property); g) false witness (in making unwarranted assertions about Dan's behaviour).[20]

One of Sayers's most well-known contributions to a theology of sin and evil is her restatement of Christian morality in "The Other Six Deadly Sins." Some may argue that Sayers was fixated on this issue because of her own sexual history and the birth of an illegitimate son, but her arguments about orthodox views of sin are much more encompassing than this. In the essay, she complains:

> Perhaps the bitterest commentary on the way in which Christian doctrine has been taught in the last few centuries is that fact that to the majority

---

18. Dorothy L. Sayers to Maurice Reckitt of Guildford, May 14, 1941, in *Letters of Dorothy L. Sayers*, vol. 2, 259.

19. Dorothy L. Sayers, "The Dogma in the Manger," *VII: An Anglo-American Literary Review* 3 (1982): 42–43.

20. Half of a handwritten letter to Monsignor Ronald Knox, no date given, Wade document 2/8.

of people the word "immorality" has come to mean one thing and one thing only. By a hideous irony, our shrinking reprobation of that sin has made us too delicate so much as to name it, so that we have come to use for it the words which were made to cover the whole range of human corruption. A man may be greedy and selfish; spiteful, cruel, jealous, and unjust; violent and brutal; grasping, unscrupulous, and a liar; stubborn and arrogant; stupid, morose, and dead to every noble instinct—and still we are ready to say of him that he is not an immoral man. I am reminded of a young man who once said to me with perfect simplicity: "I did not know there were seven deadly sins: please tell me the names of the other six."[21]

In *The Seven Deadly Sins in the Work of Dorothy L. Sayers*, Brown rightly notes that Sayers's biggest concern is for the sin of pride.[22] In "The Church's Responsibility," Sayers suggests that the church condemns only those sins it is easy to condemn. It agrees to "a definition of morality so one-sided that it has deformed the very meaning of the word by restricting it to sexual offences. And yet, if every man living were to sleep in his neighbor's bed, it could not bring the world so near shipwreck as that pride, that avarice, and that intellectual sloth which the Church has forgotten to write in the tale of the capital Sins."[23] Her concern for pride drove her play *The Zeal of Thy House*, the story of a craftsman who believed himself better than God.

Sayers recognizes that pride manifests itself not just in people's views of their work but also in their religious attitudes. In "Christian Morality," she reminds us that Jesus was hated in part because he kept company with those the religious authorities considered sinners: people who ate, drank, and were merry. But, she says:

> if we look at the Gospels with the firm intention to discover the *emphasis* of Christ's morality, we shall find that it did not lie at all along the lines laid down by the opinion of highly placed and influential people. Disreputable people who knew they were disreputable were gently told to "go and sin no more"; the really unparliamentary language was reserved for those thrifty, respectable, and sabbatarian citizens who enjoyed Caesar's approval and their own.[24]

21. Dorothy L. Sayers, "The Other Six Deadly Sins," in *Whimsical Christian*, 157.
22. Brown, *Seven Deadly Sins in the Work of Dorothy L. Sayers*, 38.
23. Dorothy L. Sayers, "The Church's Responsibility," in *Malvern, 1941: The Life of the Church and the Order of Society; Being the Proceedings of the Archbishop of York's Conference*, ed. unknown (London: Longmans, Green, & Co., 1942), 72–73.
24. Dorothy L. Sayers, "Christian Morality," in *Whimsical Christian*, 153.

Sayers proposes a revaluing of sin, beginning with reprioritizing values in other areas of life. During the interwar and wartime contexts, Sayers condemned many of the economic choices societies (her own and others) were making. Part of her goal for postwar reconstruction was that people would value different things, which would in turn change what "sins" were grounds for engagement:

> The Churches are justifiably shocked when the glamour of a film actress is assessed by the number of her love affairs and divorces; they are less shocked when the glamour of a man, or of a work of art is headlined in dollars. They are shocked when "unfortunates" are reduced to selling their bodies; they are less shocked when journalists are reduced to selling their souls. They are shocked when good food is wasted by riotous living; they are less shocked when good crops are wasted and destroyed because of over-production and under-consumption. Something has gone wrong with the emphasis; and it is becoming very evident that until that emphasis is readjusted, the economic balance-sheet of the world will have to be written in blood.[25]

The economic choices the country made were a form of gluttony, she believed, but they did not succeed without the complicity, or what in "The Other Six Deadly Sins" she calls the "co-operative gluttony," of consumers.

The wartime context, particularly given the unique totalitarianism manifest during World War II, had another consequence for people's understanding of sin: It brought good and evil into stark contrast. In her foreword to W. A. L. Elmslie's *Five Great Subjects: Broadcast Talks* published in 1943, Sayers hints at the prevailing worldview vis-à-vis evil and how confusing it becomes when world events contradict it. She writes:

> Being told either that good and evil are merely relative, or that he [the common person] can exercise no effective choice between them, he does not know what to do with his moral sense, and with that consciousness of personal inadequacy which a robust and realist Christian philosophy recognizes as a sense of sin. Looking at the world about him, he cannot get rid of the impression that there is guilt somewhere, and that perhaps he himself is not altogether what he might be. The arguments of people who "don't believe in sin" do not remove his sense of guilt; they only make him feel ashamed and guilty about feeling guilty.[26]

25. Ibid., 156.
26. Dorothy L. Sayers, foreword to *Five Great Subjects: Broadcast Talks*, by W. A. L. Elmslie (London: SCM, 1943), 7.

Redemption and Atonement

Questions about guilt and responsibility bring us to Sayers's views on redemption and atonement. In October 1942, Sayers wrote to a friend about the process of producing *The Man Born to Be King*. "One of the actors came up to me during rehearsal, just after we'd been doing the 'My Lord and My God' bit, and said, 'that's the first time I've ever heard the Atonement explained—so as to mean anything, that is.' Which shows the advantage of putting things in words of one syllable, without technical theological terms, and linking them up to the action of the story."[27] Through the vehicle of her plays and other writings, Sayers was able to clarify and explain atonement theology in ways professional theologians could not.

What can be done, given the inevitability of sin and human complicity in it? Sayers found it important to challenge those who objected to Christian theology concerning the consequences of sin. The Christian interpretation of Romans 6:23, "The wages of sin is death," is that the natural consequence of human sin is the finality of death but that the sacrifice of Christ makes it possible for people to live in eternity with God. Those who are not familiar with Christian belief often protest that to deny sinners eternity with God seems an unfair and arbitrary punishment.

Sayers is quick to distinguish between what we might call punishment and consequences. In reference to her play *The Zeal of Thy House*, where her proud lead character falls prey to a terrible tragedy, she argues, "In spite of much abominable and perverted teaching to that effect, there is no evidence that God ever uses arbitrary punishment, in this world or the next; and there is no example of it in this play."[28] William of Sens experienced what Sayers calls "consequential punishment"—the natural consequence of his prideful actions and statements. Sayers uses two analogies in describing consequential punishment: "If you put your hand in the fire, you will be burnt" and "if you drink prussic acid, you will die."[29] She is concerned that people not misunderstand Christians on this point. Human sin leads to death and separation from God as surely as fire burns, even if human sin is

---

27. Dorothy L. Sayers to Marjorie Barber, in *Letters of Dorothy L. Sayers*, vol. 2, 380.

28. Lot 290, id, folder 1/4 titled "material related to performances of *The Zeal of Thy House*." At the very back of this folder is an enticing one-page document titled "Sin and Punishment in *The Zeal of Thy House*."

29. The "hand in the fire" analogy comes from a document from the Sotheby's collection, lot 290, id, folder 1/4 titled "material related to performances of *The Zeal of Thy House*"; and *The Mind of the Maker* (San Francisco: HarperSanFrancisco, 1979), 12. The "drinking prussic acid" analogy appears in Reynolds, *Letters of Dorothy L. Sayers*, vol. 3, 276.

harder to quantify. Therefore, in choosing sin, humans are choosing separation from God; it is a result of our choices, not an arbitrary punishment imposed by God.

In the mid-1940s, Sayers wrote a play she considered her best work to date, *The Just Vengeance*. In the introduction, she calls it "a miracle-play of Man's insufficiency and God's redemptive act"—a play about the atonement.[30] The action of the play is set in wartime, with the death of an aviator who finds he must make a choice whether to receive the message of the cross. He stumbles into Lichfield, where he has an encounter with George Fox. (This is a wonderful example of Sayers's integration of history into her writing. Fox wrote in his journal in the 1600s about a vision he had of Lichfield, and Sayers included it in her play.) Fox reminds the man, "We die into something as we are born into something, but the act of death, like the act of being born, is an individual matter." A parade of dead people, all of whom died for different reasons, present themselves to the airman. Then a choice is put before him: "Son, you have come to the place of the images, as all men come, whose eyes are not shut fast against redemption, drawn to the moment of glory. . . . Wherefore you must make your answer now."[31]

Sayers draws the *Persona Dei* as a character in her play who intones:

> Nay, but the hands
> That made you, hold you still; and since you would not
> Submit to God, God shall submit to you,
> Not of necessity, but free to choose
> For your love's sake what you refused to Mine.
> God shall be man; that which man chose for man
> God shall endure, and what man chose to know
> God shall know too—the experience of evil
> In the flesh of man; and certainly He shall feel
> Terror and judgment and the point of the sword;
> And God shall see God's face set like a flint
> Against Him; and man shall see the image of God
> In the image of man; and man shall show no mercy.
> Truly I will bear your sin and carry your sorrow,
> And, if you will, bring you to the tree of life,
> Where you may eat, and know your evil as good,
> Redeeming that first knowledge. But all this
> Still at your choice, and only as you choose,
> Save as you choose to let Me choose in you.[32]

30. Dorothy L. Sayers, *The Just Vengeance* (London: Victor Gollancz, 1946), 9.
31. Ibid., 15–16, 23.
32. Ibid., 48.

Sayers's theology of the atonement focuses heavily on God's choice to submit, through Jesus' incarnation, to the rules by which God governs the world—freedom of human choice and the consequences thereof. In late 1950, Sayers was contacted by a correspondent who was concerned that Jesus was being "mixed up" with God. Her response makes it clear how Christ's full divinity and full humanity are important to the atonement:

> To me, it is essential to start by saying that Jesus is God—not just "a good man," or "a great teacher," or "a man so much after God's heart that God called Him His Son," or even "a divinely good man." If He is not personally God, the whole story of the crucifixion and atonement is only a cruel injustice, disgraceful to God and man, and of no more saving power than the death of any other victim; and all one succeeds in implanting in the mind of a child, along those lines, is the horrid notion of vicarious punishment, without explanation or justification. Children are frightfully sensitive to injustice, and this gives them a grudge against God which sticks in their minds all their lives. That the God who made the world should Himself bear the pains and penalties of the creatures He made is magnanimity and incomprehensible; that any being less than God should be allowed by God to take the blame is by no means creditable to God, and by no means helpful to man.[33]

Sayers, as a respected writer and an instructed layperson gifted with words, was an important bridge between clergy and theologians, on the one hand, and the British public, on the other, when it came to communicating theology about atonement and redemption. The bishop of Dover contacted her in 1948 on behalf of the archbishop of Canterbury, asking her to address a clergy school about atonement theology. He wrote, "What we hoped to do . . . was to consider the difficulties faced by those who are trying to present the doctrine of the Atonement to a world which thinks in different terms, and how these difficulties can be best met. . . . If Christ crucified was to the Greeks foolishness in the first century, even more so is he to the neo-pagan of to-day. And in what idiom can we get it across?"[34] The bishop refused to allow Sayers's self-proclaimed amateur status to excuse her from this speaking opportunity:

> I am never sure what is meant by the word "amateur." Does an "amateur theologian" mean a moderately competent theologian, or merely one who doesn't make a living out of being a theologian? If the first, I regard it as

33. Dorothy L. Sayers to Mrs. Cicely Hood, December 18, 1950, Wade document 3/15.

34. The bishop of Dover to Dorothy L. Sayers, February 13, 1948, Wade document 198/58.

a most unfair description of yourself. . . . If the second, that might make the Clergy School even more eager to hear what you have to tell them. Once upon a time, King George V. described President Roosevelt to me as being something of an amateur in politics.[35]

In an essay titled "Poetry, Language, and Ambiguity," Sayers provides a helpful overview of the various ways believers have understood atonement over the years, mentioning

the successive images made of the Atonement to fit the changing times. That the soul was in some sense "made free" by Christ was a fact of experience. But it was not, obviously, a historical fact. . . . Images for this were needed. The long religious experience of the Jews produced the image of the vicarious sacrifice; the ram in the thicket, the scapegoat, the Passover lamb; the burnt-offering and the sin-offering and the trespass-offering. To the Gentiles of the Roman Empire another image was suggested: to them a literal slavery was a reality only too familiar; it produced the image of the ransom. The rising bourgeois civilization of the Medieval West tended to find itself in bondage to the usurer and harassed by suits in the civil courts; the dominant image became . . . the image of the just debt. . . . In the nineteenth century, the Evangelical movement, for some reason at present obscure to me, was much obsessed with dirt, and inclined in its images to gather at the river and to be washed in the Blood of the Lamb. . . . The peculiar *Angst* of our own age—socially and financially secure by comparison, aesthetically revolted by blood-baths and crimson fountains, and too dogmatically egalitarian to desire anybody's sacrificial charity—has taken a new form, predominantly morbid and medical. This has most interestingly produced an entirely new set of Atonement images, of which the central symbol is Christ the Healer.[36]

Some of Sayers's most interesting work on the atonement appears in her essay "Forgiveness and the Enemy," a timely message published in 1941. She wrestles with humans' capacity to forgive and the relationship between atonement and forgiveness in our relationship with God. Sayers mentions that while human beings often set conditions on their forgiveness of others, "if we assert that Divine forgiveness is of this bargaining kind, we meet with a thundering denial from poet and prophet and from God Himself."[37] Forgiveness, she argues, is not fundamentally about the elimination of consequences or punishment:

35. Ibid.
36. Dorothy L. Sayers, "Poetry, Language, and Ambiguity," in *The Poetry of Search and the Poetry of Statement* (London: Victor Gollancz, 1963), 282–83.
37. Dorothy L. Sayers, "Forgiveness and the Enemy," *Fortnightly* 149 (April 1941): 379.

It may be easier to understand what forgiveness is, if we first clear away misconceptions about what it does. It does not wipe out the consequences of the sin. The words and images used for forgiveness in the New Testament frequently have to do with the cancellation of a debt: and it is scarcely necessary to point out that when a debt is cancelled, this does not mean that the money is miraculously restored from nowhere. It means only that the obligation originally due from the borrower is voluntarily discharged by the lender. If I injure you and you mulct me in damages, then I bear the consequences; if you forbear to prosecute, then you bear the consequences. If the injury is irreparable, and you are vindictive, injury is added to injury; if you are forgiving and I am repentant, then we share the consequences and gain a friendship. But in every case the consequences are born by somebody.[38]

"Forgiveness," defines Sayers, "is the re-establishment of a right relationship, in which the parties can genuinely feel and behave as freely with one another as though the unhappy incident had never taken place."[39] Sayers brings this thinking to bear upon the events of her day:

The issue is not really affected by arguments about who began first, or whether bombs or blockade are the more legitimate weapon to use against women and children, or whether a civilian is a military objective; nor need we object that no amount of forgiveness will do away with the consequences of the crimes—since we have already seen that forgiveness is not incompatible with consequence. The real question is this: When the war comes to an end, is there going to be anything in our minds, or in the minds of the enemy, that will prevent the re-establishment of a right relationship? That relationship need not necessarily be one of equal power on either side, and it need not exclude proper preventative measures against a renewal of conflict—those considerations are again irrelevant. Are there any crimes that in themselves make forgiveness and right relations impossible?[40]

Sayers challenges those among her contemporaries who believe forgiveness of their enemies is impossible by reminding them of the "monstrous and shattering paradox" in the New Testament—that the murder of God was forgiven because "they know not what they do."[41] In exploring the restoration of relationship with God, she rightly points out that right relationship is not experienced when the offender still feels guilty about the offense or still bears ill will toward the offended

38. Ibid., 380.
39. Ibid., 381.
40. Ibid., 381–82.
41. Ibid., 382.

so that, while God does not, and man dare not, demand repentance as a condition for *bestowing* pardon, repentance remains an essential condition for *receiving* it. Hence the Church's twofold insistence—first that repentance is necessary, and secondly that all sin is pardoned instantly in the mere fact of the sinner's repentance. Nobody has to sit about being humiliated in the outer office while God dispatches important business, before condescending to issue a stamped official discharge accompanied by an improving lecture. Like the Father of the Prodigal Son, God can see repentance coming a great way off and is there to meet it, and the repentance *is* the reconciliation.[42]

Sayers once described Christianity as the only religion that believed God could "wrench a positive good out of a real evil." In her poem "Obsequies for Music," Sayers draws a picture of Jesus as a gardener who comes to bury the dead hopes, hatreds, pasts, and loves of human beings:

> These therefore came with shows and sound
> Unto a hallowed space of ground,
> Wherein a young and radiant priest
> Stood. On his shoulder was a spade,
> And there with shining hands he made
> A garden, looking toward the east.[43]

42. Ibid., 381.
43. Dorothy L. Sayers, "Obsequies for Music," in *Poetry of Dorothy L. Sayers*, ed. Ralph E. Hone (Cambridge: Dorothy L. Sayers Society in association with the Marion E. Wade Center, 1996), 103.

7

Work, Vocation, and Business Ethics

Christian people . . . must get it firmly into their heads that when a man or woman is called to a particular job of secular work, that is as true a vocation as though he or she were called to specifically religious work. . . . Then all the work will be Christian work, whether it is Church embroidery or sewage farming.

Dorothy L. Sayers, Wade document 11/23–25

*A*s this chapter was being written, another dissatisfied American worker shot up his workplace, killing several coworkers and terrorizing others in a rage against . . . what? Working conditions? People he perceived had betrayed him? The economy that drove him to work there in the first place? Dorothy L. Sayers would call his workplace despair and ensuing anger a direct result of the fall. Sayers held distinct views of work, its roots in vocation, and the ramifications for workers and those supervising them. These views, in turn, depended on Sayers's theological understanding of humanity made in God's image.

One of the strongest themes throughout Sayers's writing relates to vocation and work. While Sayers's theology of work comes forth most strongly in *The Mind of the Maker*, her play *The Zeal of Thy House*, and three essays on work ("Living to Work," "Vocation in Work," and "Why Work?"), it also permeates her letters, other essays, several unpublished manuscripts, and many of her mysteries. One scholar suggested in the early 1980s that "the most important subject which Sayers chooses to consider in the detective stories is not, surprisingly, good vs. evil, or even the illumination of crime; rather, she is concerned with work."[1] Kathleen Gregory Klein notes that most of the Wimsey novels centering around a murder "show the murder committed in a manner which betrays the murderer's profession or craft. The characters who kill are thus doubly condemned by Sayers's standards: first, for not respecting life, and second, for not respecting their work."[2] Integrity in intellectual work is a central theme in one of Sayers's most popular novels, *Gaudy Night*. Sayers's letters are also filled with protests against people who invite her to write outside her perceived range and calling.

Theological Reflections on Work and Vocation

It is impossible to understand Sayers's views on work and business ethics, two central elements in her writing, without first exploring her theology of vocation. This she locates in the first chapter of Genesis. In Genesis 1:27, we learn that humanity is created in the image of God. Sayers asks what is unique about that image in which we are created; to answer this, she looks to the first twenty-six verses in Genesis. The main image of God seen in those verses is that of Creator. Sayers proposes in *The Mind of the Maker* that if most of what we know of God in verses 1 through 26 is that God creates, and we are told in verse 27 that humans are made in the image of God, then being creative (what she calls "the desire and the ability to make things") is the main characteristic common to God and humanity.[3]

For Sayers, this link between humanity and its Creator is not mere semantics or an accident of verse arrangement by biblical redactors. Being creative is a critical part of our humanity. The human being "makes things—. . . an interminable variety of different and not strictly necessary things—because he wants to. . . . He cannot fulfill his true nature if he is prevented from making things for the love of the job;

---

1. Kathleen Gregory Klein, "Dorothy Sayers," in *Ten Women of Mystery*, ed. Earl F. Bargainner (Bowling Green, OH: Bowling Green State University Popular Press, 1981), 29.
2. Ibid., 32.
3. Dorothy L. Sayers, *The Mind of the Maker* (San Francisco: HarperSanFrancisco, 1979), 22.

he is made in the image of the Maker, and he must himself create or become something less than a man."[4] According to this understanding, anything that threatens or inhibits our creativity also threatens our very humanity. The most essential human vocation, in Sayers's theology, is to make or to create.

What are the implications of Sayers's theology for workers and employers as they go about their daily lives? In Sayers's ideal world, every human being would be engaged regularly in work that has a creative component. According to what she calls "the gospel of work," all work must allow people to fulfill their vocation by being creative, or else it cheats them of their essential humanity. Sayers values work that allows people to reflect in pride and say, "Look at what I made today." Her hope is for a world in which there is little distinction between one's calling and one's work: Work is a vocation, and every worker feels called to what he or she is doing. Harriet Vane reflects in *Gaudy Night* that "to be true to one's calling, whatever follies one might commit in one's emotional life, that was the way to spiritual peace."[5] She later comments to Miss DeVine about a passionate devotion to one's calling: "When you get the thing dead right and know it's dead right, there's no excitement like it. It makes you feel like God on the Seventh Day—for a bit, anyhow."[6]

People do not bring guns to work and shoot their coworkers in Sayers's ideal world. People do such things because their work is demeaning, what Sayers calls "soul-deadening," somehow contrary to their calling as humans and as makers. Sayers recognizes that some employment, such as assembly-line work, does not often provide creative possibilities for workers.[7] In June 1943, the bishop of Pretoria challenged Sayers after reading her essay "Why Work?" He asked if she were suggesting that all factory workers should quit their jobs or whether it would actually be possible for them to see their work as a vocation. While acknowledging that a Christian worker, at least, could certainly make safety pins to the glory of God, Sayers also suggests that it would be criminal to ask someone to spend their entire life making one small part of a safety pin.[8] She would applaud those companies that allow their workers to assist one product all the way down the assembly line from start to fin-

---

4. Dorothy L. Sayers, "Vocation in Work," in *A Christian Basis for the Post-War*, ed. Albert E. Baker (New York: Morehouse-Gorham, 1942), 89–90.

5. Dorothy L. Sayers, *Gaudy Night* (New York: Avon Books, 1968), 28.

6. Ibid., 149.

7. The 2003 film *Seabiscuit* (Universal Pictures) begins with a description of the advent of the assembly line: "It was the beginning and the end of imagination, all at the same time."

8. Dorothy L. Sayers to the bishop of Pretoria, June 21, 1943, Wade document 410/33. See document 410/36 for his original letter.

ish. While this method may seem inefficient in purely economic terms, it provides variety for workers and also allows them the pride of seeing the finished product.

Sayers actually found an employer sympathetic to this way of running a business, T. M. Heron, and invited him to contribute a book to a series she was editing. Sayers said of Heron in an April 1941 letter, "He does understand what it's all about—as very few employers of labour do; and if he can't write the thing himself, he can give us the stuff, both from the men's point of view and his own."[9] Unfortunately, Heron was called into government service and never finished the book. The Bridgeheads series was, according to Sayers's biographer and friend Barbara Reynolds, "a series of books . . . on social, moral and theological subjects, aimed at encouraging the public to think creatively and constructively about the future" after World War II.[10] Sayers's *Mind of the Maker* was the first volume in the Bridgeheads series. She saw creativity as playing a vital role in postwar reconstruction in Britain. The Statement of Aims for Bridgeheads sets forth this ambitious goal: "We shall try to quicken the creative spirit which enables man to build . . . systems in the light of his spiritual, intellectual, and social needs. We aim at the Resurrection of Faith, the Revival of Learning and the Re-integration of Society."[11] In an April 1941 letter, Sayers even uses explicitly sacramental language about creativity, hoping that the other Bridgeheads writers will see their work as "the outward and visible sign of a creative reality."[12]

What of those people who are in factory labor and do not see it as something they can do "as unto the Lord"? In that same letter, Sayers recognizes the "profound gulf between the work to which we are 'called' and the work we are forced into as a means of livelihood."[13] In "Vocation in Work," she encourages these workers to find "some creative and satisfying hobby at least" as an outlet for their creative energies.[14] If work itself cannot be creative, then let what people do outside their work be. For Sayers, mystery novels were a means of supporting her family and financing other kinds of writing she preferred to do. She calls her mysteries "potboilers" and agrees that "a great deal of necessary work *is* in the nature of a pot-boiler, and . . . it ought to be arranged so as

9. Dorothy L. Sayers to V. A. Demant, April 10, 1941, in *The Letters of Dorothy L. Sayers*, vol. 2, ed. Barbara Reynolds (Cambridge: Dorothy L. Sayers Society, 1997), 248.

10. Barbara Reynolds, *Dorothy L. Sayers: Her Life and Soul* (New York: St. Martin's Press, 1993), 299.

11. Ibid., 308.

12. Sayers to V. A. Demant, April 10, 1941, in *Letters of Dorothy L. Sayers*, vol. 2, 247.

13. Ibid., 248.

14. Sayers, "Vocation in Work," 97.

to boil the pot as quickly as possible and in such a way that nobody's pot remains without a fire to boil it."[15] Sayers did not advocate doing poor work. Her own potboilers were generally of high quality, and she encourages the same for others.

In addition to challenging workers and employers alike to permit creative expression in work, Sayers confronts larger economic systems. For example, she condemns measuring human value only in financial terms. Doing so encourages a hatred of work, a lack of motivation on the workers' part, and the production of useless material just to make money. Sayers returns to her theology of vocation again in this tirade from "Vocation in Work": "Ask whether men made in the image of God can or should be required to dedicate their lives to the production of all this junk of china-dogs, patent medicines, telephone-dolls, nail-varnishes, crooner-music, trash novels, and general rubbish and nonsense with which commerce has cluttered the world."[16] She finds it insulting to God and to God's image in us for human work to be used for such low commercial ends. Sayers is especially vituperative about the kinds of items sold in Christian bookstores, seeing low-grade kitsch being made, sold, and bought in the name of the God whose image we represent.[17] But she also questions whether work should primarily be about manufacturing employment and worthless products, paying farmers not to grow crops, and wasting products or sending them to other countries because they are not good enough for our own. These practices corrupt the workers' sense of purpose so much, she writes in April 1941, that "they can neither get satisfaction from their work nor employ their labor in creation."[18] The very existence of the *Dilbert* cartoon franchise testifies that these problems are still with us.

What is it about work that makes it so hateful to some people? In "Vocation in Work" and "Why Work?" Sayers distinguishes between two main perspectives on work, what she calls "working to live" and "living to work." Some people see work as "a hateful necessity, whose only use is to make money for them, so that they can escape from work and do something else."[19] For these people, work exists only to help them live the rest of their lives, to support their leisure. Others, Sayers observes, tend to "look upon their work as an opportunity for self-fulfillment. They

15. Ibid., 96–97.
16. Ibid., 98–99.
17. Christian organizations in general often rouse Sayers's ire because she finds that they tend to do work of poor quality and are less than honest in some of their business dealings, in the name of having their minds on higher things.
18. Sayers to V. A. Demant, April 10, 1941, in *Letters of Dorothy L. Sayers*, vol. 2, 248.
19. Dorothy L. Sayers, "Living to Work," in *Unpopular Opinions* (New York: Harcourt, Brace, & Co., 1947), 150.

only want to make money so that they may be free to devote themselves more single-mindedly to their work. . . . If they were to be cut off from their work, they would feel that they were cut off from life."[20] For these people, work is life giving, fulfilling a fundamental human need.

What distinguishes the toil of those who love work from that of those who hate it? In "Living to Work," Sayers includes artists, scholars, and scientists, people passionate about making and discovering things, among those who live to work. This category also encompasses engineers, farmers, priests, teachers, doctors, skilled mechanics, explorers and sailors, craftspeople, some full-time mothers, and nurses, "in whom we recognise a clear spiritual vocation—a call to what is sometimes very hard and exacting work—. . . whose work is something more to them than a mere means of livelihood."[21]

Those who hate work are not necessarily only people doing hard, disgusting, uninteresting, or ill-paid work. Sayers also lumps the "idle rich" into this category.[22] Citing the fact that many readily invest ample time and money in hobbies with little or no economic return, she suggests that money should not be one's primary purpose for working or for evaluating work.[23] In *The Mind of the Maker*, she reminds readers that the amount of money one earns is not necessarily proportional to one's satisfaction in that work "and that what we ought to be asking is a totally different set of questions about work and money."[24] Why,

20. Ibid.
21. Ibid., 151. She acknowledges that these categories of work share three characteristics: (1) The work allows individual initiative; (2) it allows workers to "view with satisfaction the final results of their labour," however detailed or laborious the work might be; and (3) the work follows what Sayers calls the "natural rhythm of the human mind and body" without binding the worker to the "monotonous, relentless, deadly pace of an inhuman machine" (ibid., 154).
22. She suggests that what makes someone hate his or her work is the attitude that person takes toward work and money. Work haters, according to Sayers, see money as something that "saves them from the curse of work. . . . Work is something hateful, only to be endured because it makes money; and money is desirable because it represents a way of escape from work" (ibid., 151).
23. See the "Sword of the Spirit" manuscript, Wade MS-243/7.
24. Sayers, *Mind of the Maker*, 203. In "Why Work?" she elaborates on what those "different questions" might be: "We should ask of an enterprise, not 'will it pay?' but 'is it good?'; of a man, not 'what does he make?' but 'what is his work worth?'; of goods, not 'can we induce people to buy them?' but 'are they useful things well made?'; of employment, not 'how much a week?' but 'will it exercise my faculties to the utmost?' And shareholders in—let us say—brewing companies, would astonish the directorate by arising at shareholders' meetings and demanding to know, not merely where the profits go or what dividends are to be paid, not even merely whether the workers' wages are sufficient and the conditions of labour satisfactory, but loudly, and with a proper sense of personal responsibility: What goes into the beer?" (Dorothy L. Sayers, "Why Work?" in *Creed or Chaos?* [New York: Harcourt, Brace, & Co., 1949], 52).

she asks, do actors and artists so eagerly live to work, while factory workers, though often far better paid, reluctantly work to live? Sayers wonders how much money people would need, beyond the subsistence that enables them to continue working, if the world admired work more than wealth.

The possibility of work's being an enemy is not a new one. In fact, it is usually traced back to the fall. In *The Zeal of Thy House*, one of the angels states outright that "the hatred of work must be one of the most depressing consequences of the Fall."[25] French lay thinker Jacques Ellul, responding to a comment by Karl Barth about choosing one's vocation, counters that a biblical view of work "shows it to be a consequence of sin and 'the painful lot of all men' but hardly the fulfillment of one's life."[26] Ellul believes that viewing work as a vocation is not possible in a technological society "where work is governed not by personal predilections but by the rules of efficiency. . . . Work is a matter of necessity for survival."[27]

Ellul, as he writes in *The Ethics of Freedom*, does not find a biblical precedent for viewing work as a vocation.[28] In stating this point, he cites what he believes is an often misused portion of Scripture, suggesting, "How misleading it is to deduce from Genesis 1:28: 'Replenish the earth and subdue it,' the idea that work is a divine vocation! We simply have to work—that is all."[29]

Sayers, however, does not locate work as a calling in that part of Genesis but rather in our being created in God's image and therefore creative. Furthermore, she interprets the curse in Genesis 3:17, "Cursed is the ground because of you; through painful toil you will eat of it all the days of your life," differently. While Ellul and others view work per se as a curse and a consequence of sin, Sayers does not see the *fact* of work as the real curse. In "Vocation in Work," she clarifies her understanding of the curse and takes to task those who see work as a consequence of the fall: "Can we really believe that the writer of Genesis supposed the unfallen happiness of Adam and Eve to consist in interminable idle-

25. Dorothy L. Sayers, *The Zeal of Thy House* (London: Victor Gollancz, 1939), 13.

26. Darrell Fasching, *The Thought of Jacques Ellul: A Systematic Exposition* (Toronto: Edwin Mellen Press, 1942), 152. Sayers, noting that in general Scripture is not particularly explicit on the subject of work, refers to the view held by Ellul and others as "an unimaginative interpretation of the famous passage in Genesis about the curse of Adam" (Sayers, "Vocation in Work," 89).

27. Fasching, *Thought of Jacques Ellul*, 152.

28. Jacques Ellul, *The Ethics of Freedom* (Grand Rapids: Eerdmans, 1976), 496. See also Jacques Ellul, "Work and Calling," *Katallagete* 4, nos. 2–3 (Fall–Winter 1972): 8, where Ellul suggests, "Nothing in the Bible allows us to identify *work* with *calling*."

29. Ellul, *Ethics of Freedom*, 496.

ness?" Sayers finds the operative part of the curse in the phrase "through painful toil you will eat of it": "Work was to be conditioned by economic necessity—that was the new and ominous thing."[30] Economic necessity, not work itself, is the curse of the fall in Sayers's theology.

She worries that if people see work as a result of the fall, work will lose all possible sacramental value for them. "Yet the whole of Christian doctrine centres round the great paradox of redemption, which asserts that the very pains and sorrows by which fallen man is encompassed can become instruments of his salvation, if they are accepted and transmuted by love."[31] To begin with an assumption that work must be a curse or simply a means of meeting economic needs leaves God out of the realm of vocation and work entirely. Sayers's preference is to see work as a sacramental act, "the creative activity that can redeem the world."[32] She believes Christians can provide a tabernacle for God in their work, and in many ways she embodies this. Work, for Sayers, is an expression, an offering, of prayer and worship to God. As she told one audience, "Christianity demands that *all* work should be done in a Christian way—Christianity proclaims that *all* work, all that is well done, does reveal God and may be offered to God in worship."[33]

Prescience or Naïveté?

Was Sayers's view of work and vocation—and its implications for society—naïve? In a 1948 letter, she wrote, tongue in cheek, "When I first began to talk on the subject, the Gospel of Work was usually dismissed as the dream of a literary person unrelated to the needs and desires of the working man; now, serious-minded people have begun to admit that it is not undesirable but only impossible—so that we may say that some progress has been made in the right direction."[34] Sayers suggests that her role as a Christian thinker is to expose evil where it may be present, whereas it is the job of industrial experts to find workable remedies for such problems.[35] If people do not agree that existing systems are evil, there will be no support for changing them.

30. Sayers, "Vocation in Work," 90–91.
31. Ibid., 89–90.
32. Ibid., 104.
33. Dorothy L. Sayers, address delivered at St. Martin's in the Fields, February 6, 1942, Wade document 486/134.
34. Dorothy L. Sayers to Rev. W. H. J. Mercer of York, September 14, 1948, Wade document 235/14.
35. Dorothy L. Sayers to the editor of the *Manchester Guardian*, November 5, 1942, Wade document 346/30.

Admittedly, most industrial experts who *have* brought about changes along the lines Sayers recommends have done so for profit more than because of a driving theological conviction. Some factory owners have realized that, even though piecework is more "efficient," workers are ultimately more productive if their morale is higher. Higher morale comes from allowing workers to follow a product all the way down the assembly line or at least to avoid repetitive tasks in the workplace.[36] Industrial literature reveals a move toward teams, even in assembly-line environments, and warnings about repetitive-strain injuries encourage employers to add variety to the tasks their workers complete.[37] These pragmatic motives for avoiding the more "soul-deadening" aspects of factory work still accomplish some of what Sayers advocates.[38]

Many industrial firms have also been influenced by the Toyota Production System (TPS), a move away from traditional assembly-line production.[39] While this system has enabled Toyota to produce consistently excellent automobiles, the values behind it are not solely profit driven. One of the principles underlying the Toyota system is respect for humanity.[40] This principle, while clearly conditioned by financial mo-

36. Volvo's short-lived Udewalla plant is probably the most radical example of these ideas being integrated into the real world: "Instead of one long moving line, forty parallel teams built complete cars at stationary 'docks,' producing three or four cars per team each shift. . . . Team members . . . took responsibility for coordination of whole car assembly as well as three major sub-assemblies. . . . Team members also managed the monthly rotation of job assignments. . . . Wages for individual workers rose according to a pay-for-knowledge system, with the top rate corresponding to 'whole-car competence'—a status attained after . . . passing a test requiring whole-car assembly in twenty hours or less with a maximum of four minor defects" (Christian Berggren, "Are Assembly Lines Just More Efficient? Reflections on Volvo's 'Humanistic' Manufacturing," in *Lean Work: Empowerment and Exploitation in the Global Auto Industry*, ed. Steve Babson [Detroit: Wayne State University Press, 1995], 278).

37. Frits K. Pil and John Paul MacDuffie find in the literature a variety of human-resource factors that are influencing changes in manufacturing: "team-based production methods, worker participation in problem solving, job rotation, a small number of job classifications, few distinctions between management and employees, and high-training levels" ("Transferring Competitive Advantage across Borders," in *Remade in America: Transplanting and Transforming Japanese Management Systems*, ed. Jeffrey K. Liker et al. [Oxford: Oxford University Press, 1999], 42–43).

38. See also Toby D. Wall, Chris W. Clegg, and Nigel J. Kemp, *The Human Side of Advanced Manufacturing Technology* (New York: John Wiley & Sons, 1987).

39. See Jeffrey K. Liker, *Becoming Lean: Inside Stories of U.S. Manufacturers* (Portland, OR: Productivity Press, 1997). Many aspects of this system, including human-resource management, have translated well to automobile manufacturing firms in the United States. Other types of industries have adapted the system to their purposes with varying degrees of success (see Liker, *Remade in America*).

40. "Respect for humanity, which must be cultivated while the system utilizes human resources to attain its cost objectives," plays out in the TPS through giving workers

tives, represents an acknowledgment that real people, not just machines, are part of the production process and that their needs and limitations must be taken into account.

Harvard Graduate School of Education's Howard Gardner recently studied work and worker satisfaction. He and two colleagues set out to define work that is good in two senses: It exhibits a high level of expertise, and it entails regular concern with the implications and applications of an individual's work for the wider world.[41] In *Good Work: When Excellence and Ethics Meet*, Gardner and his colleagues encourage workers to embrace a sense of mission in their work—to revisit why one entered into that work and how it might serve society. These questions, while not directly asked by Sayers, are similar to the kinds of issues she raises in her theology of work.

We are also fortunate to have a comparative analysis of some of Sayers's thought and that of some of her contemporaries written fifty years after she published her writings on vocation and work. In January 1941, then-archbishop William Temple convened a conference titled "The Life of the Church and the Order of Society" at Malvern. The conference was convened to "consider from the Anglican point of view what are the fundamental facts which are directly relevant to the ordering of the new society, and how Christian thought can be shaped to play a leading part in the reconstruction."[42] There was concern that not enough thought had gone into reconstructing Britain after the First World War and that a more concerted effort should be put into this new reconstruction. One of the guiding questions of the conference was how Christianity might guide a person "in the organization of his natural activity regarding his home and family, and the political and economic realities of his nature."[43] Sayers, the only woman speaking at

---

significant work and maintaining open communication throughout the organization. This includes encouraging workers to make suggestions on how to improve production processes and involving them in quality-control teams (Yasuhiro Monden, *Toyota Production System: An Integrated Approach to Just-in-Time*, 2nd ed. [Norcross, GA: Industrial Engineering and Management Press, 1993], 185–86).

41. Howard Gardner, Mihaly Csikszentmihalyi, and William Damon, *Good Work: When Excellence and Ethics Meet* (New York: Basic Books, 2002).

42. *Malvern, 1941: The Life of the Church and the Order of Society; Being the Proceedings of the Archbishop of York's Conference*, ed. unknown (London: Longmans, Green, & Co., 1942), ix.

43. Ibid., xi. The Malvern Declaration, drafted by William Temple in an effort to synthesize the findings of the conference, speaks to work and vocation in several respects. Participants proposed a rethinking of the purposes of work so that workers "should find in the work of production a sphere of truly human activity, and the doing of it should be for the producer a part of the 'good life' and not only his way of earning a livelihood" (David Arthur, *The Malvern Declaration of 1941: The Original Text Together with a Com-*

the conference, addressed this challenge in a presentation published as "The Church's Responsibility."

One of the organizing bodies of the 1941 Malvern conference was the Industrial Christian Fellowship (ICF).[44] In 1991, a fiftieth-anniversary celebration of the Malvern conference took place, for which the ICF published a copy of the original Malvern documents along with a commentary by David Arthur, national secretary of the ICF. Arthur's commentary assesses the aims of the original Malvern conference in light of the succeeding fifty years of British history. This provides a wonderful glimpse, from an industrial perspective, of how the convictions Sayers and her contemporaries espoused may or may not have influenced the society in which they lived. Arthur begins, "It is a very different world. So we are tempted to give the Malvern Declaration merely a passing glance, and to put it aside, as a historical curiosity of passing interest. It is, however, because we believe that it contains important messages for our new world . . . that ICF has decided to re-print and re-issue" the document.[45]

Arthur's commentary does acknowledge the difficulty of discerning exactly how the Malvern conference influenced postwar reconstruction in Britain, but he believes at the very least that it affected public opinion. He observes:

The General Election of 1945 clearly signalled the nation's desire for a change, and the subsequent developments in the Welfare State, Education, the National Health Service, the redistribution of wealth through higher taxes, death duties and social benefits, and the nationalisation of major industries, were all broadly in line with the Malvern principles and

---

mentary [Orpington, UK: Industrial Christian Fellowship, 1991], 25). They called for the "restoration of man's economic activity to its proper place as the servant of his whole personal life, and the expression of his status in the natural world as a child of God for whom Christ died" (ibid., 26). Their recommendations also exhorted that "the Church should strive to keep alive in all men and in all functional groups a sense of vocation by constantly calling upon them to consider what is the purpose of their various activities, and to keep this true to the purpose of God for His people" (ibid., 27).

44. "The aim of ICF is to change attitudes towards the world of work, by helping people to find a fuller sense of God's purpose in their working lives. Particularly:

• Helping Christians to realize that in their work they serve both God and neighbour, and that Faith, Work and Worship are all one.

• Encouraging everyone to apply Christian values in their daily work, and helping people resolve the moral dilemmas which they often face.

• Exhorting the Churches to support people in their work, and to declare the importance and value of all people's work in generating wealth for the common good.

• Persuading industry, commerce and business to operate within a set of principles and moral values, based on Christian teaching" (ibid., 29).

45. Ibid., 1.

recommendations. Now, forty years on, many of these things are taken for granted.[46]

Arthur believes that contemporary Christians in Britain, at least, can concur with many of the economic sentiments of the Malvern Declaration, but the economic situation is so different that intellectual assent may not make much difference in real-world industrial and economic realities.[47] He does note the many advances made in improving conditions for factory workers:

> In parts of industry and the whole world of work, much has been learned about "what makes people tick," how to help them develop their skills and abilities and to become the best of which they are capable. . . . Many tasks have been re-designed to give more job-satisfaction, and employees have a greater understanding of how their own tasks fit in to the achievement of the overall purpose of creativity and the service which their company provides.[48]

Unfortunately, these trends are not consistent from factory to factory or from company to company, and new technologies merely raise new ethical issues.

The specific arena of vocation, and the church's ability to affirm the vocation and daily work of its people, is one area Arthur finds distinctly lacking, but he says little more about it.

Overall, it is fair to say that, while some of Sayers's specific goals may not have been realized (and perhaps are not realizable in today's economy), certainly the questions she raised about work and vocation are still important arenas of discussion. Humanity's relationship to God the Creator and how we live out our calling as "subcreators" will always be worthy of consideration. Sayers's words before World War II even drew to a close still ring true today: "We must look to it that our aims, both as individuals and as a society, shall be such that we can fittingly worship and show forth God in the work of our fingers and in the work of our brains."[49]

---

46. Ibid., 3.

47. He argues, "Most Christians today would have no problem in agreeing with the underlying principles, that the proper place of man's economic activity is as his servant and not his master, and that a way of life founded on the *supremacy* of the economic motive is contrary to God's plan for mankind" (ibid., 9).

48. Ibid., 11.

49. Sayers, address delivered at St. Martin's in the Fields, Wade document 486/140.

8

Words and Language

We must bring imagination to the task of communicating thought. The task grows harder every day because of the multitude of techniques, because of the proliferation of meaningless verbiage, and also because the younger generations have been steadily deprived of the four great traditional safeguards: formal logic and the Latin Grammar, which were a negative defence against fallacy and slipshod syntax; a dogmatic theology and the habit of great verse, which were a positive education in the handling of the magical images.

Dorothy L. Sayers, "Poetry, Language, and Ambiguity"

*O*ne of the joys of reading Dorothy L. Sayers is her mastery of the English language. She has both the creativity and the fluency to use the language with precision, grace, and humor. In 1948, her letters begin to mention the addition of a pig to her household. Sayers enjoyed the animals she kept for food, naming her chickens after Jane Austen characters (the exploits of Elinor and Marianne, complete with illustrations, are especially amusing) and calling her pigs by names like Fatima and Francis Bacon. One reads through the letters fully expecting that one day Sayers will tell someone that she and her husband have

123

eaten their first pig. This being too prosaic for her, she writes instead that "the pig has gone to a place of which Moses would not approve."[1] This vivid statement captures concisely the gifts Sayers's language and theological facility bring together.

Many frustrated readers would agree with Sayers that "a passage is not plain English—still less is it good English—if we are obliged to read it twice to find out what it means."[2] Some of Sayers's most articulate, passionate, and amusing writing is on the subject of language gone awry, not unlike Lynne Truss's recent best-seller on punctuation titled *Eats, Shoots, and Leaves*. In Sayers's essay "Plain English," written before World War II, she critiques a newspaper passage:

> With an incredulous and almost religious awe we see looming up out of this syntactical fog a whacking great participial construction, of the kind that used to terrify us when we did Latin in the fourth form, with the participle at the beginning, the verb in the middle and the subject at the end. . . . This may be vigorous—it is certainly startling and even shocking—but it is not English. Neither is it modern, nor clear, nor economical. It is a cumbersome, antiquated, outlandish, obfuscating, verbose bore and nuisance.[3]

Before the war, Sayers the literary critic may have enjoyed using her considerable linguistic skills to denigrate those not quite as gifted as she or to advocate for clarity of communication. But soon she realized that the right use of words had life-or-death implications and that we neglect language to our peril. As early as 1936, Sayers recognized the impoverishment of contemporary educational methods, which had gutted curriculum of the foundational elements of language. Before she had even composed her classical education manifesto *The Lost Tools of Learning*, Sayers observed, "The wisdom of modern educators has freed our children from the shackles of a classical training, and this is about as sensible as freeing young draughtsmen from the study of anatomy. The result in either case is the same: a drawing and an English alike spineless, nerveless, slack-sinewed, ugly, lumpy and meaningless."[4]

1. This phrase has stayed with me ever since I read through the letters in the Wade archive in 1996, although I never wrote down its specific source. See Leviticus 11:7 for the mosaic prohibitions on eating meat from animals with cloven hooves.

2. Dorothy L. Sayers, "Plain English," in *Unpopular Opinions* (New York: Harcourt, Brace, & Co., 1947), 98.

3. Ibid., 100–101.

4. Dorothy L. Sayers, "The English Language," in *Unpopular Opinions*, 108.

In *The Lost Tools of Learning*, Sayers proposes a return to the medieval educational method called the Trivium, a three-tiered structure in which basic skills build on one another:

> The whole of the Trivium was, in fact, intended to teach the pupil the proper use of the tools of learning. . . . First he learned a language . . . what it was, how it was put together and how it worked. Secondly, he learned how to use language: how to define his terms and make accurate statements; how to construct an argument and how to detect fallacies in argument (his own arguments and other people's). . . . Thirdly, he learned how to express himself in language; how to say what he had to say elegantly and persuasively.[5]

Falling Prey to Propaganda

World War II brought with it a double menace: widespread literacy combined with propaganda. If the English educational system had still taught ways of reading and using language critically, people may not have been susceptible to the linguistic machinations of propaganda. However, in the absence of adequate training in the use of words, Sayers found her country's citizens vulnerable to being manipulated by language:

> For we let our young men and women go out unarmed, in a day when armour was never so necessary. By teaching them all to read, we have left them at the mercy of the printed word. By the invention of the film and the radio, we have made certain that no aversion to reading shall secure them from the incessant battery of words, words, words. They do not know what the words mean; they do not know how to ward them off or blunt their edge or fling them back; they are a prey to words in their emotions instead of being the masters of them in their intellects. We who were scandalized in 1940 when men were sent to fight armoured tanks with rifles, are not scandalized when young men and women are sent into the world to fight massed propaganda with a smattering of "subjects"; and when whole classes and whole nations become hypnotized by the arts of the spell-binder, we have the impudence to be astonished.[6]

As early as 1939, Sayers recognized this menace and addressed it in "The Dictatorship of Words," a speech to fellow writers in the Modern Language Association. She asked them to think about whether "juggling with words at such a time" was an act of innocence (like children "stringing daisy chains" while their house burned over their heads) or

5. Dorothy L. Sayers, *The Lost Tools of Learning* (London: Methuen, 1948), 8–9.
6. Ibid., 12–13.

a powerful weapon (like "playing with detonators in a factory full of high explosive").[7] She noted that German propaganda writers were instructed to copy British propaganda methods, which had been instrumental in weakening Germany in the past. Noting that propaganda could be "used for creative and desirable ends" as well as for destructive ends, she proposed that writers in wartime "must fight the word with the word."[8]

Part of Sayers's concern was that communication methods in the mid-twentieth century had made it possible for large quantities of information to be disseminated quickly—more so than during previous wars and eras. People had a great deal of information at their disposal, and there was almost universal literacy among adults in her country at the time. This would not necessarily present a problem, but "to be *literate* is not the same thing as to be *educated*. Inflammatory and unsound rhetoric is comparatively harmless when addressed to a restricted body of people, trained in the use of words, who can detect bad reasoning and argue back. When broadcast among those untrained in analysis and argument, it is the most *powerful weapon ever placed in the hands of the unscrupulous*."[9]

The combination of an uneducated but literate public and increased amounts of information being communicated had two possible effects, Sayers observed. First, wordsmiths would be inclined to write for ever-more specialized and elite audiences, abandoning any effort to communicate to the common person. Simultaneously, anything authoritative that might be published could be lost in the sheer volume of available information, particularly because "everything appears equally good, because stated with the same air of authority."[10]

Sayers called her fellow writers to account: "It *is* up to us, if we have any feeling for the right kind of *Democracy, Liberty, Education and Order* to keep awake and do something about it." She exhorted them to "challenge ignorant and incompetent writing" wherever they encountered it and to lift up good writing by recommending books and plays that exhibited it. One of her closing comments reminded them of the power of words: "A word is like fire—a good servant, but a bad master—and like fire, it remains a servant only so long as we respect its nature and retain a wholesome dread of its potentialities." She told the wordsmiths present that if they did not rise to the challenge, nobody would, "for no

7. Dorothy L. Sayers, "The Dictatorship of Words," January 5, 1939, Wade MS-67.
8. Ibid.
9. Ibid.
10. Ibid.

one else can. It is not an easy task, but it is well worth doing. We really cannot sit about until the catastrophe happens."[11]

Sacramental Uses of Language

Sayers's convictions about language affected not only her political writings but also her religious work. In one of her BBC addresses, for example, she explains the importance of using the right words in sacramental acts. She argues that for any action to be truly sacramental, it must be made up of three things: "the right material means, the right words, and the right intention."[12] Words, then, can be holy if used in the proper context. They can also be unholy and damaging, as we have already seen. Sayers condemns exploitive advertising in her writings about business ethics. While translating Dante's *Divine Comedy*, Sayers notes how words can be misused, "that abuse and corruption of language which destroys communication between mind and mind" when people "exploit others by playing upon their desires and fears."[13] She notes that while Dante did not live to see political propaganda, commercial advertisement, and sensational journalism in their fullest form, he nonetheless prepared a place for them in one of the circles of hell.

Sayers was careful to use language in a way that would not cause harm. In 1943, a listener took her to task over part of her translation in *The Man Born to Be King*, accusing her of not believing in eternal punishment because she did not translate the word *everlasting* consistently in two contexts. Sayers reminded him that she was originally commissioned to write the play for children, and therefore

> I boggled at the use of the word "eternal" or "everlasting" in connection with death, and damnation. Eternal and damnation is all right, if and when one is old enough to realize the meanings of the two words, but enough children have already suffered from horrifying notions about tortures going on for ever to make one chary of frightening the rising generation.
>
> Everlasting, or eternal life, on the other hand, though they may not understand it is not likely to produce any dangerous reaction in their little minds.[14]

11. Ibid.

12. Dorothy L. Sayers, "The Sacrament of Matter," BBC radio addresses delivered in 1940, lot 292, iii of the Sotheby's collection, Wade Center.

13. Dante Alighieri, *Hell*, trans. Dorothy L. Sayers (London: Penguin, 1949), 185.

14. Dorothy L. Sayers to J. P. Valentin, April 29, 1943, lot 290, ivc, folder 2/3, Wade Center.

Simple linguistic correctness is not enough if the chosen words manipulate the audience unfairly. Sayers articulates in her "Poetry, Language, and Ambiguity," "From battered words and meaningless clichés we are led to words which, though they still possess perfectly clear and well-defined meanings as purely descriptive terms, are nevertheless currently used as mere incantations for the calling-up of passions." She recognizes the "always dangerous and (potentially) evil" abuse of words merely to rouse such passions.[15]

Many expressed gratitude to Sayers for using her linguistic abilities to bring life to familiar doctrines. A vicar in Paignton preached a series of sermons in 1943 reflecting on the various *Man Born to Be King* broadcasts. A newspaper clipping about his sermons notes, "Many leaders of the Church were profoundly grateful to the gifted author. Certainly she used her imagination, but they needed imagination in reading the Bible. One of the great hindrances to the conversion of souls was unreality, which showed itself in the parsonic voice, conventional language and the inability to put religion into life."[16] Sayers saw a need to breathe fresh air into established pronouncements in the church. As she wrote in "The Execution of God":

> It has often been observed that if we say a thing often enough, we shall end by believing it. But it is equally true that if we say a thing often enough, we shall end, not perhaps by disbelieving it exactly, but by losing all awareness of what we are saying; the more particularly, if the language we use is not only familiar to us, but also a little out of date. Thus it becomes possible to repeat placidly, Sunday after Sunday, "Very God of Very God . . . He was crucified under Pontius Pilate," and find nothing very remarkable in the statement.[17]

Technical Terms

As noted earlier, Sayers was frustrated with the lack of linguistic capability among the clergy of her day. For her, clear communication took precedence over exactitude of theological terminology. As she wrote in March 1942, "The theologian must, when assessing popular expositions, consider not so much: 'are the words exact?' as 'is the right impression being conveyed?'"[18] She remained energized, too, about technical lan-

---

15. Dorothy L. Sayers, "Poetry, Language, and Ambiguity," in *The Poetry of Search and the Poetry of Statement* (London: Victor Gollancz, 1963), 269, 276–77.

16. Press clipping from *Torquay Directory*, August 5, 1943.

17. Dorothy L. Sayers, "The Execution of God," *Radio Times*, March 23, 1945, 3.

18. Dorothy L. Sayers to J. H. Oldham, March 4, 1942, Wade document 341/22.

guage used without precision. Observing that societies had become ever-more interdependent at the same time that information and knowledge were exploding and becoming increasingly specialized, she complained in her address to the Socratic Club, "It is rapidly becoming more and more difficult for individual men to understand each other. Whenever two persons attempt to converse on any subject more abstruse than the weather or the wearing properties of nylon, a point may be reached—and reached only too quickly—when the speakers cease to communicate, and merely utter mutually unintelligible sounds."[19] Sayers also found the lack of facility with technical vocabulary in the church maddening. A reader contacted her about *The Mind of the Maker*, and she responded:

> Like you I become irritated by the refusal to re-interpret the past. The effort to bring theology and philosophy up to date by continually inventing new vocabulary for experience tends to give the impression that the experience of to-day has no connection with the experience of yesterday—so ready have we become to accept the word for the thing. It seems to me much more fruitful to take the expressions of the past, and to say this universal experience is what these old people meant by these words, and so illuminate the present by the past, and the past by the present.[20]

Sayers advocated teaching the people in the pew technical terminology, suggesting that clergy underestimate laypeople's intelligence when they assume that technical language will necessarily be off-putting to them. Despite the challenge of competing technical vocabularies, Sayers did not propose making language more rigid—indeed, she saw this as an impossible task. One of her more vivid analogies states:

> The desperate attempts of scientists to reduce language to a kind of algebraic formula in which the same symbol has always the same meaning resemble the process of trying to force a large and obstreperous cat into a small basket. As fast as you tuck in the head, the tail comes out; when you have at length confined the hind legs, the fore paws come out and scratch; and when, after a painful struggle, you shut down the lid, the dismal wailings of the imprisoned animal suggest that some essential dignity in the creature has been violated and a wrong done to its nature.[21]

Instead, she called for an acknowledgment of the organic nature of language by those who use it. Indeed, the dynamic nature of words and

19. Sayers, "Poetry, Language, and Ambiguity," 264.

20. Dorothy L. Sayers to H. J. Massingham of Bucks, September 16, 1941, Wade document 151/78.

21. Dorothy L. Sayers, "Creative Mind," in *Unpopular Opinions*, 49.

word meanings makes it possible to write more evocatively, as she told
the Socratic Club:

> Language is by its nature ambiguous. We receive it, loaded with all
> its accrued associations; we use it in varying contexts which modify
> its significance, as a colour shows modified by the colours which sur-
> round it; we alter it by our use of it; and we pass it on, thus altered
> and enriched—or, it may be, impoverished—by our treatments of it,
> to those who come after. All new ideas, all new systems of thought are
> compelled to communicate themselves, as best they can, not in a lan-
> guage fresh-minted for the occasion, but in this ancient currency. To
> the poet this is an advantage, for it makes of every word a storehouse
> of accumulated power.[22]

As shown in previous chapters, Sayers proposed a partnership between clergy and those gifted with language. She was particularly
concerned not to leave theological instruction solely in the hands of
amateurs because it would be easy for people to be led astray. She
mentioned in a letter to Alec Vidler, head of the Theological Literature
Association:

> It is because theologians can't write English—and don't know how the
> English they do write sounds to the ordinary man—that you get the
> ordinary man turning for religious instruction to popular scientists,
> or the popular press, or to popular writers of detective fiction. And it's
> all wrong. Most of us popular writers . . . are apt to make mistakes.
> Also, not all of us are honest. I am fairly honest; I take some pains to
> tell people, "this isn't what I say; it's what the Church says." But if I
> wasn't honest, I could start some putrid little anti-clerical sect of my
> own to-morrow.[23]

One of the blessings of Sayers's religious writing is her clarity of
speech. She wrote in 1939 to a clergy acquaintance:

> It isn't that some people aren't saying and writing quite a lot of good
> stuff—I've read a good bit of it lately—but it seems to lurk about in
> ecclesiasticl [sic] papers and books published under devout titles and
> never get out to the common man. For one thing, most of it isn't well
> enough written, the thought is often all right, but it's tied up in dull
> words. If they want to say, "Brood of vipers," why the blazes don't they
> say "Brood of vipers"? Christ didn't say "a whole community infected by

22. Sayers, "Poetry, Language, and Ambiguity," 275.
23. Fragments of a letter from Dorothy L. Sayers to Fr. Alec Vidler, date unknown,
Wade document 398/43ff.

an unsound ideology"—He said "vipers" and meant "vipers." If they mean that the Church must either be crucified or disappear, why not say so? It's no good saying that "a time of trial is possibly in store for us."[24]

When Sayers meant "brood of vipers" in her work, she said it clearly, which makes her religious (and other) writings so refreshing to read. Who else would title an essay "The Other Six Deadly Sins"? Who else would write with such pungency that several essays were "suppressed before they appeared"?[25] Who else would call the church to account for its dilution of the gospel in such a provocative way?

24. Dorothy L. Sayers to Rev. John Shirley, December 28, 1939, Wade document 254/68.
25. As Sayers notes in her foreword to *Unpopular Opinions*, v.

9

Creativity and Art

A bad play is a bad play, and though, like some bad statuary and abominable stained glass, it may assist the prayers of the faithful, it will do nothing to convince the world at large that the Christian religion is worthy of intelligent consideration. And I am not altogether sure even about the faithful: does bad art really do for them anything that good art would not do better?

Dorothy L. Sayers, "Playwrights Are Not Evangelists"

*N*othing has done more to fasten the stigma of insincerity and stupidity upon the Christian religion," acknowledged Dorothy L. Sayers, "than the horrid florescence of 'religious' art."[1] Sayers, like many Christian artists, thought deeply about the relationship between the church and the arts. She worried in a letter to the bishop of Coventry that "the reason why one doesn't *expect* a professing Christian as such to be witty or intelligent or artistic or lively is that we don't really believe that God is any of these agreeable things or the source of them."[2] It angered her that churches did not respect artists as being

1. Dorothy L. Sayers to the editor of the *Church Times*, May 6, 1941, Wade document 347/39.
2. Dorothy L. Sayers to the bishop of Coventry, June 26, 1944, in *The Letters of Dorothy L. Sayers*, vol. 3, ed. Barbara Reynolds (Cambridge: Dorothy L. Sayers Society, 1999), 28.

called to their work and instead insisted on co-opting them for the work of explicit evangelism. She personally believed it never benefited an artist or the church to make art out of duty or evangelistic intent. Certainly, art could have evangelistic influence and effect, but one should never write or paint or compose music specifically for that purpose:

> The integrity of the artist is autonomous, and if Art is again to serve the Church, the Church must again learn to serve the Arts. She must observe a decent humility towards the artist, and acknowledge that his is a true vocation, whose demands are paramount. To instruct the painter about draughtmanship or the playwright about dramatic construction is not her rightful business; to require that he should wrest his work into alien and artistically unsatisfactory shapes "to edification" is the surest recipe for producing—not good religious art, but plainly and simply bad art, which is a betrayal of vocation and an abomination to God and man. . . .
>
> Nor, may I add, are ecclesiastics wise in trying to "get hold of" any artist who happens to be a Christian, in order to make him lecture to youth groups, preach sermons, or open Church bazaars. In doing so, they are merely hindering the artist in his vocation, which is to glorify God by his technique and not by theirs.[3]

Creativity and Inspiration

We have already seen significant elements of Sayers's theology of creativity in two other chapters. The chapter on vocation revealed that Sayers believed the basic calling of every human being is to create. In her essay "What Do We Believe?" Sayers succinctly articulates this view:

> The great fundamental quality that makes God, and us with Him, what we are is creative activity . . . and by implication, man is most godlike and most himself when he is occupied in creation. . . . The men who create with their minds and those who create (not merely labour) with their hands will, I think, agree that their periods of creative activity are those in which they feel right with themselves and the world.[4]

Sayers's convictions about vocation probably drove her artistic theology most. They reflect how, why, and when an artist creates. In an undated letter, she sets forth how she understands the calling of workers and, in particular, writers:

3. Sayers to the editor of the *Church Times*, May 6, 1941, Wade document 347/39.
4. Dorothy L. Sayers, "What Do We Believe?" in *Unpopular Opinions* (New York: Harcourt, Brace, & Co., 1947), 15.

The duty of Man in general and as a worker in particular is to:
   a. Serve God (if you don't believe in God, of course, that's your funeral, and you will have to carry on with the rest of the programme without any rational grounds, but I can't help that).
   b. Serve his fellow-man, but only in such a way as enables them both to serve God. . . .
   c. See that his work serves God. . . .
   d. Serve the work. . . .
The duty of the writer in particular is to
   e. Make writing his job, and perform his service to God and man, in terms of his own skill and not other people's.
   f. Write because he has something he wants to say (and not in order to act up to his notion of what THE WRITER ought to be like, or because his public expects it, or because somebody says he ought, or that it would "do good," or "give so much pleasure," or even to make a living, though this is the next most respectable motive after having something he wants to say. But if he *really* has nothing to say he had better choose another job).
   g. Write well—or at any rate as well as he can, or at the very least write grammatically.[5]

Sayers's insistence that a writer compose only "because he has something he wants to say" forms the centerpiece of a well-known series of correspondence with C. S. Lewis, who disagrees with her on this point.[6] She and Lewis, both deeply passionate about their craft, trade accusations of sin and idolatry and remain persuaded of their own positions. In an article written several years later called "Playwrights Are Not Evangelists," Sayers reiterates her convictions on this matter, reflecting some of her own struggles as a writer in high demand. She discusses what happens when an author is asked to write on a particular topic and refuses (as she refused Lewis when he requested a specific type of writing from her).

There is, to be sure, no harm in suggesting a theme for a play; but if the writer replies that it does not appeal to him, then it is both wicked and unwise to undermind [sic] his resistance by appeals to his vanity ("nobody could do it so well as you"), his missionary zeal ("you have so much influence"), or his duty to the brethren ("we look to you for help"). . . . Better leave it at that, and not try to lead him into temptation. For unless he possesses a very tough defence-mechanism, he may be over-persuaded by your two-pronged attack delivered simultaneously upon his baser pas-

5. Dorothy L. Sayers to Mr. Ould, undated, lot 292, vii, folder 3/16, Wade Center.
6. For more on her disagreement with Lewis on this subject, see Diana Pavlac Glyer and Laura K. Simmons, "Dorothy L. Sayers and C. S. Lewis: Two Approaches to Creativity and Calling," *VII: An Anglo-American Literary Review* 21 (2004): 31–46.

sions and his tender conscience, and so fall into the most disastrous of all errors—that of writing outside the range of his spiritual experience. Then he will begin to ape the emotions which you have told him he ought to feel, in the effort to communicate to his audience the light which he has not himself received: you will have made his work bogus and himself a hypocrite—all to no purpose, since bogus plays are without power.[7]

Sayers believed that Lewis was guilty of writing occasionally beyond his range. She preferred to see artists and writers work out of what she calls the "enkindled imagination" so that all their work is fueled by passion and creativity, not by duty. She sees wrong motives both corrupting the artist and ruining the art. In the same essay, she argues that a playwright who "writes with his eye on a kind of spiritual box-office . . . will at once cease to be a dramatist, and decline into a manufacturer of propagandist tracts." She believes the calling of the playwright is "not to save souls but to write good plays,"[8] tasks that are often mutually exclusive. Sayers does acknowledge that "many men, such as Dante or John Bunyan, have written immortal works with the avowed intention of communicating to others the illumination which they have themselves received. True: but then they first received it. The fire which fell upon them was of a sort to kindle their artistic imagination, so that they could not rest till they had spoken."[9] Not waiting for the fire of inspiration is, for Sayers, somehow lazy and prideful.

For Sayers the playwright, this attention to good work influenced the entire production of a play. When James Welch of the BBC reminded her that Val Gielgud, her producer of choice for *The Man Born to Be King*, was not a Christian, she hastily responded that she did not want a Christian; she wanted a producer. She said consistently of her plays, "It is (let us face it) far more important that the actors should be good actors than they should be good Christians."[10] In the third installment of "Sacred Plays," she shed light on her aversion to mixing evangelistic intent with artistic integrity: "Every work of art has its own proper Truth, which is a Truth of structure and proportion and direction; and it will not suffer the mixture of other kinds of Truth."[11] She believed that any inspired work that was well done could, on its own, point a reader or a viewer to God without any additional help from the artist or

7. Dorothy L. Sayers, "Playwrights Are Not Evangelists," *World Theatre* 5, no. 1 (Winter 1955–56): 62–63.

8. Ibid., 61.

9. Ibid., 62.

10. Dorothy L. Sayers, "Sacred Plays: III," *Episcopal Churchnews*, February 6, 1955, 24.

11. Ibid.

performer. She exhorted Christian artists to "trust the work itself to do its job—which it will do, if they make it as good as they can. If they do not make it as good as it can be, it will fail of its effect, and no amount of pious intention will make up for that failure. This is always a hard thing for the Children of light to understand."[12]

Sayers's language about artistic integrity is often quite strong. In "The Church's Responsibility," she even argues that "if a statue is ill-carved or a play ill-written, the artist's corruption is deeper than if the statue were obscene and the play blasphemous. Deeper, because the artist is being false to his own vision of the Truth; because it is a sapping from within of that disinterested integrity which is the point at which men can touch the truth that is outside space and time."[13] This echoes Miss Shaw's statement in *Gaudy Night* that "a bad picture by a good painter is a betrayal of truth—his own truth."[14]

Undoubtedly, some would question whether there really is such a thing as "disinterested integrity" by which an artist can be inspired. However, Sayers may really be saying that it is God's job to inhabit an inspired work of art, not the artist's job to force some sort of spiritual connection with the audience. Indeed, in the introduction to her translation of *Hell*, Sayers draws a distinction between art used by the *artist* to evangelize and art used by *God* to shape a person. She observes that Virgil, the image in Dante of poetry and art, morality and philosophy, "cannot himself enter Heaven or bring anyone else there (art and morality and philosophy cannot be made into substitutes for religion) but he can (and they can), under the direction of the Heavenly Wisdom, be used to awaken the soul to a realization of its own sinfulness," and therefore can assist the soul toward that "state . . . in which it is again open to receive the immediate operation of Divine Grace."[15]

Aesthetic Theology

In her essay "Towards a Christian Aesthetic," Sayers articulates a need for Christians to think more about the arts:

12. Ibid.
13. Dorothy L. Sayers, "The Church's Responsibility," in *Malvern 1941: The Life of the Church and the Order of Society; Being the Proceedings of the Archbishop of York's Conference*, ed. unknown (London: Longmans, Green, & Co., 1942), 75.
14. Dorothy L. Sayers, *Gaudy Night* (New York: Avon Books, 1968), 286.
15. Dorothy L. Sayers, introduction to *Hell*, by Dante Alighieri (London: Penguin, 1949), 67.

Oddly enough, we have no Christian aesthetic—no Christian philosophy of the Arts. The Church as a body has never made up her mind about the Arts, and it is hardly too much to say that she has never tried. She has, of course, from time to time puritanically denounced the Arts as irreligious and mischievous, or tried to exploit the Arts as a means to the teaching of religion and morals—but I shall hope to show you that both these attitudes are false and degrading, and are founded upon a completely mistaken idea of what Art is supposed to be and do. . . . If we commit ourselves to saying that the Christian revelation discovers to us the nature of *all* truth, then it must discover to us the nature of the truth about Art, among other things.[16]

What then, for Sayers, was art supposed to be and do if its purpose was not to be evangelistic? She wanted to see a uniquely Christian artistic philosophy developed, suggesting a way to establish "the principles of 'Art Proper' upon that Trinitarian doctrine of the nature of Creative Mind which does, I think, really underlie them."[17] On this foundation, she proposed, it may be possible to develop a Christian aesthetic that, "finding its source and sanction in the theological centre, would be at once characteristically Christian and of more universal application than any aesthetic whose contact with Christianity is made only at the ethical circumference."[18] (*The Mind of the Maker* was Sayers's attempt to set forth this trinitarian doctrine about the creative process.) She believed the "mutilated limbs and withering branches" of the arts in Britain could be healed and revitalized by "re-grafting [them] into the main trunk of Christian tradition."[19]

Sayers believed the failure to ground one's philosophy of the arts in a trinitarian and incarnational theology encouraged people to ground it instead in secular ideals. However, these ideals could conflict with one's theology. "Where the conflict between them became too noisy to be overlooked, we have tried to silence the clamour by main force, either by brutally subjugating Art to religion, or by shutting them up in separate prison cells and forbidding them to hold any communication with one another."[20] Sayers's hope was to create a theology of art and of creativity that would allow the church to embrace the arts as a natural extension of the church.

Sayers located the problems of Christians' views of the arts in the work of Plato—although she suggested he was not to blame for others'

16. Dorothy L. Sayers, "Towards a Christian Aesthetic," in *Unpopular Opinions*, 31.
17. Ibid., 30.
18. Ibid.
19. Ibid.
20. Ibid., 31.

misuse of his thought: "He was one of the greatest thinkers of all time, but he was a pagan; and I am becoming convinced that no pagan philosopher could produce an adequate aesthetic, simply for lack of a right theology."[21] She differed with Plato and with others who reduced art to either representation or imitation. She suggested that a true work of art was not primarily a copy or a representation of anything but was in some way new. It may involve representation, but "that is not what makes it a work of art." Sayers cited as an example Aeschylus's *Agamemnon*, arguing that it was more than a copy or a representation of

> something bigger and more real than itself. It is bigger and more real than the real-life action it represents. . . . When it is shown to us like this, by a great poet, it is as though we went behind the triviality of the actual event to the cosmic significance behind it. . . . His art was that point of truth in him which was true to the eternal truth, and only to be interpreted in terms of eternal truth.[22]

For Sayers, then, there was a quality behind "true" art that brought it beyond simple mimesis, or imitation, to a higher level of communicating truth via the art itself. This was accomplished not by evangelistic intent in the artistic presentation but by the significance of the "eternal truth" that was the subject of the art.

Sayers believed that only Christianity offered an adequate philosophical—and theological—basis for the creative task. Her interpretation of Genesis suggests that the desire and the ability to make things are what make humans most like God and that we are closest and truest to the image of God within us when we are engaged in the act of creation.

Incarnating the Truth

Her theology of creativity, as expressed in *The Mind of the Maker*, relates closely to her understanding of incarnation. The "idea" in her trinitarian model is actualized in the process of composing, painting, writing—an incarnation of sorts. Because the incarnation is central to Christian theology, Sayers locates this as the fulcrum of a Christian theology of the arts and as the major contribution Christian artists can make to a philosophy of the arts in general. She suggests in "Towards a Christian Aesthetic," "Let us take note of a new word that has crept into the argument by way of Christian theology—the word *Image*. Sup-

21. Ibid., 33.
22. Ibid., 39.

pose, having rejected the words 'copy,' 'imitation' and 'representation' as inadequate, we substitute the word 'image' and say that what the artist is doing is to *image forth* something . . . something which, by being an image, *expresses* that which it images."[23]

Image and the expression of image are crucial in Sayers's theology of art. In a 1944 letter to the bishop of Coventry, Sayers comments on the ongoing discussion about the purpose of art. "Art is to Experience as the Son is to the Father: not the 'representation of fact' but the image of the truth."[24] Expression of an image is also important to Sayers's view of the relationship between theology and writing. For Sayers, writing is predicated upon neither "art for art's sake" nor "art for truth's sake," in the sense of using art or literature as an evangelistic or moralistic tool. Her goal as a writer, be it poet or playwright or novelist, was to express an image, to create and to incarnate the creative idea God had planted in her (not simply an imitation of an existing idea). This is what she meant when she wrote about *Agamemnon's* expressing an eternal truth that could be beheld only through eternal truth. Thus, in creating *The Man Born to Be King,* Sayers wanted not to evangelize Britain (although the plays did have this effect for some) but to tell a story she found particularly vivid and exciting.[25] Likewise, she did not write *The Emperor Constantine* to convince the populace of the truth of Christ's divinity but rather to show them how exciting dogma could be.[26]

23. Ibid., 40.
24. Sayers to the bishop of Coventry, June 26, 1944, in *Letters of Dorothy L. Sayers,* vol. 3, 27.
25. In the introduction to the plays, Sayers wrote, "I say that this story is a very great story indeed, and deserves to be taken seriously. I say further . . . that in these days it is seldom taken seriously. It is often taken, and treated, with a gingerly solemnity: but that is what honest writers call frivolous treatment. . . . It is, first and foremost, a story—a true story, the turning point of history" (Dorothy L. Sayers, *The Man Born to Be King* [Grand Rapids: Eerdmans, 1943], 21). Barbara Reynolds states that Sayers's "coherent visualisation of the story, both as theologian and as dramatist, is summed up in a further masterly statement: 'The history and the theology of Christ are one thing: His life is theology in action, and the drama of his life is dogma shown as dramatic action'" (Barbara Reynolds, *Dorothy L. Sayers: Her Life and Soul* [New York: St. Martin's Press, 1993], 328). This is as true for the Old Testament, presented on screen, as it was for the New Testament, presented on the radio. Steve Hickner, codirector of Dreamworks' movie *The Prince of Egypt,* spoke about the choices he and his staff made in bringing the story of the exodus to the screen. There were several points at which they wanted to change details of the story but eventually chose not to: "We found that a lot of times, the closer we stayed with the . . . [original story], the better dramatically it actually was" (David Kronke, "Leading Man," *Southwest Airlines Spirit,* December 1998, 106).
26. When an American wrote to her of his intention to produce *The Emperor Constantine* in Washington, D.C., she strongly advised him that, if he needed to cut anything (it is a very long play), it *not* be the Nicea scene: "Strange as it may appear, and despite

While Sayers believed a non-Christian artist could make art that edifies God, she also believed a Christian foundation was important to the artist (as to other professionals), as she told the bishop of Coventry: "'We can do our science, or our painting, or our doctoring quite well without Christ'—that sounds a very reasonable thing to say, if we forget or were never told that Christ is precisely the truth we are discovering, the beauty we are expressing, the life we are restoring, and the energy and skill we put to all these things."[27] Sayers contrasts art made by non-Christians with art made by Christian artists—and art made by well-meaning but untalented Christians who want to evangelize:

Art that is the true image of experience is true art, even though the experience is ugly or immoral (as the image of God is still the image of God, even in a wicked man); but you can't make untrue, or venal, or incompetent art into good art, by putting it in church or extracting morals from it, any more than you can get the Holy Spirit out of a tin of petrol. If you want a more conventional symbol as a reminder that God was crucified, two lines scratched in the wood are better than a tawdry and sentimental crucifix: they don't pretend to be art, and they don't tell lies. You can get a good crucifix from a good artist who, without being a Christian, has some experience in his soul which can express itself in the form of a crucified man; you can get a better crucifix from an *equally* good artist with the *same* experience, who is also a Christian; but you can't get a good crucifix *either* from the Christian who is not an artist, *or* from the artist who is merely doing for money something that doesn't express his experience. The worst frame of mind in which to make crucifixes is the one in which one says, "I will now make a crucifix for the express purpose of correcting and improving other people"; the best is when one says: "I share with my fellow-men a passionate experience which is expressing itself in this crucifix for myself, and also for them, because they, though inarticulate, will know their own experience in the expression which I am giving it." The error into which moralists fall lies in saying to the artists, "It would do people good to have this or that feeling: make them have it." That is not art but propaganda, and whatever its immediate success, it falsified the art and degrades, in the end, both the artist and the people. And the error the people fall into is to say to the artist: "We want to have this nice

whatever anybody may urge to the contrary, that scene is absolutely sure-fire theatre from start to finish. I have known it [to] exercise an uncanny fascination on the hard-headed, uninstructed people who don't know the homo-öusion from the pelargonium, and who have never in their lives heard a theological dogma debated. (That is probably the secret of its spell.) . . . If the eye is satisfied and the playing swift, the audience will listen spellbound to forty minutes of clotted theology—at least, they will in England" (Dorothy L. Sayers to Charles M. Bruch, July 4, 1956, Wade document 526/34).

27. Sayers to the bishop of Coventry, June 26, 1944, in *Letters of Dorothy L. Sayers*, vol. 3, 26.

feeling; make us have it." That is not art but trade ("fulfilling a public demand"), and it debauches both the artist (because he is then not knowing his own experience in its image, but merely making an idol) and the people (because what they then recognise in the idol is not the expression of their experience but only a projection of their own desires). What most people ask for when they think they are asking for art (apart from mere entertainment) is usually either propaganda or idols.[28]

Search and Statement

Sayers's convictions about the creative process also manifest themselves in an address late in her life titled "The Poetry of Search and the Poetry of Statement." In defining the differences, she articulates, "Both are concerned with personal experience; but the poetry of Search concentrates on the 'gropings.' . . . The poetry of Statement, on the other hand, is not written till the journey is ended: it maps the true route from tentative beginning to triumphant arrival."[29] The poetry of search contains "all the false steps, blind alleys, and pits of confusion into which . . . [the poet] may fall by the way."[30] If the poetry of statement, on the other hand,

> mentions the false wanderings it is only to warn people off them; but it is concerned to get somewhere and to show other people the way. The poet must of course have plodded every step of the journey himself: he must not merely announce other people's conclusions. . . . But the poet is concerned with the truth he has discovered about things in general, not merely with the workings of his own mind.[31]

Sayers's own work reflects both search and statement. *The Mind of the Maker* would probably fall into the category of the poetry of search. Sayers herself calls it both an "odd sort of exercise of applied theology"[32] and an "odd theological adventure."[33] In various letters, she describes

28. Dorothy L. Sayers, from a fragment of a letter, addressee and date not given, but part of a June 26, 1944, letter to the bishop of Coventry. A slightly different version of this letter is published in Reynolds, *Letters of Dorothy L. Sayers*, vol. 3, 24–32. This portion is taken from lot 292, vii, folder 3/16, Wade Center.

29. Dorothy L. Sayers, *The Poetry of Search and the Poetry of Statement* (London: Victor Gollancz, 1963), 8–9.

30. Ibid.

31. Ibid.

32. Dorothy L. Sayers to Dr. J. H. Oldham, June 16, 1941, Wade document 341/27.

33. Dorothy L. Sayers to Rev. Dom Ralph Russell, October 28, 1941, Wade document 406/81.

the process of trying to explain something she has vague ideas about in ways that would make sense and contribute to others' thinking about both creativity and theology. *The Man Born to Be King*, on the other hand, might be considered poetry of statement, not merely because the denouement of the story was already known but because Sayers knew from the beginning exactly what she wanted to accomplish through the work.

Ultimately, one of Sayers's most enduring contributions to thinking Christianly about creativity and art is her exhortation to do these things well. Art done "merely by pious persons intent on edification" is nothing but a devotional exercise for uncritical congregations.[34] Even if its flaws are "excused by the pious (though by nobody else) on the grounds that it was not intended to be drama, but 'religion,'" a bad play is a poor witness.[35] Art, Sayers contends, stays with people in ways that written or spoken words often do not—and this makes it that much more dangerous when done poorly:

> That is the whole case for religious drama—and also the whole case against bad religious drama. You may preach yourself blue in the face about distinction between the Divine Personality and the Human Nature "of a reasonable soul and human flesh subsisting" without achieving the conviction produced by one vivid and dramatic moment in a Mystery-Play; and similarly, if one of the wrong conceptions has been vividly and dramatically imprinted on the imagination, you will have hard work to preach it out again.[36]

34. Sayers, "Playwrights Are Not Evangelists," 61.
35. Ibid., 62.
36. Dorothy L. Sayers, "Sacred Plays: II," *Episcopal Churchnews*, January 25, 1955, 25.

10

Women's Issues

Nothing is more startling, and indeed horrifying, than the contrast between the perfect simplicity of Jesus in His relations with women, . . . His complete silence as to any special duties, frailties, mysteries, dangers, or dirt connected with their sex, and the self-consciousness and interminable chatter of His followers on the subject.

Dorothy L. Sayers, notes on the "Oecumenical Penguin"

*I*n July of 1948, C. S. Lewis wrote to Dorothy L. Sayers to express his concerns and solicit her opinion regarding the movement to ordain women in the Anglican Church. Little did he know that six years before, one of Sayers's editors had complained to her about unequal treatment of men and women, writing disconcertingly, "Why, to put it in a nutshell, should you not be Archbishop of Canterbury?"[1] Sayers's response to Lewis was telling:

Obviously, nothing could be more silly and inexpedient than to erect a new and totally unnecessary barrier between us and the rest of Catholic Christendom.

1. Barbara Reynolds, ed., *The Letters of Dorothy L. Sayers*, vol. 2 (Cambridge: Dorothy L. Sayers Society, 1997), 349n3.

I fear you would find me a rather uneasy ally [in opposing it]. I can never find any logical or strictly theological reason against it. In so far as the Priest represents Christ, it is obviously more dramatically appropriate that a man should be, so to speak, cast for the part. But if I were cornered and asked point-blank whether Christ Himself is the representative of male humanity or all humanity, I should be obliged to answer "of all humanity"; and to cite the authority of St. Augustine for saying that woman also is made in the image of God.[2]

Sayers's insistence on women's equality with men in the eyes of God came through with remarkable consistency in her writings. With the exception of a comment about the need for male actors to play the angels in *The Zeal of Thy House* (because of the weight of the wings), Sayers did not suggest that women should not do anything that men are qualified to do. When this position is found in her work, in fact, it is articulated by a woman on the verge of madness. As Annie complains in *Gaudy Night*:

"You broke him and killed him—all for nothing. Do you think that's a woman's job?"

"Most unhappily," said Miss De Vine, "it was my job."

"What business had you with a job like that? A woman's job is to look after a husband and children. . . . I wish I could burn down this place and all the places like it—where you teach women to take men's jobs. . . . It's women like you who take the work away from the men and break their hearts and lives. No wonder you can't get men for yourselves and hate the women who can. God keep the men out of your hands, that's what I say. You'd destroy your own husbands, if you had any, for an old book or bit of writing."[3]

Sayers addresses this question a few years later in "Are Women Human?" when she articulates, "The only decent reason for tackling any job is that it is *your* job and *you* want to do it."[4] Harriet Vane exemplifies this position, suggesting in *Gaudy Night*, "I know what you're thinking—that anybody with proper sensitive feeling would rather scrub floors for a living. But I should scrub floors very badly, and I write detective stories rather well."[5] Sayers's voice on this matter was clear, insightful for her time, and both controversial and influential.

2. Dorothy L. Sayers to C. S. Lewis, July 19, 1948, in *The Letters of Dorothy L. Sayers*, vol. 3, ed. Barbara Reynolds (Cambridge: Dorothy L. Sayers Society, 1999), 387.

3. Dorothy L. Sayers, *Gaudy Night* (New York: Avon Books, 1968), 372.

4. Dorothy L. Sayers, "Are Women Human?" in *Are Women Human?* (1971; reprint, Grand Rapids: Eerdmans, 1992), 23.

5. Sayers, *Gaudy Night*, 30.

In introducing the essays in *Unpopular Opinions*, Sayers writes that the BBC actually told her once, "Our public do not want to be admonished by a woman" (regarding her essay "Living to Work").[6] What the BBC missed out on, the church was privileged to receive. Sayers was invited to speak on vocation at the 1941 Malvern conference (the only woman out of fifteen speakers), where nearly 80 percent of the 227 attendees were male—most of them clergy and other Christian leaders. Sayers acknowledged a willingness to correspond with and speak to clergy in part because she believed the clergy occasionally needed to hear the views of laypeople. Part of her role in clarifying doctrine was to bring clarity to issues, topics, and language the clergy had mystified or muddied unnecessarily.

Human? Or Not Quite?

One such area had to do with women and men and the relationship between them. In a set of notes she prepared for the "Oecumenical Penguin" project, Sayers included a section on the theology of the virgin birth and the ways it had been misunderstood by God's people: "I should like to put on record my conviction that the whole attitude of the Churches to the man-woman question needs scouring and sweetening, and that until this is done it is quite hopeless to expect that any enthusiasm for the reform of 'morals' will be aroused by the agitated shrieks of the clergy."[7] She found the church and society at large all too ready to set women apart as somehow special, unique, fragile, or otherwise alien to humanity. As she wrote to the bishop of Coventry:

> I think the real charge against the Churches' attitude to the "woman question" is that it is apt to be cold and coarse, and that the fashionable eulogies of the "Christian home" too often (when freed from the sentiment and silver paper) bear an embarrassing resemblance to extracts from the *Stockbreeder's Gazette*. The Church of Rome is by far the worst offender. I don't mean that there should be any reaction towards the preposterous deification of "love" and the autonomy of the emotions; what is wrong, I am quite sure, is the insistence on assessing one half of humanity in terms of a single function. (The only other animals we treat in this way are sheep, cows, domestic poultry, etc. The cat, for instance, is respected as a good mouser, irrespective of sex; a bitch-pack is not called upon to impart a feminine touch to its hunting, but simply to hunt. The nervous ambivalence of our public attitude to women M.P.'s: if they confine them-

6. Dorothy L. Sayers, *Unpopular Opinions* (New York: Harcourt, Brace, & Co., 1947), v.
7. Lot 292, i, one of the recently acquired Sotheby's folders at the Wade Center.

selves to dealing with "women's questions," their constituents protest, very justly, that they want a member who will deal with *general* questions, such as trade, agriculture, and foreign policy; if, on the other hand, they address themselves like intelligent persons, to these "homo" interests, critics complain that their presence in the House has created no revolution in Parliamentary thinking—the implication being that there is some kind of female view to be taken on such questions as the Curzon Line or Bancor, which female M.P.'s should put forward, not as a personal opinion, but as part of a sexual function).[8]

Sayers's reference to "'homo' interests" is clarified in her essay "The Human Not-Quite-Human," in which she discusses the Latin words for male (*vir*), female (*femina*), and human (*homo*). She points out in this pungent essay that *homo* refers to both men and women but that many people hear "humanity" and think "male" (similar terms *aner* and *anthropos* in Greek are the source of much consternation when discussing the need for inclusive language Scripture translations). Sayers observes that "man is always dealt with as both *Homo* and *Vir*, but Woman only as *Femina*"—the "human not-quite-human" of the essay's title.[9] Women's choices are not assessed as human choices but always in relation to the woman's sex, Sayers complains. Men's choices, on the other hand, define human choices. She wonders what it would be like if these were reversed: "Probably no man has ever troubled to imagine how strange his life would appear to himself if it were unrelentingly assessed in terms of his maleness; if everything he wore, said, or did had to be justified by reference to female approval; if he were compelled to regard himself, day in day out, not as a member of society, but merely . . . as a virile member of society."[10]

Jesus and Women

The difficulty with these views of men and women, for Sayers, is that they do not match the model set forth by Jesus. At the end of "The Human Not-Quite-Human," she contrasts with startling clarity his relationship with women and that of society and the church by describing Jesus as someone who "never treated them either as 'The women, God help us!' or 'The ladies, God bless them!'"[11] This essay was published in

8. Dorothy L. Sayers to the bishop of Coventry, June 26, 1944, in *Letters of Dorothy L. Sayers*, vol. 3, 30.

9. Dorothy L. Sayers, "The Human Not-Quite-Human," in *Are Women Human?* (Grand Rapids: Eerdmans, 1971), 37.

10. Ibid., 39.

11. Sayers, "Human Not-Quite-Human," 47.

1941, but women in the twenty-first century still find themselves forced into the categories (and stereotypes) of helpful ladies and threatening women. Sayers went into more detail in a 1944 letter to the bishop of Coventry, whom she applauded for "saying that the Church ought not to treat women as dogsbodies, and plead[ed] further that she ought not to treat them as cows-bodies either, but as human beings, whose activities are not all and always comprised within their sexual function."[12] She wrote concerning Jesus' interactions with women that

> alone among teachers and founders of religion, he did and said nothing special about them. He never said they were tempters, or snares, or weaklings, or imbeciles, or inspirations, or angels; he never mapped out a special sphere of duties for them, or told people to keep clear of them or shut them up; when they asked him intelligent questions he replied seriously and intelligibly, and when Martha wanted to hike Mary off on the ground that women's place was in the kitchen He told her to leave her alone; He never patronised, or condescended, or scolded, or nagged at women for being women, or turned shy or silly or self-conscious or superior on them, and not one teaching or parable of his ever turns on funny stuff about wives or horrid warnings about women; you could read the whole Gospel from end to end without learning from it that there was anything peculiar about women, or that mankind was divided into two sections, the one consisting of complete human beings with certain sexual functions, and the other of perambulating sex-organs with a distant resemblance to humanity. You don't realise, perhaps, how extraordinary that is It's unparalleled. There has been nothing like it before or since. There has certainly never been anything like it in Christ's Church.
>
> All other religions and gods and ethical systems have been preoccupied with sex one way or the other, whether the upshot of the thing is a ferocious asceticism or "nameless orgies." But when you get hold of God personally, you come up against a blank wall. He just doesn't bother about it. He doesn't seem to notice it. If you force the subject on His attention, he merely observes that a dirty look is as bad as the whole hog and that men are in no position to cast stones at the women. . . . Otherwise, not a word—only a few incidental pictures of women harmlessly engaged in looking after children, making bread, mending garments and sweeping the house for lost sixpences, and pleading for justice in the courts, and a long, serious, and polite discussion on theology with a nondescript female by a well. (It is true, he suggested that she should fetch her husband, but not, apparently, to enlighten the feebleness of her female understanding, for He clearly didn't really want the man, didn't get him, and was content to continue the conversation without him.) This refreshing absence of hysteria is unique in religious history.

12. Sayers to the bishop of Coventry, June 26, 1944, in *Letters of Dorothy L. Sayers*, vol. 3, 28.

Consequently, while welcoming the "no dogsbody" notion, I should like to see something said about encouraging women to have *human* interests as well as "women's interests," and human needs instead of merely "women's needs." There are presumably special "male needs" also. By all means let us have all these things attended to. But when we have dealt specifically with *vir* and *femina*, there is still *homo*—even *homo sapiens*. It's not *good* for women to be everlastingly forced to think of themselves in terms of sex.[13]

The difficulty in encouraging women to have human interests, Sayers points out in "Are Women Human?" is that women are often tied to the home but that all interesting work has been removed from the home.[14] She lists spinning, dyeing, weaving, brewing and distilling, catering, milking, pickling, bottling, and bacon curing, as well as "the management of landed estates," as jobs women had been doing that were removed from the home and "handed . . . over to big industry, to be directed and organized by men at the head of large factories."[15] Why do we wonder that women are not satisfied at home when all the interesting work has been relocated outside it? Sayers asserts, "It is perfectly idiotic to take away women's traditional occupations and then complain because she looks for new ones. Every woman is a human being—one cannot repeat that too often—and a human being *must* have occupation, if he or she is not to become a nuisance to the world."[16] Sayers argues for people doing those jobs they do best. If men can

brew and bake as well as women or better, then by all means let them do it. But they cannot have it both ways. If they are going to adopt the very sound principle that the job should be done by the person who does it best, then the rule must be applied universally. If the women make better office-workers than men, they must have the office work. If any individual woman is able to make a first-class lawyer, doctor, architect or engineer, then she must be allowed to try her hand at it.[17]

Sayers calls society on its double standards about men's and women's work, noting that comparatively few people are passionately involved in their work, but "if that one person in a thousand is a man, we say, simply, that he is passionately keen on his job; if she is a woman, we say she is a freak."[18] She does acknowledge some difference between the

13. Ibid., 28–29.
14. Sayers, "Are Women Human?" 24.
15. Ibid.
16. Ibid., 25.
17. Ibid.
18. Ibid., 27. This comment bears a striking resemblance to Teresa Heinz Kerry's observation during the 2004 Democratic National Convention that when a man speaks his

sexes in this essay, suggesting that "it is stupid to insist that there are as many female musicians and mathematicians as male—the facts are otherwise . . . [and] what we must *not* do is to argue that the occasional appearance of a female mechanical genius proves that all women would be mechanical geniuses if they were educated. They would not."[19]

Marriage, Sexuality, and Divorce

Sayers's thoughts on marriage and divorce follow naturally from her expectations about work and other societal roles. In a "vitae" of sorts found in her papers, she writes about her views on marriage:

Women and Marriage: consider that chief difficulties in most cases are economic. Extremely keen that all women, married or not, should be able to make money for themselves and take their share in the upkeep of the home. Consider that it will soon be thought as degrading to be "kept" by a husband as "kept" in any other way. Would welcome legislation to abolish husband's liability for wife's income-tax, personal debts and other unfair distinctions.[20]

Barbara Reynolds suggests that this was written in 1928, only two years after Sayers's marriage to Mac Fleming, who evidently chafed at being a "kept man" with a wife who made more money than he.

Sayers found the church's views on marriage often inappropriate and even dangerous. In writing about the virgin birth for the "Oecumenical Penguin" project, Sayers notes:

Whatever we say or do not say about this there is one point that *must* be dealt with. Almost every non-Christian, together with a great many Christians believe that this doctrine implies a total condemnation of sex and marriage as being in themselves dirty, disgusting and defiling. . . . In face of the Churches' historic record in the treatment of women and the handling of sexual matters, it cuts no ice whatever to point to the fact that Catholics recognise marriage to be a sacrament and that everybody babbles a great deal about the sanctity of Christian motherhood and the Christian family. Nor, of course, is the Anglican marriage service very helpful, with its "remedy against fornication." The widely felt repugnance to this dogma is not, I am sure, caused by—though it finds support and

---

mind, we call him smart and well informed, whereas when a woman does, we call her opinionated—or worse, one might add.

19. Ibid., 29–30.

20. "Vitae" of sorts, undated (Barbara Reynolds labels it 1928), Wade document 21/9ff.

rationalisation in—scientific difficulties about miracles; plenty of people will accept the resurrection who boggle at the Virgin Birth. It is due to a retching discomfort about what is commonly thought to be the rationale of the doctrine.[21]

Sayers seems to wish that the church would elevate its view of both marriage and sexuality rather than subscribe to superstition and misinterpretations of Christian doctrine. She does not let divorced people off the hook either. In 1953 and 1954, Sayers and some friends published a satirical series called "The Pantheon Papers" in *Punch.* In addition to those items that made their way into publication, Sayers's papers contain some that did not. Part of "The Pantheon Papers" was a fictitious calendar, a parody of the church year containing "unholy" days and feast days. Sayers proposes celebrating on February 14 the Feast of the Broken Home—including the following hymn sung to the tune of "Hyfrydol."[22] She notes that "this hymn should not be wasted on persons of modest means or demeanor":

For a Solemn Divorce
Alimony! Sing to Mammon! His the bed and his the board
Alimony! His the judgment, his the whacking great award;
Hark! The songs of Social Science roaring like a water-chute
Mammon, lord of mixed relations, whose decrees are absolute!

[Female voices:] Alimony! No more cast-offs left to moulder on the
    shelf
Every girl's a speculator doing better for herself
[Male voices:] Alimony! No more shirkers flinching from a task
    undone—
Only free and lordly spenders who can pay to have their fun!

Praise to Mammon! Though we flourish far too thick upon the ground,
Though statistics seem to furnish too few husbands to go round
Even so great Mammon brings us healing balm for all our ills,
Where the wrongs of all the ringless blossom into dollar bills.

21. From "Notes 3" from "Oecumenical Penguin" documents, lot 292, i, Wade Center. Sayers suggests that the church's view of sexuality is too closely tied to its understanding of sin: "The real trouble here is the misconception of what is meant by sin. It is one thing, and a perfectly right thing, to say that sex, like every other human function, partakes the corruption of the Fall. Everybody can understand that, provided you have explained what the Fall is. It is even possible to make clear to people that sex exhibits in a very marked manner the cleavage and duality introduced, by the Fall, into human nature. But if you give people the impression that sex *is* the Fall and the sin of sins (whether in marriage or out of it), you are producing an atmosphere in which the Virgin Birth appears as a rather dirty story, told by nasty old Puritans" (ibid.).
22. "Hyfrydol" is the tune for "Come, Thou Long Expected Jesus" and other hymns.

Superstition shall not bind us spouse to spouse for all our lives;
Year by year let Mammon find us richer husbands, dearer wives:
Swift Romance shall run its ranges still, though pope and parson
    frown,
Till the ringing of the changes ring their rotting steeples down.

Alimony! Sing to Mammon! Every woman has her price!
Every time a heart is broken gold puts in another splice;
Alimony squares the audit, sets the fancy free to roam:
Leave to those that can't afford it faith and truth and home sweet home!

Alimony! Sing to Mammon! His the board and his the bed;
When you've cut out all the gammon, bring the bacon home instead;
Where your treasure, there your heart is—chase it while you have the
    breath,
For the only thing, my smarties, mammon can't buy off is death.[23]

Sayers and Feminism

In spite of her influential writings on women and the preponderance
of women scholars who have used her work to bolster feminist agendas,
Sayers was uneasy about being considered a feminist. Her well-known
address "Are Women Human?" began with this admission to her audience, a women's society:

> When I was asked to come and speak to you, your Secretary made the
> suggestion that she thought I must be interested in the feminist movement.
> I replied—a little irritably, I am afraid—that I was not sure I wanted to
> "identify myself," as the phrase goes, with feminism, and that the time
> for "feminism," in the old-fashioned sense of the word, had gone past.
> In fact, I think I went so far as to say that, under present conditions, an
> aggressive feminism might do more harm than good. As a result I was,
> perhaps not unnaturally, invited to explain myself.[24]

One of the concerns Sayers has with feminism is the temptation to replace
male domination with female domination. She argues that women be
accepted as human beings, "not as an inferior class and not, I beg and
pray all feminists, as a superior class."[25] There is a persistence among
contemporary feminists to read Sayers through a feminist lens, despite
her own discomfort with this tendency. Elizabeth Trembley notes that

23. Material on "The Pantheon Papers," lot 292, v, folder 2/5, Wade Center.
24. Sayers, "Are Women Human?" 17.
25. Ibid., 33.

feminists attribute to Sayers a feminist agenda she never had, becoming upset by Harriet's acceptance of Peter's marriage proposal in *Gaudy Night*.[26] Sayers does see how "for certain purposes it may still be necessary . . . for women to band themselves together, as women, to secure recognition of their requirements as a sex" but cautions, "Do not let us run into the opposite error of insisting that there is an aggressively feminist 'point of view' about everything."[27]

In 1943, having been faced with the question of women's ordination, Sayers returned to the question of whether women were accorded the basic courtesy of being considered human. In July, she wrote to a correspondent:

> As matters stand it is almost impossible to get the clergy to tackle the subject of the status of women, because they always think it is going to be something or other about Orders; and the agitation about this has only succeeded in side-tracking the dispute and confusing the issues. I think that to clamour for admission to the priesthood (whether or not it is desirable) is to throw the whole thing out of proportion; it is bound to look like just one more effort to get women into a paid profession, whereas the real controversy is about something much more fundamental.[28]

In "Are Women Human?" Sayers articulates, "The question of 'sex-equality' is, like all questions affecting human relationships, delicate and complicated." She recognizes its complexity and asks her readers to acknowledge it as well, to avoid generalizations about either men or women. "What is unreasonable and irritating," she continues, "is to assume that *all* one's tastes and preferences have to be conditioned by the class to which one belongs. That has been the very common error into which men have frequently fallen about women—and it is the error into which feminist women are, perhaps, a little inclined to fall about themselves."[29] While men and women are quick to categorize themselves and one another, she finds, Jesus is not. "Perhaps it is no wonder," she suggests, "that the women were first at the Cradle and last at the Cross. They had never known a man like this Man—there has never been such another."[30]

---

26. Elizabeth A. Trembley, "'Collaring the Other Fellow's Property': Feminism Reads Dorothy Sayers, in *Women Times Three: Writers, Detectives, Readers*, ed. Kathleen Gregory Klein, 81–99 (Bowling Green, OH: Bowling Green State University Popular Press, 1995).

27. Sayers, "Are Women Human?" 36.

28. Dorothy L. Sayers to Miss J. Hodgson, July 8, 1943, in *Letters of Dorothy L. Sayers*, vol. 2, 421.

29. Sayers, "Are Women Human?" 17, 20.

30. Sayers, "Human Not-Quite-Human," 47.

PART *3*

*Sayers
for the
Twenty-first
Century*

11

Reclaiming Sayers
for the People of God

It must be made clear to people that theological language is intended to mean something—that it is not "just an abstraction," but an abstraction from experience. . . . I wish I could make clear how unrelated to anything the basic Christian dogmas appear to the common man. It's not that they are difficult or even that they are unintelligible, but that they aren't expected to have any relevance. . . . For the common man, religion goes off into theology and stays there. He doesn't think it's expected or even intended to come back in any apprehensible result.

Dorothy L. Sayers to J. H. Oldham, April 1, 1942

Dorothy L. Sayers proposed a partnership between the church and professional writers, citing the church's lack of clarity in communicating its beliefs.[1] What does she offer the people of God in the

1. She wrote in April 1942, "Theologians and ecclesiastics should make intelligent use of the kind of layman who is trained in the current and poetic use of words. These are the people who can interpret theology to the common man, and clear up ambiguities" (Dorothy L. Sayers to Dr. J. H. Oldham, *Christian News-Letter*, April 1, 1942; the original is Wade document 341/20).

twenty-first century? Are her questions and concerns still valid? How are her responses to the conditions of her day valuable now?

This chapter assesses how believers can appropriate Sayers's theological wisdom and methods according to the classifications of clarification/restatement, exploring traditional doctrines, and theological reflection on themes in everyday life. Sayers wrote in February 1943, "What is in question, you see, is not a revision of doctrine, but a *metanoia*—a determination to recognise the Logos wherever he is found, week-days as well as Sundays; in the carpenter's shop as well as in the theologian's truth, to do so in practice, and not only in theory."[2] It is clear from her many cautions that she did not set out to revise doctrine.[3] Instead, she sought to clarify it, to identify misunderstandings people might have about basic Christian convictions. What function did her clarifications serve if not to bring about the *metanoia* she wrote of in this letter? As a layperson and as a professional writer, Sayers reflected how to "recognise the Logos" in a variety of places both within and beyond church walls.[4]

Sayers the lay theologian modeled the ability and the desire to bring her faith to bear on "week-days as well as Sundays." The topics on which she reflected theologically were not simply traditional church doctrines; they were also issues of work, economics, leisure, and creative hobbies. One of Sayers's most frequent concerns with the church was its tendency to confuse people with what one might call "Sunday language"—including theological jargon that was often outdated, misleading, or unnecessarily complex. She instead advocated using "weekday language" to explain the things of God to people—the language of the everyday, of "cats and cabbages," as she put it.[5] *The Man Born to Be King*, with its

---

2. Dorothy L. Sayers to Rev. Canon S. M. Winter, February 2, 1943, Wade document 235/40. A slightly different version of this letter was published in Barbara Reynolds, ed., *The Letters of Dorothy L. Sayers*, vol. 2 (Cambridge: Dorothy L. Sayers Society, 1997), 389. *Metanoia* is a Greek word meaning "a change of mind" or "turning," usually understood as a 180-degree turn, not a minor change. It is often translated into English as "repentance." See William F. Arndt and F. Wilbur Gingrich, eds., *A Greek-English Lexicon of the New Testament and Other Early Christian Literature* (Chicago: University of Chicago Press, 1967), 513–14. *Logos* is one of the terms used in the Gospel of John to describe Jesus. Usually translated "Word," it is based on the Greek concept of word or reason (ibid., 478–79).

3. Over and over again, Sayers found it necessary to remind people that she was not inventing a new set of beliefs but rather restating the historical convictions of the church.

4. As early as 1918, Sayers was exploring how to "recognise the Logos" in areas outside the church. Her 1918 poem "Sacrament against Ecclesiasts" was written from the point of view of a priest who encounters Christ in an unexpected form and does not recognize him. Later Christ chides the priest for not understanding (Ralph E. Hone, ed., *Poetry of Dorothy L. Sayers* [Cambridge: Dorothy L. Sayers Society in association with the Marion E. Wade Center, 1996], 90–91).

5. The terminology of "Sunday language" and "weekday language" is my own. The "cats and cabbages" comment is quoted in Barbara Reynolds, *The Passionate Intellect* (Kent,

contemporary language and controversial slang, is perhaps the most obvious example of this.

One could also interpret Sunday language as referring to language specifically about religious topics, and weekday language as referring to subjects not traditionally within the purview of the activities of the church or its reflection. Sayers protested the tendency of the church to require that Christian "celebrities" speak and write for the church's own purposes.[6] Part of her protest was that by requiring Christian professionals to speak chiefly on traditionally religious themes or occasions, the church was narrowing Christians' language and contributions. Sayers refused to be limited only to Sunday language; her protests grew in both intensity and frequency the more she felt pressured to give up her weekday language.

How this played out in Sayers's life is evident from the volume of writing she did about her own vocation. She reflected on art, writing, plays, and poetry, all through the lens of her Christian faith. She suggested repeatedly that the church permit Christian professionals to focus on their own vocations, whatever they might be. She called for a body of Christians who would think and write and speak about their own subjects with Christian assumptions behind them. Sayers wished the church would embrace, say, an expert in frogs as simply that—an

---

OH: Kent State University Press, 1989), 141. These comments also appear in Dorothy L. Sayers, introduction to *Purgatory*, by Dante Alighieri (New York: Penguin, 1955), 54. Sayers, like C. S. Lewis, was also gifted at crafting analogies, although she did not use them nearly as often as he did. Two of her best have to do with the exclusive claims of Christianity. In the chapter "The 'Laws' of Nature and Opinion" in *The Mind of the Maker* (San Francisco: HarperSanFrancisco, 1979), Sayers discusses the difference between laws and arbitrary conditions. She gives the example of arguing that to make an omelette one must wear a top hat (an arbitrary condition) versus arguing that to make an omelette one must first break the eggs (a law). In another context (Barbara Reynolds, ed., *The Letters of Dorothy L. Sayers*, vol. 3 [Cambridge: Dorothy L. Sayers Society, 1999], 276), Sayers refines this, citing the difference between saying, "If you drink prussic acid, you will die" (a law) and "If you drink prussic acid, I will kill you" (an opinion). Sayers was impatient with those who understood the Christian position on sin and death as an opinion, not as a law of certain consequences.

6. In a letter to Rev. Canon S. M. Winter, Sayers wrote about the church's "pathetic astonishment and gratification over any person with a reputation in secular affairs who will condescend to approve or patronise Christianity in public. 'Here,' she cries, waving flags, 'is actually an intelligent person—an astronomer, novelist, diplomat, stockbroker, painter, somebody with a proper job—who nevertheless is a Christian, or almost a Christian, or at least not actively anti-religious; how unexpected and complementary!' . . . Her next step is to do all she can to distract and impede him in the exercise of that job by taking him away to address meetings, write apologetics, and generally exhaust himself in ecclesiastical work which is *not* his proper job" (Sayers to Rev. Canon S. M. Winter, February 2, 1943, in *Letters of Dorothy L. Sayers*, vol. 2, 389).

expert in frogs rather than a Christian to be exploited for specifically religious purposes. She mentioned the trap of setting frog expertise opposite Christianity, arguing that instead the church must "take it for granted that Christianity and intelligence go together, and that all truths serve Truth; and so piously rejoice in froghood."[7] Sayers specifically mentioned frog experts, but her suggestion is worth considering for Christians in any profession. What would it look like for Christian physicians, film directors, teachers, homemakers, politicians, or scientists to reflect on their vocations through the eyes of faith as extensively as Sayers did?

Sayers, in mentioning "the carpenter's shop as well as the theologian's truth," also identified a larger problem among believers: the unwillingness to accept lay or "secular" vocations as valuable. This was not a new issue for the church. From the early centuries and increasingly in the Middle Ages, religious leaders and thinkers tended to elevate those with explicitly clerical or religious vocations (monks, priests, nuns) above the laity. When the church expected Sayers to write and speak on themes such as "What the Christian Faith Means to Me," it was asking her to take time away from the things God had given her to write or to say, which she felt denied her calling as a professional writer. Instead, she elevated her vocation, refusing to have it either denied or co-opted by the church.

In her writings, Sayers asserted the value of all vocations. Her essays "Vocation in Work," "Living to Work," and "Why Work?" asserted the need for every person to have meaningful work. Even if someone were in a largely mundane job, Sayers argued, there should be room for creativity and meaning, either in the job or in that person's outside hobbies. Sayers's convictions about creativity, as rooted in humanity's reflection of God's image, elevated all creative work to the level of godly work.

Sayers's criticism of the church's views vis-à-vis secular vocation was scathing, especially in "Why Work?":

> In nothing has the Church so lost her hold on reality as in her failure to understand and respect the secular vocation. She has allowed work and religion to become separate departments, and is astonished to find that as a result, the secular work of the world is turned to purely selfish and destructive ends, and that the greater part of the world's intelligent workers have become irreligious or at least uninterested in religion. But is it astonishing? How can anyone remain interested in a religion which seems to have no concern with nine-tenths of his life?[8]

7. Dorothy L. Sayers to Noel Davey, October 18, 1945, Wade document 28/105–6.
8. Dorothy L. Sayers, "Why Work"? in *Creed or Chaos?* (New York: Harcourt, Brace, & Co., 1949), 56.

She criticized the church for failing to see secular vocations as sacred, challenging church and clergy to acknowledge that when someone is called to a particular secular job, it is as true a vocation as specifically religious work. Her own "No More Religion" was a constant reminder to correspondents that she believed her calling from God was not to be an ever-present "Christian celebrity" addressing mission societies or opening church gatherings. She was to serve God through her work.

How did Sayers's own work interact with her church involvements? Late in life she was a churchwarden for the parish of St. Thomas, Regent Street, in London. Her involvement with this parish was connected with its mission to intellectuals through the St. Anne's Society, also called St. Anne's House.[9] This organization was founded in 1943 by Rev. Patrick McLaughlin and Rev. Gilbert Shaw as "a centre of liaison between the Christian Faith at its most intelligent . . . level, and the Secular Intellect at that point where it is most conscious of social and ethical responsibilities."[10] St. Anne's provided an opportunity for thinking people to hear the Christian faith explained intelligently and to have their questions considered and discussed with thoughtfulness and integrity. Sayers described one of the events of St. Anne's House in a letter to the editor of the *Daily Sketch*:

> A number of Christian priests and laymen will make it their business to explain how the Christian revelation does "make sense" of the universe and of the lives of individual men and women. There will be services, lectures and discussions; and in addition, the message of the Faith will be presented through the arts of drama, music, etc. Every effort will be made to deal with questions of today in terms relevant to the needs of twentieth-century people.[11]

9. See Dorothy L. Sayers, "Saint Anne's Day," presentation given on July 26, 1957, from the article file of the Wade Center. For more detailed information about St. Anne's House, see James Brabazon, *Dorothy L. Sayers* (New York: Charles Scribner's Sons, 1981), 239–42, 267–68.

10. Ibid.

11. Dorothy L. Sayers to the editor of the *Daily Sketch*, March 1, 1946, in *Letters of Dorothy L. Sayers*, vol. 3, 202–3. In her "Saint Anne's Day" presentation, Sayers spoke in more detail about the special needs of the contemporary audience, saying that the work of St. Anne's House "may be called part of the work of evangelisation; but it is evangelisation of a very special kind, addressed to a very special set of people, and that in conditions quite unprecedented in the history of Faith. . . . It is a new kind of heathendom. It is not merely a question of preaching Christ to those who know little or nothing of Him and dislike what they know; nor even of persuading agnostics that there is a God who creates and judges. We are dealing with a generation who literally do not believe that there is any judgment at all."

Thus, she managed to combine her church involvement with some of her strongest vocational gifts, those of artistic expression and "sanctification of the intellect."

Sayers was also committed to keeping the experiences and perspectives of the everyday soul in view when discussing, formulating, and communicating her convictions and ideas.[12] Her complaints about the failure of the clergy to communicate with the person in the pew reflected her perception that the clergy was not sufficiently in touch with parishioners' lived experiences. Sayers's own contributions were founded in the real world. For example, her speeches and writings about postwar reconstruction were rooted firmly in her own experiences and in her observations about life in England during the war. Sayers's theory of a trinitarian creative process and her arguments about the worth of work also came out of her personal work history.

Sayers for Today

Given Sayers's concerns about being co-opted by the church, it may be risky to use the language of "appropriation" vis-à-vis her theological contribution. Does calling attention to her as a lay theologian and encouraging the people of God to use her work for theological purposes violate her desire to be appreciated as a professional writer? Not necessarily, given the connection between her professional writing and her effectiveness as a lay theologian.[13] Calling attention to her explicitly theological work does

12. In 1936, Sayers gave an address titled "The Importance of Being Vulgar" to benefit the British Red Cross Hospitals Library fund. According to a February 13 review in the *Daily Telegraph*, "by vulgarity Miss Sayers meant the feelings and emotions of the common people, and she had no difficulty making her point that the great writer must be able to understand and share those emotions" (London Staff, review of "Being Vulgar," *Daily Telegraph*, February 13, 1936, page unknown). Interestingly, Sayers's later research about Dante unearthed the fact that he had begun writing a document (never finished) called "Writing in the Vulgar Tongue" (Dante Alighieri, *Hell*, trans. Dorothy L. Sayers [London: Penguin, 1949], 39).

13. Sayers herself invited the church to make use of cultural contributions, warning that if the church did not, they would be used for other purposes. In "Types of Christian Drama," she wrote, "If there is any strong natural urge which the Church neglects to baptize and incorporate into her own life, it will not conveniently atrophy and disappear. It will go on its own way, becoming increasingly secularized, and eventually putting itself at the service of any rival religion which is ready to make use of it. And in the meanwhile, the Church itself will become impoverished for lack of that natural power and vivacity. . . . She has vacated a particularly dominating pulpit and has no right to appear pained and surprised if she finds it occupied by other preachers with powerful lungs" (Dorothy L. Sayers, "Types of Christian Drama, with Some Notes on Production," *VII: An Anglo-American Literary Review* 2 [1981]: 85). While it is unlikely that "rival religions" would

not negate the rest of what she wrote. If anything, it provides a balance to the volumes of work already published about her mysteries and her Dante translation. Further, as explored in chapter 2, Sayers was effective as a lay theologian largely because of her experience as a professional writer. Had the church succeeded in forcing Sayers to write according to its own agenda, her work may have lacked the inspiration that gives it life and therefore would not be at all useful to the church or the world.

Perhaps Sayers's concerns should shape *how* we use her, though. Her protests about her lack of theological training, for example, remind us not to see Sayers as an ultimate authority and not to look to her on every topic of interest to Christians. She does provide, however, an important dialogue partner for academic theology. Where the people of God are intimidated by theologians, Sayers can provide clarity and infuse dogma with life. Professional theologians can learn from Sayers how to communicate their ideas with clarity and style. Where Sayers herself is unsure of her theological reach, people with theological backgrounds can testify to her orthodoxy.[14]

While it is appropriate to remain mindful of Sayers's protests, perhaps using Sayers's idea of a partnership between the church and professional writers is a helpful way of thinking about utilizing her work. After all, Christians already use the writings of C. S. Lewis and other writers in their personal devotions and for corporate study. With that partnership in mind, we return to how the people of God can learn from Sayers's work. These suggestions will focus mainly on writings that are in print, as it is difficult for large numbers of people to gain access to her other publications.[15]

A recent reading/discussion group in Wheaton, Illinois, provides an interesting example of how Sayers's writings can be used by the people of God. We are fortunate to have a detailed description of the genesis, formation, and study process of this group, courtesy of Marjorie L. Mead of the Marion E. Wade Center.[16] Sayers's Dante translation is still in use

---

get very far by trying to make use of Sayers without tripping over her strong Christian convictions, it *is* true that the church has neglected to baptize and incorporate Sayers's theological contribution into its life.

14. In fact, Sayers told a correspondent that she had theologically trained colleagues check the theology of her work to make sure that what she was writing was orthodox (see Dorothy L. Sayers to Rev. W. A. W. Jarvis, January 10, 1946, in Reynolds, *Letters of Dorothy L. Sayers*, vol. 3, 194).

15. Some of the writings mentioned herein may have recently gone out of print, but it may be possible to find them in bookstores. Other out-of-print materials are readily available in public and university libraries. To locate out-of-print books, see www.bibliofind.com and www.abebooks.com.

16. I am indebted to Ms. Mead, who was gracious enough to describe this group in detail to me via email. The information and much of the phraseology in these next paragraphs are hers.

in universities, and evidently more people read *The Divine Comedy* in the first forty years after she translated it than in all the decades and even centuries between Dante's time and the mid-1950s.[17] Dante is intimidating to many, but Sayers took a great story and made it accessible even to those afraid of the material. The essays and notes accompanying Sayers's Dante translations provide a literary introduction to medieval and scholastic theology, among other topics.

Mead, associate director of the Wade Center at Wheaton College, invited a group of people to join her in reading and studying Sayers's Dante translation, beginning in 1997.[18] The group included current and former Wheaton College staff and faculty; certain members were invited because they had expertise in particular areas that would benefit the discussion.[19] Many group members had never read Dante before; most had not used Sayers's translation even if they had read it. The group met weekly in the Wade Center reading room during a lunch hour. The members read aloud and discussed two cantos a week. The group read through roughly one volume a semester, taking a break in the summer.

Because people from different departments and vocations participated, there was a "very genuine interplay" and an "interesting, significant discussion" that few other campus opportunities offered. Mead describes the group this way: It was "a perfect example of what the academic en-

---

17. Barbara Reynolds lauds this "remarkable cultural event. . . . Since the publication of *Hell* in 1949, followed by *Purgatory* in 1955 and by *Paradise*, which came out posthumously in 1962, Dante has had more English-speaking readers in the last forty years than he had in the preceding six and a quarter centuries" (Reynolds, *Passionate Intellect*, xii). *The Letters of Dorothy L. Sayers*, vol. 3 is largely a celebration of this "cultural event."

18. The genesis of the group was a suggestion by a colleague about starting a group to read Dante aloud. Mead, because of her interest in Dante's and Sayers's ideas and the impressions their work had on their readers, broadened the group to include both reading and discussion.

19. This particular group included representatives familiar with philosophy, theology, literature, and music. In addition, one group member knew Italian. Group members represented both Protestant and Catholic traditions. Mead shares, "All of these variables really enhanced our discussion times" (conversation via email). In addition, this particular group was helped by the membership by fax of Barbara Reynolds, who is an Italianist and who completed Sayers's translation of *Purgatory*. Reynolds faxed the group each week with comments on the cantos they were scheduled to read and answered questions generated by the group. This is a nice example of how an "expert" can be involved, even if he or she is not nearby or not able to participate regularly. Mead notes that in the case of Dante, "much of this could be gained by those who do not have access to . . . [Reynolds], however, by simply using her *Passionate Intellect* as a secondary source" (conversation via email). Groups meeting to study the theology in Sayers's novels could similarly use Janice Brown, *The Seven Deadly Sins in the Work of Dorothy L. Sayers* (Kent, OH: Kent State University Press, 1998); and William David Spencer, *Mysterium and Mystery: The Clerical Crime Novel* (Ann Arbor: UMI Research Press, 1989) as resource materials.

terprise should be but all too rarely is—people of various backgrounds gathering for the sheer delight of learning."[20] Much of Sayers's work can be used in similar cross-disciplinary scholarly groups and also in church adult education contexts, home groups, seminary courses, and even informal gatherings of friends. The possibilities are legion.[21] Reading and discussion groups are quite common in recent years.

Groups formed for other reasons can also benefit from reading Sayers. The Southern California C. S. Lewis Society makes a point of reading one episode of Sayers's *Man Born to Be King* together every year. The society also hosted a 2001 summer workshop on C. S. Lewis's and Dorothy L. Sayers's perspectives on creativity and calling. Sayers's work also makes regular appearances in gatherings of the Mythopoeic Society, a group whose intended purpose is to study the writings of C. S. Lewis, J. R. R. Tolkien, and Charles Williams.

Clarification/Restatement

Certainly, basic Christian beliefs are still misunderstood, for a variety of reasons. Because of the proliferation of nondenominational church movements and the increasing population of nonchurched people, the traditional creeds are no longer in use or familiar to parishioners except in the most liturgical churches.[22] Furthermore, since the last decade or two of the twentieth century, both the religious-political right and the

20. Conversation via email.

21. While there will be some guidelines proposed for appropriating Sayers's work, I am hesitant to be too specific in suggesting what kinds of people and/or groups should use her various writings. Readers are encouraged to be creative, forming reading/study/discussion groups across church, neighborhood, generational, and vocational lines. For example, a speaker at the 1998 Wheaton Theology Conference made a particularly compelling presentation about a group that had formed in her home to study C. S. Lewis's Chronicles of Narnia. The group included teenagers, parents, and "grandparent" figures, one of whom was a retired minister and could help interpret the theology in Lewis's work (Gretchen Erhardt, "Aslan Counters Relativism: The Importance of Theology in the Dining Room" [paper presented at the Wheaton Theology Conference, 1998, Wheaton, IL]). If I am not mistaken, the group continued to meet for additional book study and discussion after completing the Narnia series.

22. Sayers would find this state of affairs lamentable, as she saw the creeds as the best way to make sure that what one was articulating was "actually Christianity, and not some private religion one has invented out of one's own taste and fancy, which are so apt to run away with one" (Dorothy L. Sayers to G. F. Littleboy, February 19, 1951, in Barbara Reynolds, ed., *The Letters of Dorothy L. Sayers*, vol. 4 [Cambridge: Dorothy L. Sayers Society, 2000], 3.) I have said "traditional creeds" here because even the least liturgical churches often observe some oft-implicit form of creed, be it a statement of faith or some other body of convictions and standards.

religious-political left have identified various cultural values with Christian beliefs, making it difficult for churched and nonchurched alike to distinguish between Christian doctrine and cultural conviction.

Some of Sayers's clarifying writings could be used by entire churches, with pastors or theologically educated members taking the lead in helping parishioners understand and grapple with orthodox and historical belief and doctrine. This is perhaps especially true in newer churches that do not have strong historical or credal roots.[23] However, other of her writings are just as useful for the individual Christian (and, in some cases, non-Christian) as for group or congregational use.

Some of Sayers's explicitly theological work is eerily relevant today. For example, her essay "The Other Six Deadly Sins" anticipates by several decades the current myopia in some parts of the church regarding sexual sin (to the exclusion of other, potentially more deadly, sins).[24] This analysis of the deadly sins challenges both beliefs about sin and how they influence subsequent actions. One venue in which this essay could be used is the community in which a member has "fallen" into some sort of sexual sin. In such situations (as when a member of a Christian community becomes pregnant out of wedlock, as did Sayers, although her community was not aware of it), community members often succumb to gossip and condemnation. Jesus' response to this was to challenge his audience, "If any one of you is without sin, let him be the first to throw a stone at her" (John 8:7). Sayers's essay, in clarifying how the church has historically understood various kinds of sin, reminds believers that "there is no one who does good, not even one" (Pss. 14:3; 53:1, 3; Rom. 3:10). Studying the essay together, whether as a congregation,

---

23. This requires, of course, that church leaders grapple with Sayers's writings in the first place. John Thurmer's concerns about how the theological "guild" often fails to respect the amateur or the interdisciplinary writer may come into play here. Are seminaries willing to use Sayers's writings in educating pastors? Are pastors willing to use her work in their own personal development and in that of the people they lead? As it is appropriate, I will make suggestions about using Sayers's essays, plays, and letters in the seminary classroom as well as in congregational or small-group settings.

24. Janice Brown's analysis of Sayers's understanding of the deadly sins reflects the latter's view, like that of others before her, that pride is the deadliest sin of all (Brown, *Seven Deadly Sins in the Work of Dorothy L. Sayers*, 38). Sayers, in explaining the image of the lustful in Dante's second circle of hell, says of lust, "Dante, with perfect orthodoxy, rates it as the least hateful of the deadly sins. (Sexual sins in which love and mutuality have no part find their place far below)" (Dante, *Hell*, 101). Sayers's essay "Christian Morality" also examines the difference between, in particular, Christ's morality and the ways the church has interpreted—or misinterpreted—it (Dorothy L. Sayers, "Christian Morality," in *The Whimsical Christian* [New York: Collier, 1978]). Ralph Hone cites in his collection of Sayers's poetry her whimsical rhyme, "As years come in and years go out, I totter toward the tomb, / Still caring less and less about who goes to bed with whom" (*Poetry of Dorothy L. Sayers*, 152).

a church staff or board, or a small group, allows the sexual sin to be put in perspective and requires other members of the community to face issues and sins, such as pride, in their own lives.[25]

"The Other Six Deadly Sins" and "Christian Morality," which is not as readily available, could also be useful in the instruction of new Christians. Because Christianity is perceived as being about particular do's and don'ts, it can be helpful to examine a more systematic way of viewing morality. Many Christians are unaware of the church's historical stance on sin, its consequences, and how it can or should be addressed by the body of Christ. Janice Brown's *Seven Deadly Sins in the Work of Dorothy L. Sayers* provides some historical material and a helpful context for understanding these essays.

"The Dogma Is the Drama" contrasts what the church believes, according to its creeds, with how the typical Christian is perceived, "in the likeness of a crashing and rather ill-natured bore," as mentioned in chapter 3. This essay is largely an exhortation to Christian believers about how they present Christianity to the outside world. Sayers's mock "catechism" reveals how limited and/or distorted the average Christian's understanding of his or her faith is. This is not necessarily an appropriate source of study for those just joining the church. Rather, it is perhaps best used either in adult education or in small groups of those who have been Christians for some time. This document, in particular, has a certain amount of shock value in that Sayers challenges the Christian status quo in no uncertain terms. Therefore, it is necessary to frame its use in a way that helps those studying the essay to receive it without being defensive. It is also easy for people to dismiss some of Sayers's more prophetic commentary simply because it is funny. Once the laughter has died down, it is important to take seriously what she has observed about Christians' naïveté and occasional apathy. It may take some intentional guidance from a group leader for those reading the essay to dig to a deeper level.

"The Greatest Drama Ever Staged" addresses some of the same issues as "The Dogma Is the Drama" but would be useful to nonbelievers as well as believers. This would be an interesting essay with which to begin an investigative Bible discussion or a dialogue between intelligent Christians and thinking nonbelievers who wonder exactly what the Christian faith is about. Interestingly, a group of British churches courted controversy several years ago by advertising its Easter services using a

---

25. The American church failed grievously in 1998 when it so readily condemned President Clinton for his peccadilloes, however inappropriate, but was absolutely silent on the single largest act of gossip in human history, the online posting and publication of the Starr report.

poster of Jesus looking like a well-known painting of revolutionary Che Guevara with the caption "Meek. Mild. As If. Discover the Real Jesus. Church. April 4." Sayers's message in "The Greatest Drama Ever Staged" is singularly appropriate to this endeavor and could easily be used in Easter sermons or in follow-up discussions for interested visitors. She too identified Jesus as a revolutionary, reminding believers that

> the people who hanged Christ never, to do them justice, accused Him of being a bore—on the contrary; they thought Him too dynamic to be safe. It has been left for later generations to muffle up that shattering personality and surround Him with an atmosphere of tedium. . . . To those who knew Him, however, He in no way suggested a milk-and-water person; *they* objected to him as a dangerous firebrand.[26]

Again, this essay could make Christians defensive, but Sayers would suggest that perhaps they need to be.[27] The dialogue between nonbelievers discovering Christ's revolutionary side and believers who have obscured it, however unintentionally, could prove quite dynamic.

"Creed or Chaos?" reminds the people of God that forms of Arianism and other early church heresies recur throughout history.[28] Some of Sayers's letters make this point even more strongly. In her correspondence with Father D'Arcy about a handbook of heresies, for example, she wrote:

> One's always wanting to say of some bright new brand of religion that this is nothing new, but simply dear old Eutychianism or Apollinarianism or what not, that everybody was already tired of in the year dot, but by the time one's hunted around to be quite sure what precise brand of irregularity it represents, the moment for effective repartee has gone by. . . . They are always sneering at "Neo-Orthodoxy"—let's have a little "Neo-Heresy" for a change. "Professor Dash and the other Neo-Sabellians"—"Mr. Blank's somewhat austere Neo-Nestorianism"—"the vapourings of Mrs. Asterisk and the Neo-Manichees"—"Dr. Obelisk and the Neo-Patripassian revival" would look very good in a review.[29]

26. Dorothy L. Sayers, "The Greatest Drama Ever Staged," in *Creed or Chaos?* (New York: Harcourt, Brace, & Co., 1949), 5.

27. How well some of Sayers's more blunt commentary is accepted by God's people may depend on how it is presented. If a respected individual comes to those with whom he or she worships and presents Sayers's challenges as important for all believers, a study endeavor may work better than if a new pastor imposed them on a resistant congregation, for example.

28. Both Jehovah's Witnesses and Mormons reflect Arianism in their belief systems, but most Christians are not aware of this, nor have they been educated about exactly why it is heretical to suggest that Jesus was a created being.

29. Dorothy L. Sayers to Rev. Father D'Arcy, July 19, 1941, Wade document 205/19.

Studying "Creed or Chaos?" along with certain of Sayers's letters would allow Christians to clarify their own orthodoxy and convictions while learning how to confront heresy in its modern forms. This essay, however, needs to be used either in conjunction with some good references on early church history and patristic thought or in the presence of an individual who can explain the various heresies as Sayers raises them. Thus, it may be suited for use in a short-term adult education course or a cross-disciplinary scholarly discussion group such as the one that studied Dante. "Creed or Chaos?" would also make a nice addition to a seminary course on patristic theology.

Sayers's letters, some volumes of which are available through online booksellers or through the Dorothy L. Sayers Society, place her frustrations, corrections, and convictions in context. They also present her thought in small, discrete amounts, ideal for individual or group reflection. The letters are also a useful way for those interested primarily in her mysteries to be introduced to Sayers's thought more broadly and to her more extensive theological reflection.

Sayers's works that focus on clarifying doctrine are useful not only in articulating orthodoxy but also in confronting misunderstanding. In an age in which some branches of the church are increasingly anti-intellectual, her challenge to engage in disciplined thought is essential.[30] Her "Letter to Average People," for example, rebukes those who either practice or deny Christianity without a clear understanding of it. So does the essay "The Greatest Drama Ever Staged," which takes a slightly more gentle approach: "Before we dismiss Christ as a myth, an idealist, a demagogue, a liar or a lunatic—it will do no harm to find out what the creeds really say about him. What does the church think of Christ?"[31]

The cultural do's and don'ts embraced by many Christians have often contributed to the tendency of the world to reject Christianity. Believers today need to be challenged to articulate their beliefs clearly and to separate basic convictions from cultural expectations. Sayers's essays and letters, given their clear statement of right belief and mistaken impres-

30. Sayers remarked in 1942 that "my theology is much too intellectual to get over to the man in the street. I find it very difficult to view the matter in those terms of personal relationship which mean so much to most people" (Dorothy L. Sayers to the bishop of Derby, February 25, 1942, Wade document 112/4). Her thoughts about the common person's emphasis on personal relationship over solid theology, while articulated nearly sixty years ago, would be just as appropriate today. While Sayers perceived her theology as too intellectual for the person on the street, however, it was at least clearer than what that person might hear in church. Dorothy L. Sayers, "The Contempt of Learning in Twentieth Century England," *Fortnightly* 153 (April 1940): 373–82 offers a fascinating analysis of why anti-intellectualism has been on the rise in the last century.

31. Sayers, "Greatest Drama Ever Staged," 3.

sion, contribute to that challenge in both content and method. Further, her lifetime commitment to intellectual integrity models what it looks like for a thinking Christian to dialogue with other intellectuals.[32]

Exploring Traditional Doctrine

While clergy in most mainline denominations undergo extensive seminary training, including the study of both church history and theology, these subjects are not always communicated to the person in the pew. A number of assumptions may contribute to this circumstance. For example, people would not find these subjects interesting, or there are more important things in which to invest a congregation's time. In nondenominational churches, where seminary education is often optional or conducted on an irregular basis, clergy *and* congregations are even less likely to be well versed in the history of the faith and traditional doctrine. Churches that do teach theology and history often focus on their own traditions, neglecting the history and convictions of the wider Christian movement.

Sayers's work is especially valuable in teaching both church history and doctrine because it makes these subjects accessible to the common person. *The Emperor Constantine*, for example, has educational value in regard to both the doctrine of the Trinity and the context in which those beliefs were clarified. The scene about the Council of Nicea was especially successful in exciting audiences about trinitarian doctrine. The council scene could be read corporately in the context of adult education or congregational study or used in a seminary class on early church history or patristic theology. Again, it would be helpful to consult reference works or to have group members research various aspects of the Nicene controversy.[33]

The Mind of the Maker is a more analytical and explicitly theological study of the Trinity. One way to make it more accessible is to begin with the analogy about creative art and invite artists—lay or professional—in the group to apply the analogy to their forms of art. A group of students

32. Her letters provide perhaps the best example of this. In them, we often see extensive discussions with people whose convictions were quite different from Sayers's. She did not shy away from these challenges unless they were simply not well supported by logic and reason.

33. If a group planned to meet for several weeks, one useful approach might be to study "Creed or Chaos?" using the glossary to clarify the various theological controversies mentioned. If the group were interested in more detail, members could each research a particular conflict and report back. Then the group could read—or even act out—the Council of Nicea scene from *The Emperor Constantine*.

at Fuller Seminary tried this in 1999 with fascinating effect. Each student was invited to bring a creative item he or she had made and to discuss it in light of Sayers's Idea/Energy/Power model. One student brought several quilts to show. As she displayed each quilt, she mentioned the ways in which it was "scalene" in its trinity. She then unfolded one while saying, "I think this one balances the Idea, Energy, and Power the best." She was right—the entire class gasped as they saw it. The experience was a perfect depiction of the strength of Sayers's model and of the power of the Holy Spirit to use art to communicate.[34]

A group could also pursue an artistic project together and reflect on the Idea, Energy, and Power manifested in that project. Beginning with a tangible situation and moving to the theological analogue mirrors how Sayers herself composed the book and indeed how much of her theological understanding grew out of real life. Artists' groups could also benefit from reading parts of *The Zeal of Thy House*, as the Lewis Society 2001 creativity and calling workshop did. Given Sayers's concerns about the lack of an intelligent Christian theology of the arts, a group of artists and theologians could be brought together around several of her writings on the arts for the purpose of formulating a more coherent theology in this area.

The Man Born to Be King is useful in a study of the incarnation. It could be read in conjunction with the Gospels over the course of several months in an academic, small-group, or larger church setting. Seminarians are familiar with Kurt Aland's *Synopsis of the Four Gospels*; Sayers's radio plays often serve a similar function.[35] The introduction to the play series provides a fascinating analysis of how Christ's dual nature challenged those staging the plays; as such, this portion could be used in a course on christological doctrine.

As shown in chapter 3, Sayers managed to bring what many thought was dead to life, both through translation and incarnation.[36] *The Man*

---

34. An artists' or writers' group might further benefit from *The Mind of the Maker* by analyzing their own art or writing according to Sayers's "scalene Trinities" and seeking to improve its balance. Dorothy L. Sayers, "Towards a Christian Aesthetic," in *Unpopular Opinions* (New York: Harcourt, Brace, & Co., 1947) would also provide a helpful undergirding for their work—as it would for Christian institutions grappling with the place of art in the church.

35. In fact, one of her letters reveals that Sayers made her own four-column diagram of the Gospels in preparation for writing *The Man Born to Be King* (Reynolds, *Letters of Dorothy L. Sayers*, vol. 3, 273).

36. For many, it seems, the faith of their fathers and mothers is dead. A California university newspaper in the mid-1980s advertised a support group for "Adult Children of Catholics" (this announcement appeared in the *California Aggie*, the campus paper for the University of California at Davis). The shaping (and potentially destructive) power of being raised in the church is reflected in contemporary book titles as well: *Growing Up*

Born to Be King took one of the oldest and most-told stories in human history and made it new. Reading it today can make it new for contemporary readers and listeners too.[37] The play has often been a part of Christians' Lenten preparation for Easter. For a group that wants to read *The Man Born to Be King* in the weeks leading up to Easter, the schedule according to which Sayers suggested the various parts be aired is included in appendix C.[38] Dramatic experience or ability is not as important as the ability to read well aloud. Some of the plays even include children, making *The Man Born to Be King* particularly suitable for use by families and home churches.

Sayers's nativity play *He That Should Come* was rereleased in 1998 in the volume *Two Plays about God and Man*, along with *The Devil to Pay*. The 1998 volume contains production suggestions for those wishing to perform these plays. *He That Should Come* was originally a radio play, and this is suitable for simple reading in groups of fifteen or more. The action takes place at the inn in whose stable Mary gave birth. Because of the subject

Born-Again (by Patricia Klein); and *The Dangers of Being Raised in a Christian Home* (by Donald Sloat, who has since written *Growing Up Holy and Wholly: Understanding and Hope for Adult Children of Evangelicals*). One finds in the more "alternative" belief systems and trends a reaction to traditional forms and practices of faith. Pop singer Madonna, who has combined yoga and Eastern spirituality with kaballah, a mystical branch of Judaism involving the study of sacred texts, is just one example of the trajectory of postmodern faith and practice. While the recent spiritual resurgence has benefitted the Christian church somewhat, seekers are also exploring myriad options beyond traditional Christianity. Recent polls have found a 10 to 20 percent decline in church attendance in this country over the last thirty years. While this data is confounded by the fact that Americans tend to overreport their church attendance, certain studies have been formatted in such a way as to control for the factors related to overreporting. For more on both the decline in attendance and the difficulty in interpreting these statistics, see Andrew Walsh, "Church, Lies, and Polling Data," *Religion in the News* 1, no. 2 (Fall 1998): 9–11.

37. I have listened to one of the early BBC broadcasts (but not the first) of *The Man Born to Be King* and have heard both American and British casts read individual plays at the 1997 Sayers Society meeting at Wheaton College. One of the most vivid readings I have heard, however, was in the context of a seminary class in California in early 1997, where an international and multicultural cast read one of the first plays in the series. To a native Californian for whom a multicultural context is both natural and expected, this reading brought the story to life as no other reading had. By contrast, hearing the BBC production—with which Sayers had even been involved—in solely British accents was not particularly inspiring for me. The American cast for the 1997 Sayers Society meeting was taken from Wheaton College's drama department and showed how a well-rehearsed and professional group of actors can bring this material to life. At the beginning of 2004, a theater company in Cambridge, England, performed the plays to similar effect.

38. When the Southern California C. S. Lewis Society reads them annually, members simply read around the table—no parts are assigned. While this is both necessary and appropriate given the format of their meetings, I find it much more enlivening to assign different participants to different parts so that the same character is being voiced by the same reader each time.

matter, this play is especially appropriate for Advent reading. However, in light of Sayers's suggestion to teach doctrine also in the summer months, one might use this play in the "off-season" as a change of pace.

Having *The Devil to Pay* back in print is a special treat. Taken in combination with "Strong Meat" and "The Triumph of Easter," both of which are published in *Creed or Chaos?* this play provides an important exploration of evil. While Sayers often had Hitler (and occasionally Mussolini) in mind when writing on this subject, the actions of leaders such as Hussein and Milosevic and of repressive governments worldwide and inner-city conflicts at home bring questions about evil to the forefront of every generation.

Theological Reflection on Everyday Life

History and doctrine are not the only arenas in which Sayers's work contributes to the education of God's people. "Are Women Human?" provides excellent material for discussion on women's issues, either in women's groups or (preferably) in mixed groups. Sayers's analysis of how meaningful work was removed from the home with the growth of industry is grist for valuable conversations between spouses when one partner works chiefly at home. Many who choose to stay home to raise children have never known home life to be as meaningful as it was in the preindustrial era, but there are modifications one can make to one's activities and purchasing habits to restore some of that meaningful activity. For example, baking one's own bread or growing/raising one's own food rather than buying commercial products brings some of the meaningful activity that industry removed back to the home. "The Human-Not-Quite-Human" also raises helpful issues about how we assess the value of women's and men's contributions. Catherine Kenney's biography of Sayers, *The Remarkable Case of Dorothy L. Sayers*, contains a section on Sayers's treatment of women in her writings. This could be used as a companion to women's study of Sayers.[39]

39. Many analyses of Sayers's views on women, written from a wide variety of perspectives, have been published. See, for example, Elizabeth Say, *Evidence on Her Own Behalf: Women's Narrative as Theological Voice* (Savage, MD: Rowman & Littlefield, 1990); Carolyn Heilbrun, *Writing a Woman's Life* (New York: Ballantine Books, 1988); idem, "Dorothy L. Sayers: Biography between the Lines," in *Dorothy L. Sayers: The Centenary Celebration*, ed. Alzina Stone Dale, 1–14 (New York: Walker & Co., 1993); Mary Ellen Ashcroft, "Exorcising the Angel by Craft: Writing as Incantation/Incarnation in the Work of Dorothy L. Sayers" (Ph.D. diss., University of Minnesota, 1992); and studies on Sayers specifically as a woman novelist: Shona Elizabeth Simpson, "Making Scenes: Modernism and the Romance in 1930s Fiction by British Women Writers" (Ph.D. diss., Duke University, 1996); and Rhonda Jean Rockwell, "All's Fair: Gender, Imagination, and World War" (Ph.D. diss., University of California at Berkeley, 1993). See also Elizabeth A. Trembley, "'Collaring the Other Fellow's

The Lost Tools of Learning sets out Sayers's educational views, which are intriguing in and of themselves.[40] The realm of education was one in which Sayers conceded a desire to exercise "a little quiet influence in the right direction," as she wrote in November of 1948.[41] This Oxford address continues to be held up as a model for educational reform in the United States.[42] In fact, at a 2000 Sayers conference in Pennsylvania, one scholar shared that at classical education gatherings, many present are unaware that Sayers wrote anything other than *The Lost Tools of Learning*! Even students would eagerly participate in discussions about Sayers's influential essay.

Sayers's treatment of intellectual integrity, work, and pride, as communicated in *Gaudy Night*, *The Zeal of Thy House*, and *The Mind of the Maker*, has relevance to students, teachers, craftspeople, and workers in other fields as well. *Gaudy Night* would be especially beneficial for study in academic contexts. It provides a not-too-didactic way of addressing both integrity in conducting research and responsibility in supervising it. While Sayers argued that she understood the things of God via her intellect, *Gaudy Night* emphasizes the balance between the head and the heart and how each needs the other.

Sayers's convictions about work and vocation ("Why Work?" "Living to Work," "Vocation in Work," as well as material from many of her letters, especially volume 2, pp. 247–50 and volume 3, pp. 252–60) remain among her most underutilized and underappreciated writings. Ever-changing working conditions may make it difficult to establish an exact correspondence between her suggestions and contemporary work environments.[43] However, it behooves every worker to think through his

---

Property': Feminism Reads Dorothy Sayers," in *Women Times Three: Writers, Detectives, Readers*, ed. Kathleen Gregory Klein, 81–99 (Bowling Green, OH: Bowling Green State University Popular Press, 1995); Jennifer H. Disney, "Being Human: Dorothy Sayers on Vocation and the Feminine," *Mars Hill Review* 13 (Winter/Spring 1999): 53–61; and Kathleen Gregory Klein, "Dorothy Sayers," in *Ten Women of Mystery*, ed. Earl F. Bargainner, 10–39 (Bowling Green, OH: Bowling Green State University Popular Press, 1981).

40. See Reynolds, *Letters of Dorothy L. Sayers*, vol. 3, 336 for more information on the context in which *The Lost Tools* was presented. While the essay itself is not in print, one can often find it in libraries and online. My understanding is that it may have been placed online without permission.

41. Dorothy L. Sayers to Eric Partridge, November 29, 1948, in *Letters of Dorothy L. Sayers*, vol. 3, 410.

42. See Barbara Reynolds's editorial note in *Letters of Dorothy L. Sayers*, vol. 3, 489. She cites Douglas Wilson's 1991 book, *Recovering the Lost Tools of Learning*, and David B. Warner's 1994 Sayers Society presentation on the context and legacy of *The Lost Tools of Learning*.

43. This in itself raises an important question about working in contemporary society. One of Sayers's convictions was that every worker should be allowed a certain measure of creativity in his or her work. She wrote of the importance of being able to reach the

or her beliefs about work: its purpose, its theological justification, its limitations. By setting forth a comprehensive theology of vocation and work, Sayers provides the Christian worker with material for discussion, if not for a work-related *metanoia*.

"Why Work?" is still in print in *Creed or Chaos?* Combining it with the broader case study on vocation and work from chapter 7 offers several promising possibilities. Because Sayers's convictions challenge employers, employees, the public, and the church, people could gather in each of these configurations to study and discuss the implications of her writing on their behavior. Christian workers in general could benefit from a theological foundation for work. The church as a whole reflects far too little on the ethical implications of what we purchase and choose not to purchase and how we value workers and the worth of their work.

A logistically difficult but potentially valuable application of Sayers's writings could take place in a gathering of employers, business owners, and employees. For example, they could meet to hear a panel presentation on "A Christian Perspective on Work and Vocation according to Dorothy L. Sayers." The panel should include at least one owner/employer, at least one employee, and at least one economist, all of whom have familiarized themselves with Sayers's writings on these subjects. Each panelist could discuss, from his or her professional perspective, the implications and feasibility of applying Sayers's thought. The audience could then be broken into small groups for additional discussion, perhaps at one point separated into groups of employees, employers, and economists, and at another point divided so that each group contains a combination of people. If the employers and employees come from a variety of work situations, they could also be divided by type of work (e.g., all postal workers in one group, all university employees in another, all auto-industry plant workers in another).

It is quite possible that today's economists would see most of Sayers's views as either impractical or naïve.[44] Yet the fact remains that she pro-

---

end of the day and say, "Look at what I made today." In an increasingly service-oriented workplace, what is the equivalent of creative craft? Are there ways to encourage and accept creativity in today's workplace? Do owners and managers see the value of fostering such creativity, even in service industries?

44. Sayers faced these accusations even at the time she was writing about these subjects. She would protest, however, that her critics were beginning at the wrong point—an economic view of the worth of work rather than one endeavoring to understand human vocation. Economic realities do often force people into employment that is not fulfilling, but Sayers's own trajectory of work shows that, for her at least, it was possible to approach the "potboiling" work with dignity and integrity, and she did it long enough and successfully enough that she was able to move on to work that was more fulfilling.

pounded a uniquely Christian view of vocation and work. Perhaps her most powerful contributions to the people of God, in fact, are the value she placed on secular vocations and the way she brought her faith to her own work. How she lived out her Christianity in the context of her vocation is a model for others not called to explicitly religious work. By reflecting as much as she did on her vocation, on creativity, and on work and vocation as a whole, Sayers left a legacy to be mined by working Christians everywhere.

Inspiring the Laity

Given that lay theology involves reflecting Christianly on the data of everyday life, Sayers's material on vocation and work in particular inspires in several ways. For example, her insistence on the sacred nature of secular work allows laypeople to find meaning—even Christian meaning—in activity outside the church.[45] For those who feel ambivalent about working, Sayers elevated the value of work. For those confused about their divine purpose, she emphasized the importance of both identifying one's calling and honoring it. By challenging the church to honor secular vocations, Sayers provided a measure of freedom for laypeople whose church demands conflict with their work demands.

Sayers was not suggesting that people prioritize work over church attendance and involvement.[46] She was, rather, asking the church not to call people away from their true vocations to work for it unless such work was a part of their calling.[47] By emphasizing that different people

45. A friend once asked whether Sayers emphasized work to the exclusion of, for example, stay-at-home mothers. Sayers included this form of work among the vocations of those who "live to work." She was concerned about the home not being a meaningful *place* to work because industrialization had removed so many activities from the home, as she mentioned in *Are Women Human?* (Grand Rapids: Eerdmans, 1971). However, there seems to be a revival in recent years of home-based activity and industry. *Citizen* magazine published an article in 1999, "Modem Mamas," about people who choose to telecommute (work from home by computer) in order to be at home with their children (13, no. 1 [January 1999]: 20–21).

46. When she was writing, there was probably less overt conflict between attending church and going to work, as fewer businesses would have been open on Sundays, and churches would not have been offering as many weeknight and Saturday services as today's churches do.

47. Did Sayers articulate these ideas in contexts in which the people of God could hear them? We do not know who composed the audience for all of Sayers's addresses on work, although at least one of them, "Why Work?" was also published as a pamphlet after it was given. We know some local residents attended that speech (see Reynolds, *Letters of Dorothy L. Sayers*, vol. 2, 361). The address at the Dome, Brighton, was advertised to the public, so there were probably both laypeople and clergy present. One address was to a

are called by God to different work (both inside and outside the church), Sayers's writings restore a sense of vocation to believers who are less and less familiar with that concept.

Sayers also provides inspiration for the lay theologian. She was not a professional theologian, yet many of her insights and essays are unique, striking, and vitally important. Furthermore, Sayers demonstrated how God can be brought into the midst of both one's work and one's play or hobbies. Writing was her craft, and she used it skillfully and consistently in ways that glorified God and pointed God's people heavenward—even when that was not her overt goal. She never seemed to separate her writing from her faith, even when she was not writing directly about Christianity.

Sayers also modeled theological reflection in ways that inspire even those who are not professional writers. Throughout her work, her faith informed how she understood and thought about her world and her life. Few if any aspects of everyday existence were removed from Christian reflection. This is perhaps most evident in her letters, which may be why editor Barbara Reynolds believes they will outlast her other work.[48] How Sayers thought intelligently and faithfully about relationships; church and culture; questions about how we spend our money and our leisure time; how art—popular, professional, and commercial—is used for God's purposes (or confounds them); what the purposes and methods of education are; how the government and the church relate; and many other details of life witness to what she calls the sanctification of the intellect. We might also credit Sayers with "sanctifying" the laity, the arts, and work as well.

Sayers's willingness to chide both clergy and laity for making Christianity less appealing than it should be is also exemplary for lay thinkers. Her insistence that laypeople not be left out of theological discourse is a too-often-unheard cry. She cast a vote of confidence by speaking slightly above the heads of her readers and demanding that they rise to her level, if only for brief discussion.[49] She wanted

---

mixed gathering of Christians (the "Sword of the Spirit" group). "Are Women Human?" was delivered to a women's group and has since been widely reprinted. Sayers also mentioned to a friend, "I always seem to be expounding the Faith in pubs" (see ibid., 68).

48. In December 1945, C. S. Lewis wrote to Sayers suggesting this very possibility: "Although you have so little time to write letters you are one of the great English letter-writers. (Awful vision for you: 'It is often forgotten that Miss Sayers was known in her own day as an Author. We, who have been familiar from childhood with her Letters, can hardly realise' . . .)" (C. S. Lewis to Dorothy L. Sayers, in reply to her December 8, 1945, letter, in *Letters of Dorothy L. Sayers*, vol. 3, 182).

49. Biographer James Brabazon notes, "For her day and age, Dorothy calculated her readership with great accuracy. A few protested at the time about her snobbishness, but

the church to live its faith as abundantly as Jesus promised, and she was not shy of risking her reputation (or her pocketbook) to make sure that happened.[50]

Sayers can inspire the laity in other ways too. Her dismay at the clergy's misrepresentations of the Christian life and church history challenges church members to seek out truthful Christian and historical witnesses. She heard the needs of the people in the pew: their questions, their concerns, their misunderstandings about Scripture and of dogma. Her writings refuse to let laypeople rest on ignorance or plead theological naïveté. Laypeople must continue to question what is taught and to put it in its proper framework. Likewise, laypeople also bear some responsibility for misrepresenting Christianity, and Sayers's overall body of work presents us with an important challenge. Are we willing to look closely at what we believe and say about our faith and how that affects others' views of Christ and Christianity?

Sayers challenged and inspired churchgoers of her day, but virtually every challenge and inspiration also has a place in today's church. Several aspects of her character infuse her writings with additional life. She was inherently curious, excited about learning, with a keen dramatic flair even at a young age.[51] Her realization that the Bible depicted events that really happened and people that really existed meant that Sayers's biblical convictions were rock solid. Her confidence in the truth of what she believed was not shaken by all she knew about biblical criticism. How can we cultivate that curiosity and intellectual rigor in ourselves? Sayers's "Note on Creative Reading" from *Begin Here* (see appendix D) explains how to discipline our reading and thinking in ways that fully engage the material. In an age that is not reading based, these encouragements are more helpful than ever.

---

a great many more rejoiced in the sense that they were being allowed to share in the author's elevated viewpoint" (Brabazon, *Dorothy L. Sayers*, 124).

50. For example, Sayers earned relatively little money for writing *The Man Born to Be King* (although she probably earned royalties once the play was published). It was commissioned for the Children's Hour program on the BBC, and Sayers had some conflict with one of the BBC representatives over it. In at least one of her letters during this season, she wrote, "I shall now proceed to be autocratic—as anyone has a right to be, who is doing a hundred pounds' worth of work for twelve guineas" (Dorothy L. Sayers to May E. Jenkins, November 22, 1940, in Reynolds, *Letters of Dorothy L. Sayers*, vol. 2, 196).

51. Even in her very early letters, we find traces of embellished detail, seemingly included for its storytelling value. Reynolds's introduction to volume 1 of *Letters of Dorothy L. Sayers* points out that in many of the letters "the creative writer is plainly to be discerned: in her eye for a significant detail (an umbrella-stand stuck full of swords in France at the outbreak of World War I), her skill in bringing an episode to life by casting it in dialogue (Purfield and the pound of bacon), her satisfaction in making the most of a good tale (the wedding of her cousin Gerald Sayers)" (xviii).

John Thurmer observes in *Reluctant Evangelist* that Sayers's status as a layperson also afforded her some advantages that others did not have: "Whatever else may be said about Sayers's theology, she was positive. She did not need to be cautious, like an academic, or edifying, like a preacher."[52] While he bemoans the unwillingness of the theological "establishment" to give credence to lay thinkers such as Sayers, he recognizes that laypeople do not share the same limitations as theologians. The tendency of laypeople is often to assume that because they are not trained theologians, they therefore have nothing to offer in the theological realm. Sayers expressed this concern, but it did not deter her from communicating her theological reflections. The characteristics Thurmer identifies in the establishment—caution and a need to edify—were impediments against which Sayers protested. Rather than be intimidated by those with theological training, then, perhaps the laity can learn from Sayers about being less cautious, less deliberately didactic in their explorations of the Christian life—while still following faithfully where God is leading.

52. John Thurmer, "Sayers on the Trinity," in *Reluctant Evangelist: Papers on the Christian Thought of Dorothy L. Sayers* (W. Sussex: Dorothy L. Sayers Society, 1996), 42.

Epilogue

Directions for Future Research

*B*ecause relatively few people in the church are familiar with Sayers's writings beyond her mysteries, they miss out on the refreshing and pungent commentary she offers on religious themes. Sayers wrote in *Begin Here* that "the only thing that matters about a writer is whether he is qualified to deal with his subject or not, and whether what he says is false or true."[1] This study has examined, in part, Sayers's qualifications to write on theological themes and the truth of her teaching. Having examined those things that matter about Sayers, we can say confidently that it is time for the church to rediscover, or to encounter for the first time, the unclaimed treasure that lies very close to the surface of the Sayers corpus.

How can the scholarly establishment contribute to this rediscovery? This book has attempted to provide an overview of Sayers's contributions as a lay theologian, but one study cannot comprehensively illuminate such a rich field of inquiry. Recent technological advances make it possible to locate more of Sayers's published articles locally, which may inspire more scholarship among those who cannot travel to England or to Wheaton for further study. The publication of several volumes of her letters and access to others in the Wade archive allows—and, hopefully, encourages—more scholars to make use of her letters. Studying

---

1. Dorothy L. Sayers, *Begin Here: A Statement of Faith* (London: Victor Gollancz, 1940), 117.

unpublished documents remains important, as not all of her letters and manuscripts appear in published volumes. The lack of access to Sayers's larger library, however, may always impede further study on some level.

There are many topics on which we have touched only briefly here but which could easily be expanded into other volumes.[2] Janice Brown's analysis of the seven deadly sins in Sayers's work provides a model of how to trace one theological doctrine throughout the Sayers corpus—just as various scholars have explored Sayers's views of women or aspects of her creative theory. Any one of the traditional doctrines Sayers explored or the everyday topics on which she reflected theologically could be expanded into a full-length book.

Suzanne Bray has written a dissertation for the University of Lille on the influence of a variety of lay thinkers, Sayers included, on Britain during wartime.[3] One tantalizing area of study is the relationship of church and state in Sayers's work; this theme recurs in *The Emperor Constantine* and in her Dante work, as well as intermittently in other venues.

The field of Sayers studies is still relatively young, and her theological writings in particular are the one genre that has remained relatively untapped by scholars. It is hoped that this study will provoke further scholarship in the field as well as an interest in Sayers's writings in the church.

2. For example, Ralph Hone has written a literary biography of Sayers. It might also be appropriate to write a "theological biography," especially as most of her biographers are not theologically trained. Some careful and sustained exploration in England may be necessary to locate the exact source of Sayers's education on the ecumenical councils and the early church heresies. I have visited England twice, spoken with Anglican clergy, attempted to gain access to Sayers's library and to the sermons to which she was exposed at Oxford—with no success in tracking down this information.

3. While influence is a difficult area of study, one could certainly explore further Sayers's influence in a number of areas: theological, political, and social among them. Barbara Reynolds cites, for example, one study of the influence of *The Lost Tools of Learning* on educational reform in America (Barbara Reynolds, ed., *The Letters of Dorothy L. Sayers*, vol. 3 [Cambridge: Dorothy L. Sayers Society, 1999], 235).

Appendix A

Sayers's Explicitly Religious Writings

The following is a chronological digest of explicitly religious (mostly) published writings by Dorothy L. Sayers (dates are from Colleen Gilbert, *A Bibliography of Dorothy L. Sayers* [Hamden, CT: Archon Books, 1978]).

"Epiphany Hymn," 1917
Catholic Tales and Christian Songs, 1918
"Obsequies for Music," 1921
The Zeal of Thy House, 1937
"The Greatest Drama Ever Staged," 1938
"The Dogma Is the Drama," 1938
"The Triumph of Easter," 1938
"What Do We Believe?" 1939
"Is This He That Should Come?" 1939
"Strong Meat"/"The Food of the Full-Grown," 1939
The Devil to Pay, 1939
"Religious Drama and Production," 1939
He That Should Come, 1939
"The Alternatives before Society," 1939–40

Begin Here: A Statement of Faith, 1940
Creed or Chaos? 1940
"Creed or Chaos?" BBC Home Service broadcasts, 1940
"The Feast of St. Verb," 1940
"Devil, Who Made Thee?" 1940
"The Technique of the Sermon," 1940[1]
"Divine Comedy," 1940
"The Church in a New Age," 1941
"The Church's Responsibility," 1941
"The Religions behind the Nation," 1941
"God the Son," 1941[2]
"Forgiveness and the Enemy," 1941
"Introducing Children to the Bible," 1941
The Mind of the Maker, 1941
"Living to Work," 1941[3]
"Religious Education," 1941
"Vocation in Work," 1941
"Lord, I Thank Thee," 1942
"Why Work?" 1942
"The Other Six Deadly Sins," 1943
"The Christian Faith and the Theatre," 1943
The Man Born to Be King, 1943
"Towards a Christian Aesthetic," 1944
"The Execution of God," 1945
"The Faust Legend and the Idea of the Devil," 1945
"A Drama of the Christian Church," 1945[4]
"A Letter Addressed to 'Average People,'" 1946
The Just Vengeance, 1946
Unpopular Opinions, 1946
"Making Sense of the Universe," 1946

1. Review of *The Art of Preaching*, by Charles Smyth, *Spectator*, no. 5823, February 2, 1940, 150.
2. BBC talks for the Forces program: "Lord and God," "Lord of All Worlds," "The Man of Men," "The Death of God," "The World's Desire," and "The Touchstone of History."
3. Originally published as "Work—Taskmaster or Liberator?" *Homes and Gardens* 24, no. 1 (June 1942): 16–17, 62.
4. Review of *The House of the Octopus*, by Charles Williams, *International Review of Missions* 34, no. 136 (October 1945): 430–32.

"Problems of Religious Broadcasting," 1947[5]

Creed or Chaos and Other Essays, 1947

"The Meaning of Heaven and Hell," 1948

"The Meaning of Purgatory," 1948

The Emperor Constantine, 1951

"Canterbury and Religious Drama," 1951[6]

"Types of Christian Drama, with Some Notes on Production," 1952

"Is There a Definite Evil Power That Attacks People in the Same Way as There Is a Good Power That Influences People?" 1953[7]

"The Pantheon Papers," 1953–54

The Days of Christ's Coming, 1953

Foreword to *St. Anne's House*, 1953

"The Story of Easter," 1955

"The Story of Adam and Christ," 1955

"Christianity Regained," 1955[8]

"Sacred Plays," 1955 (republished as "Types of Christian Drama")

"The Story of Noah's Ark," 1955

"Playwrights Are Not Evangelists," 1955–56

"Christian Belief about Heaven and Hell," 1957[9]

Christian Letters to a Post-Christian World, 1969

"The Dogma in the Manger," 1982

"Worship in the Anglican Church," 1995

The Letters of Dorothy L. Sayers, vol. 2, 1997; and vol. 3, 1999

5. A letter in the *BBC Quarterly* 2 no. 1 (April 1947): 29–31. According to Colleen Gilbert, it discusses how "Christian programmes should lead 'to a practical increase of belief in God or of Charity to one's neighbour'; they should not be solely entertainment" (Colleen Gilbert, *A Bibliography of the Works of Dorothy L. Sayers* [Hamden, CT: Archon Books, 1978], 187). It was followed by "Problems of Religious Broadcasting: A Further Letter from Miss Sayers," *BBC Quarterly* 2, no. 2 (July 1947): 104, where Sayers evidently wrote, "The fight is about the Faith, and . . . I am fighting (a) those critics of his [referring to Kenneth Grayson, who had evidently written in response to her first letter] department, without the Church who demand that it should broadcast propaganda for anti-Christian religions; (b) those critics of his department, within the Church, who would like to reduce its teaching to an endless emotional orgy with no nasty dogma about it; (c) the enemies of Christianity, who and wheresoever" (ibid., 187–88).

6. See Gilbert, *Bibliography of the Works of Dorothy L. Sayers*, 212.

7. In Ronald Selby Wright, ed., *Asking Them Questions*, Third Series (London: Oxford University Press, 1953).

8. Review of *Surprised by Joy*, by C. S. Lewis, *Time and Tide* (October 1, 1955): 1263–64.

9. In *The Great Mystery of Life Hereafter* (London: Hodder & Stoughton, 1957).

Appendix B

Text of the Apostles', Athanasian, and Nicene Creeds

The Apostles' Creed

I believe in God, the Father almighty, creator of Heaven and earth.
I believe in Jesus Christ, His only Son, our Lord.
He was conceived by the power of the Holy Spirit and born of the Virgin Mary.
He suffered under Pontius Pilate, was crucified, died, and was buried.
He descended into Hell.
On the third day He rose again.
He ascended into Heaven and is seated at the right hand of the Father.
He will come again to judge the living and the dead.
I believe in the Holy Spirit, the holy catholic Church,
the communion of saints, the forgiveness of sins,
the resurrection of the body, and life everlasting.

The Athanasian Creed

Whosoever will be saved, before all things it is necessary that he hold the Catholic Faith. Which Faith except everyone do keep whole and undefiled, without doubt he shall perish everlastingly. And the Catholic

Faith is this: That we worship one God in Trinity, and Trinity in Unity, neither confounding the Persons, nor dividing the Substance. For there is one Person of the Father, another of the Son, and another of the Holy Ghost. But the Godhead of the Father, of the Son, and of the Holy Ghost is all one, the Glory equal, the Majesty co-eternal. Such as the Father is, such is the Son, and such is the Holy Ghost. The Father uncreate, the Son uncreate, and the Holy Ghost uncreate. The Father incomprehensible, the Son incomprehensible, and the Holy Ghost incomprehensible. The Father eternal, the Son eternal, and the Holy Ghost eternal. And yet they are not three eternals, but one eternal. As also there are not three incomprehensibles, nor three uncreated, but one uncreated and one incomprehensible. So likewise the Father is Almighty, the Son Almighty, and the Holy Ghost Almighty. And yet they are not three Almighties, but one Almighty. So the Father is God, the Son is God, and the Holy Ghost is God.

And yet they are not three Gods, but one God. So likewise the Father is Lord, the Son Lord, and the Holy Ghost Lord. And yet not three Lords, but one Lord. For like as we are compelled by the Christian verity to acknowledge every person by Himself to be both God and Lord, so are we forbidden by the Catholic Religion, to say, There be three Gods, or three Lords. The Father is made of none, neither created nor begotten. The Son is of the Father alone, not made nor created, but begotten. The Holy Ghost is of the Father and of the Son, neither made, nor created, nor begotten, but proceeding. So there is one Father, not three Fathers; one Son, not three Sons; one Holy Ghost, not three Holy Ghosts. And in this Trinity none is afore or after other; none is greater, or less than another; but the whole three Persons are co-eternal together and co-equal. So that in all things, as is aforesaid, the Unity in Trinity and the Trinity in Unity is to be worshipped. He therefore that will be saved must thus think of the Trinity.

Furthermore, it is necessary to everlasting salvation that he also believe rightly the Incarnation of our Lord Jesus Christ. For the right Faith is, that we believe and confess, that our Lord Jesus Christ, the Son of God, is God and Man; God, of the Substance of the Father, begotten before the worlds; and Man, of the Substance of His Mother, born in the world; perfect God and perfect Man, of a reasonable soul and human flesh subsisting; equal to the Father, as touching His Godhead; and inferior to the Father, as touching His Manhood. Who although He be God and Man, yet He is not two, but one Christ; one, not by conversion of the Godhead into flesh, but by taking of the Manhood into God: one altogether; not by confusion of Substance, but by unity of Person. For as the reasonable soul and flesh is one man, so God and Man is one Christ; who suffered for our salvation, descended into Hell, rose again the third day from the dead. He ascended into Heaven; He sitteth on the right hand of the Father, God Almighty, from whence He shall come to judge the quick and the dead. At whose coming all men shall rise again with their bodies and shall give account for their own works. And they that have done good shall go into life everlasting; and they that have done evil into everlasting fire.

This is the Catholic Faith, which except a man believe faithfully, he cannot be saved.

The Nicene Creed

We believe in one God, the Father, the Almighty, maker of Heaven and earth, of all that is, seen and unseen. We believe in one Lord, Jesus Christ, the only Son of God, eternally begotten of the Father, God from God, Light from Light, true God from true God, begotten, not made, one in being with the Father. Through Him all things were made.

For us men and for our salvation He came down from Heaven: by the power of the Holy Spirit He was born of the Virgin Mary and became man. For our sake He was crucified under Pontius Pilate; He suffered, died, and was buried. On the third day He rose again in fulfillment of the Scriptures; He ascended into Heaven and is seated at the right hand of the Father. He will come again in glory to judge the living and the dead, and His kingdom will have no end. We believe in the Holy Spirit, the Lord, the giver of life, who proceeds from the Father and the Son. With the Father and the Son He is worshipped and glorified. He has spoken through the Prophets. We believe in one holy catholic and apostolic Church. We acknowledge one baptism for the forgiveness of sins. We look for the resurrection of the dead, and the life of the world to come.

For further information on the establishment of the creeds, consult:

Chadwick, Henry. *The Early Church*. New York: Penguin, 1967.

Kelly, J. N. D. *Early Christian Doctrines*. San Francisco: HarperSanFrancisco, 1978.

Norris, Richard A., Jr., ed. *The Christological Controversy*. Philadelphia: Fortress, 1980.

Rusch, William G., ed. *The Trinitarian Controversy*. Philadelphia: Fortress, 1980.

Appendix C

Sayers's Suggested Dates for Airing
The Man Born to Be King *during Lent*

February 28	Sexagesima Sunday	Kings in Judaea
March 7	Quinquagesima Sunday	The King's Herald
March 14	1st Sunday in Lent	A Certain Nobleman
March 21	2nd Sunday in Lent	The Heirs to the Kingdom
March 28	3rd Sunday in Lent	The Bread of Heaven
April 4	4th Sunday in Lent	The Feast of the Tabernacles
April 11	Passion Sunday	The Light and the Life
April 18	Palm Sunday	Royal Progress
April 21	Wednesday in Holy Week	The King's Supper
April 22	Maundy Thursday	The Princes of This World
April 23	Good Friday	King of Sorrows
April 25	Easter Day	The King Comes to His Own

Dorothy L. Sayers to Rev. J. W. Welch, October 30, 1942, Wade document 434/28.

Appendix D

"A Note on Creative Reading" from Begin Here

*R*eading being one of our principal occupations on long, dark evenings, I should like to explain what I mean by saying that it ought to be done creatively. (Here, by the way, I am on my own special ground, and shall take leave to speak with authority.)

Do not, I implore you, continue in that indolent and soul-destroying habit of picking up a book "to distract your mind" ("distract" is the word for it) or "to knock down time" (there is only too little time already, and it will knock us down soon enough). The only respectable reason for reading a book is that you want to know what is in it.

Do not choose your literature by the half-witted process of asking the young woman at the library for "a nice book" and enquiring anxiously of her, "Shall I like it?" Subscribe to a decently serious paper, read the reviews and order what you think will interest you. (Study the publishers' lists too, by all means, bearing in mind that the "blurb" is written to sell the book and is therefore *not* an expression of free criticism. Do not be too much put off either; many a good book has a sickening blurb.)

If the book, when obtained, does not interest you, ask yourself why; and have the elementary politeness to give yourself a sensible answer. Does the subject displease you?—and if so, is it by any chance one of those disquieting things that you "would rather not know about," though you really ought not to shirk it? Does the author's opinion conflict with some cherished opinion of your own?—If so, can you give reasons for your own opinion? (Do try and avoid the criticism that begins: "We do not like to think" this, that or the other; it is often so painfully true that we do not like to think.) Or is it that the author is ignorant, illogical or superficial? (Are you sure? Have you taken the trouble to verify his references? Can you support your own view from your reading or experience?) Or is his style dull, obscure, or ugly? Does he write bad English? If you think so, justify yourself by examples and be sure you know why they are bad. (And don't trust those horrid little manuals all about how to write correct English; they are nearly always wrong or hopelessly pedantic; consult the people who know real literature when they see it, like H. W. Fowler, Quiller-Couch or A. P. Herbert. Language is a *live* thing; you can't confine it in little primers.)

If, on the other hand, the book does interest you, don't leave it at that. Go on and read other books bearing on the subject, and collect illuminating experience of your own; go out and *get* the experience. See whether, in view of what the books say, you can't and ought not to *do* something about it; make the books part of your life. And if the author's style appeals to you, do make a point of enjoying it. Get the feel of balance in a beautiful sentence, rejoice in the lovely appropriateness of the exact right word and thank your gods that the author had the wit and industry to choose that word, out of a whole dictionaryful of less adequate words, for the express purpose of pleasing you. Entertain yourself by finding other words yourself and discovering why they sound so feeble by comparison.

Pray get rid of the idea that books are each a separate thing, divided from one another and from life. Read each in the light of all the others, especially in the light of books of another kind. Try and see—this is the most fascinating exercise of all—whether a statement in one book may not be a statement of the same experience which another book expresses in quite different terms. (I tried to make a "synthesis" of this kind about biological man and the theological doctrine of the Fall.) Try the experiment of putting a statement of one kind into the terms of another. Try especially putting statements made in old-fashioned language into modern terms. You will often find that things you have taken all your life for incomprehensible dogmas turn out to be perfectly intelligible observations of truth. Take, for instance, those dark pronouncements in the Athanasian Creed that God is uncreate, incomprehensible and eternal, and re-state them like this: "The standard of Absolute Value is not limited by matter, not limited by space, not limited by time." It may seem more acceptable that way. . . .

Or if you read somewhere a reference to "Aristotle's three Dramatic Unities—unity of time, unity of place and unity of action," do not (as some writers do who should know better) dismiss Aristotle as a tedious old classic of two thousand years ago who tried to tie up dramatic form in red-tape of his own manufacture. What he said was a statement of fact about the plays he had observed to be successful, and he meant exactly what your favourite dramatic critic means when he says: "The interest in this play is too much scattered, and confused with side-issues. There are far too many scenes, and the story drags on over a period of three generations, so that we have to be continually consulting the programme to know what year we have got to."

Which reminds me: please burn all your book-markers—even the pretty one Aunt Mabel sent you last Christmas (or at least put that one away and only bring it out when she comes to call). You cannot possibly be so bird-witted as to be unable to discover which page you got to by looking at it.

If the author mentions some other book in terms which make it seem important, whether he approves or refutes it, don't take his word for it: get the other book and read it, and judge for yourself. If he refers to something, or uses some word, which you don't understand, get a dictionary or work of reference and look it up. (Don't write and ask the author to explain; he is not required to be an Encyclopaedia, and you will only give him a poor idea of your industry and intelligence.) Especially, examine the *sources* of what he writes; to read Mr. Somebody's critical valuation of Milton's prose or his examination of the economic effects of the Peace Treaty is quite valueless if you have never read any Milton and do not know what the Peace Treaty actually said.

Discuss the books you read. If your husband or your wife is bored with your opinions (they very often are), persuade some friend to read the same books and talk them over. By discussion I mean discussion: not just saying, "Oh, I thought it was *frightfully* interesting, didn't you?" Nor do I mean exchanging gossip about the author's personality and private life and saying he must be a delightful (interesting, un-pleasant, dangerous, irritating, fascinating, entertaining) person to know. (It is well to remember that the best of a writer's energies goes into his writing; he may not have much charm or virtue left over for private use. This does not invalidate his opinions; it merely means that he is liable to be disappointing when encountered in person.)

And do please realise that words are not just "talky-talk"—they are real and vital; they can change the face of the world. They are a form of action—"in the beginning was the Word . . . by Whom all things were made." Even the spate of futile words that pours out from the ephemeral press and the commercial-fiction-mongers has a real and terrible power; it can become a dope as dangerous as drugs or drink; it can rot the mind, sap the reason, send the will to sleep; it can pull down empires and set the neck of the people under the heel of tyranny. "For every idle word that ye speak ye shall render account at the day of judgment." I do not think that means that we shall have to pay a fine in a few million years' time for every occasion on which we said "dash it all" or indulged in a bit of harmless frivol; but I do think it was meant as an urgent warning against abusing or under-rating the power of words, and that the judgment is eternal—that is, it is here and now.

Glossary

Adoptionists. Those who believed Jesus was not really divine but was a exemplary man "adopted" by God as his son.

Apollinarianism. A heresy suggesting Jesus had only one nature, leading to disbelief in his full manhood.

Aquinas, Thomas. Representative of medieval/scholastic theology.

Arius/Arianism. Arius believed and taught that Jesus Christ was a created being.

Athanasius. He opposed Arius. The Athanasian Creed is specific in defining orthodox teaching on Christ's divinity.

Augustine of Hippo. One of the best-known theologians of the patristic period.

Chalcedon, Council of. The Council of Chalcedon (A.D. 451) was one of the great ecumenical church councils at which the early church defined the boundaries of orthodoxy concerning the person of Christ.

Christology/ical. Related to Christ's dual (fully divine and fully human) nature.

Constantine. Became sole head of the Roman Empire in A.D. 323 and convened the Council of Nicea.

Docetism. A heresy suggesting that Jesus only seemed (*dokein*, "to seem") to be human.

Ebionites. A Judaizing movement within Christianity that denied the divinity of Christ.

Eutychianism. Stressed the divinity of Christ at the expense of his humanity.

filioque. The *filioque* clause in the Nicene Creed articulates that the Holy Spirit "proceeds from the Father *and the Son*" (*filioque*). The Eastern Church believes the Holy Spirit proceeds only from the Father.

Gnosticism. An ancient philosophical movement characterized by an extreme dualism between matter and spirit. The body was seen as evil and the spirit as good.

Justinian. Head of the Roman Empire from A.D. 527 to 565.

kenosis. A Greek word meaning "emptying," used in New Testament studies to refer to Christ's self-emptying in Philippians 2.

Manichaeans. Like Gnostics, they practiced an extreme dualism.

Marcionites. Followers of Marcion, a teacher with Gnostic-like sympathies.

Monophysite. A heresy that suggested that Jesus was not fully human and had only one nature (divine).

Monothelites. Believed Christ had only one will, and it was divine.

Nestorians. Suggested that Christ had two distinct persons, one divine and one human.

Nicea, Council of. The Council of Nicea (A.D. 325) was one of the great ecumenical church councils at which the early church defined the boundaries of trinitarian orthodoxy.

Origen. A theologian writing in the third century.

Patripassianism. Proposed that the Father, not the Son, suffered.

patristic. Refers to the early Christian church (literally, to the period "of the fathers").

Pelagianism. Suggested that human beings can cooperate with God in their salvation by choosing to do good instead of evil.

Sabellianism. A heresy that denied the distinction between the Father and the Son. Each was only a name applied to God at different times.

Theopaschites. Similar to the Patripassians.

trinitarian. Refers to the three-in-one nature of God (Father, Son, and Holy Spirit).

Bibliography

Primary Sources

Published Works

Alighieri, Dante. *Hell.* Translated by Dorothy L. Sayers. London: Penguin, 1949.
———. *Paradise.* Translated by Dorothy L. Sayers and Barbara Reynolds. London: Penguin, 1962.
——— *Purgatory.* Translated by Dorothy L. Sayers. London: Penguin, 1955.
Hone, Ralph E., ed. *Poetry of Dorothy L. Sayers.* Cambridge: Dorothy L. Sayers Society in association with the Marion E. Wade Center, 1996.
Reynolds, Barbara, ed. *The Letters of Dorothy L. Sayers.* Vol. 1. New York: St. Martin's Press, 1997.
———. *The Letters of Dorothy L. Sayers.* Vol. 2. Cambridge: Dorothy L. Sayers Society, 1997.
———. *The Letters of Dorothy L. Sayers.* Vol. 3. Cambridge: Dorothy L. Sayers Society, 1999.
———. *The Letters of Dorothy L. Sayers.* Vol. 4. Cambridge: Dorothy L. Sayers Society, 2000.
Sayers, Dorothy L. ". . . And Telling You a Story." In *Essays Presented to Charles Williams*, 1–37. Grand Rapids: Eerdmans, 1981.
———. *Are Women Human?* Grand Rapids: Eerdmans, 1971.
——— "Aristotle on Detective Fiction." In *Unpopular Opinions.* New York: Harcourt, Brace, & Co., 1947.
———. *Begin Here: A Statement of Faith.* London: Victor Gollancz, 1940.
———. *Busman's Honeymoon.* New York: Harper Perennial, 1937.
———. *Catholic Tales and Christian Songs.* Oxford: Blackwell, 1918.
———. "Christian Morality." In *The Whimsical Christian.* New York: Collier, 1978.
———. "The Church's Responsibility." In *Malvern, 1941: The Life of the Church and the Order of Society; Being the Proceedings of the Archbishop of York's Conference*, ed. unknown, 57–78. London: Longmans, Green, & Co., 1942.
———. *Clouds of Witness.* New York: Harper Perennial, 1993.

———. "The Contempt of Learning in Twentieth-Century England." *Fortnightly* 153 (April 1940): 373–82.

———. "Creative Mind." In *Unpopular Opinions*. New York: Harcourt, Brace, & Co., 1947.

———. "Creed or Chaos?" In *The Whimsical Christian*. New York: Collier, 1978.

———. *Creed or Chaos?* New York: Harcourt, Brace, & Co., 1949.

———. "The Dates in *The Red-Headed League*." In *Unpopular Opinions*. New York: Harcourt, Brace, & Co., 1947.

———. *The Days of Christ's Coming*. New York: Harper, 1960.

———. *The Devil to Pay*. In *Two Plays about God and Man*. Connecticut: Vineyard Books, 1977.

———. "Divine Comedy." In *Unpopular Opinions*. New York: Harcourt, Brace, & Co., 1947.

———. "The Dogma in the Manger." *VII: An Anglo-American Literary Review* 3 (1982): 35–45.

———. "The Dogma Is the Drama." In *Creed or Chaos?* New York: Harcourt, Brace, & Co., 1949.

———. Dorothy L. Sayers to Dr. J. H. Oldham, March 4, 1942. *Christian News-Letter*, April 1, 1942, page unknown. Wade document 341/20–22.

———. Dorothy L. Sayers to the editor. *British Weekly*, September 3, 1951, page unknown. Wade document 342/37.

———. Dorothy L. Sayers to the editor. *Church of England Newspaper*, April 18, 1955, page unknown. Wade document 338/30.

———. Dorothy L. Sayers to the editor. *Church of England Newspaper*, May 2, 1955, page unknown. Wade document 338/27.

———. Dorothy L. Sayers to the editor. *Church Times*, April 6, 1938, page unknown. Wade document 349/32.

———. Dorothy L. Sayers to the editor. *Church Times*, August 25, 1951, page unknown. Wade document 525/27.

———. Dorothy L. Sayers to the editor. *Church Times*, May 6, 1941, page unknown. Wade document 347/39.

———. Dorothy L. Sayers to the editor. *Drama*, June 11, 1952, page unknown. Wade document 342/31.

———. Dorothy L. Sayers to the editor. *Evening Dispatch* (Edinburgh), January 19, 1942, page unknown. Wade document 346/51.

———. Dorothy L. Sayers to the editor. *Manchester Guardian*, November 5, 1942, page unknown. Wade document 346/30.

———. Dorothy L. Sayers to the editor. *Punch*, April 6, 1938, page unknown. Wade document 349/29.

———. Dorothy L. Sayers to the editor. *Spectator*, July 13, 1940, page unknown. Wade document 348/62.

———. Dorothy L. Sayers to the editor. *Times* (London), August 22, 1945, page unknown. Wade document 347/20.

———. Dorothy L. Sayers to the editor. *World Review*, May 13, 1941, page unknown. Wade document 347/35.

———. "Dr. Watson's Christian Name." In *Unpopular Opinions*. New York: Harcourt, Brace, & Co., 1947.

———. "Dr. Watson, Widower." In *Unpopular Opinions*. New York: Harcourt, Brace, & Co., 1947.

———. "The Eighth Bolgia." In *Further Papers on Dante*. London: Methuen, 1957.

———. *The Emperor Constantine*. Grand Rapids: Eerdmans, 1951.

———. "The English Language." In *Unpopular Opinions*. New York: Harcourt, Brace, & Co., 1947.

———. "The Execution of God." *Radio Times*, March 23, 1945, 3.

———. "The Faust Legend and the Idea of the Devil." In *The Poetry of Search and the Poetry of Statement*. London: Victor Gollancz, 1963.

———. "The Feast of St. Verb." *Sunday Times*, March 24, 1940, page unknown.

———. Foreword to *Five Great Subjects: Broadcast Talks*, by W. A. L. Elmslie, 6–8. London: SCM, 1943.

———. Foreword to *What Is Christian Education?* by Marjorie Reeves and John Drewett, vii–xii. London: Sheldon Press, 1942.

———. "Forgiveness." In *Unpopular Opinions*. New York: Harcourt, Brace, & Co., 1947.

———. "Forgiveness and the Enemy." *Fortnightly* 149 (April 1941): 379–83.

———. "Fourfold Interpretation of the *Comedy*." In *Introductory Papers on Dante*. New York: Harper & Brothers, 1954.

———. *Further Papers on Dante*. London: Methuen, 1957.

———. *Gaudy Night*. New York: Avon Books, 1968.

———. "God the Son: 4. The Death of God." BBC Forces Programme. Lot 292, iii. Wade Center.

———. "God the Son," 5th talk. (No date, but one would assume it was the Sunday after June 29, 1941, when the fourth talk was broadcast.) Lot 292, iii. Wade Center.

———. "The Greatest Drama Ever Staged." In *Creed or Chaos?* New York: Harcourt, Brace, & Co., 1949.

———. "The Gulf Stream and the Channel." In *Unpopular Opinions*. New York: Harcourt, Brace, & Co., 1947.

———. "Helen Simpson." *Fortnightly* 155 (January 1941): 54–59. Wade document 15/16.

———. *He That Should Come*. London: Victor Gollancz, 1939.

———. "Holmes' College Career." In *Unpopular Opinions*. New York: Harcourt, Brace, & Co., 1947.

———. "How to Enjoy the Dark Nights." *Star* (London), September 14, 1939, 2.

———. "The Human-Not-Quite-Human." In *Are Women Human?* Grand Rapids: Eerdmans, 1971.

———. "The Image of God." In *The Whimsical Christian*. New York: Collier, 1978.

———. "Introducing Children to the Bible." *Housewife* 3, no. 11 (November 1941): 81–83, 146. Wade document 486/125ff.

———. Introduction to *Great Short Stories of Detection, Mystery, and Horror, Third Series*, 11–18. London: Victor Gollancz, 1934.

———. Introduction to *Great Tales of Detection*, vii–xiv. London: Dent, 1984.

———. Introduction to *Tales of Detection and Mystery from "The Omnibus of Crime,"* 7–40. New York: MacFadden Books, 1962.

———. Introduction to *The Surprise*, by G. K. Chesterton, 5–9. New York: Sheed & Ward, 1953.

———. *Introductory Papers on Dante*. New York: Harper & Brothers, 1954.

———. "Is There a Definite Evil Power That Attacks People in the Same Way as There Is a Good Power That Influences People?" In *Asking Them Questions*, edited by Ronald Selby Wright, 127–36. London: Oxford University Press, 1950.

———. "Is This He That Should Come?" *Christian Newsletter* 8 (December 20, 1939): supplement.

———. *The Just Vengeance*. London: Victor Gollancz, 1946.

————. "Letter to Average People." Written originally to Eric Fenn. Published as "Monthly Letter, No. 4," newsletter of the Ilkley Council of Christian Citizenship, April 1946. Wade document 28/45–46.

————. "Living to Work." In *Unpopular Opinions.* New York: Harcourt, Brace, & Co., 1947.

————. *The Lost Tools of Learning.* London: Methuen, 1948.

————. *The Man Born to Be King.* Grand Rapids: Eerdmans, 1943.

————. "The Meaning of Purgatory." In *Introductory Papers on Dante.* New York: Harper & Brothers, 1954.

————. *The Mind of the Maker.* San Francisco: HarperSanFrancisco, 1979.

————. *Murder Must Advertise.* New York: Avenel, 1982.

————. "The Mysterious English." In *Unpopular Opinions.* New York: Harcourt, Brace, & Co., 1947.

————. *The Nine Tailors.* New York: Harcourt, Brace, & World, 1934.

————. "Obsequies for Music." In *Poetry of Dorothy L. Sayers,* edited by Ralph E. Hone, 98–103. Cambridge: Dorothy L. Sayers Society in association with the Marion E. Wade Center, 1996.

————. *Op. 1.* Oxford: Blackwell, 1916.

————. "The Other Six Deadly Sins." In *The Whimsical Christian.* New York: Collier, 1978. Also published in *Creed or Chaos?* New York: Harcourt, Brace, & Co., 1949.

————. "The Pantheon Papers." In *The Whimsical Christian.* New York: Collier, 1978.

————. "The Piscatorial Farce of the Stolen Stomach." In *Lord Peter.* New York: Avon Books, 1972.

————. "Plain English." In *Unpopular Opinions.* New York: Harcourt, Brace, & Co., 1947.

————. "Playwrights Are Not Evangelists." *World Theatre* 5, no. 1 (Winter 1955–56): 61–66.

————. "Poetry, Language, and Ambiguity." In *The Poetry of Search and the Poetry of Statement.* London: Victor Gollancz, 1963.

————. *The Poetry of Search and the Poetry of Statement.* London: Victor Gollancz, 1963.

————. "The Poetry of the Image in Dante and Charles Williams." In *Further Papers on Dante.* London: Methuen, 1957.

————. "The Psychology of Advertising." *Spectator* 5708 (November 19, 1937): 896–98.

————. "The Religions behind the Nation." In *The Church Looks Ahead: Broadcast Talks,* edited by J. H. Oldham, pages unknown. London: Faber & Faber, 1941.

————. "Religious Education." *Times* (London), August 26, 1941, 5.

————. Review of *Christian Doctrine,* by J. S. Whale. *International Review of Missions* 31 (January 1942): 117–20.

————. "Sacred Plays: I." *Episcopal Churchnews,* January 9, 1955, 20–22, 35. This article was adapted and published in 1981 as "Types of Christian Drama."

————. "Sacred Plays: II." *Episcopal Churchnews,* January 25, 1955, 24–25, 34. This article was adapted and published in 1981 as "Types of Christian Drama."

————. "Sacred Plays: III." *Episcopal Churchnews,* February 6, 1955, 24, 31–33. This article was adapted and published in 1981 as "Types of Christian Drama."

————. "Socialism Means Tyranny." *Evening Standard* (London), date/page unknown. Dorothy L. Sayers Society archive document 1.44.

————. *Song of Roland.* New York: Penguin, 1957.

————. "St. Anne's Day." Address delivered July 26, 1957. Marion E. Wade Center, Wheaton, IL.

————. *The Story of Adam and Christ.* London: Hamish Hamilton, 1955.

———. "Strong Meat." In *Creed or Chaos?* New York: Harcourt, Brace, & Co., 1949.

———. "The Technique of the Sermon." Review of *The Art of Preaching*, by Charles Smyth. *Spectator* 5823 (February 2, 1940): 150.

———. "The Theologian and the Scientist." *Listener* 44, no. 1132 (November 9, 1950): 496–97, 500.

———. "They Tried to Be Good." In *Unpopular Opinions*. New York: Harcourt, Brace, & Co., 1947.

———. "Towards a Christian Aesthetic." In *Unpopular Opinions*. New York: Harcourt, Brace, & Co., 1947.

———. *Tristan in Brittany*. London: E. Benn, 1929.

———. "The Triumph of Easter." In *Creed or Chaos?* New York: Harcourt, Brace, & Co., 1949.

———. "Types of Christian Drama, with Some Notes on Production." *VII: An Anglo-American Literary Review* 2 (1981): 84–99.

———. *The Unpleasantness at the Bellona Club*. New York: Harper Perennial, 1993.

———. *Unpopular Opinions*. New York: Harcourt, Brace, & Co., 1947.

———. "Vocation in Work." Address delivered March 1941 at the Dome, Brighton. Published in *A Christian Basis for the Post-War World*, edited by Albert E. Baker, 88–103. New York: Morehouse-Gorham, 1942.

———. "A Vote of Thanks to Cyrus." In *The Whimsical Christian*. New York: Collier, 1978.

———. "What Do We Believe?" In *Unpopular Opinions*. New York: Harcourt, Brace, & Co., 1947.

———. *Whose Body?* New York: Harper & Row, 1923.

———. "Why Work?" In *Creed or Chaos?* New York: Harcourt, Brace, & Co., 1949.

———. "Wimsey Papers—I." *Spectator* 5812 (November 17, 1939): 672–74.

———. "Wimsey Papers—II." *Spectator* 5813 (November 24, 1939): 736–37.

———. "Wimsey Papers—III." *Spectator* 5814 (December 1, 1939): 770–71.

———. "Wimsey Papers—IV." *Spectator* 5815 (December 8, 1939): 809–10.

———. "Wimsey Papers—VI." *Spectator* 5817 (December 22, 1939): 894–95.

———. "Wimsey Papers—VII." *Spectator* 5818 (December 29, 1939): 925–26.

———. "Wimsey Papers—VIII." *Spectator* 5819 (January 5, 1940): 8–9.

———. "Wimsey Papers—IX." *Spectator* 5820 (January 12, 1940): 38–39.

———. "Wimsey Papers—X." *Spectator* 5821 (January 19, 1940): 70–71.

———. "Wimsey Papers—XI." *Spectator* 5822 (January 26, 1940): 104–5.

———. "Worship in the Anglican Church." *VII: An Anglo-American Literary Review* 12 (1995): 34–48.

———. "Writing a Local Play." *Farmer's Weekly*, August 26, 1938, 42–43.

———. *The Zeal of Thy House*. London: Victor Gollancz, 1939.

———, and Barbara Reynolds. "Like Aesop's Bat." *VII: An Anglo-American Literary Review* 1 (March 1980): 81–93.

Unpublished Works

Bates, S. S. Bates to Dorothy L. Sayers, July 16, 1948. Wade document 28/7–9.

Bosky, L. E. W. L. E. W. Bosky to Dorothy L. Sayers, May 19, 1942. Wade document 12/15.

Child, Harold. Harold Child to Dorothy L. Sayers, date unknown. Wade document 19/66–67.

Dawson, Dorothy. Dorothy Dawson to Dorothy L. Sayers, August 1, 1942. Wade document 158/58.

Dover, Bishop of. Bishop of Dover to Dorothy L. Sayers, February 5, 1948. Wade document 198/62.

———. Bishop of Dover to Dorothy L. Sayers, February 13, 1948. Wade document 198/58.

Ehrhardt, Arnold. Arnold Ehrhardt to Dorothy L. Sayers, September 1945. Wade document 9/9–9/10.

Fenn, Eric. Eric Fenn to Dorothy L. Sayers, date unknown, maybe March 1946. Wade document 28/51.

Hall, James S. James S. Hall to Dorothy L. Sayers, July 27, 1943. Wade document 11/39.

Heenan, John. John Heenan to Dorothy L. Sayers, January 19, 1942. Wade document 212/2.

Johnson, Howard. Howard Johnson to Dorothy L. Sayers, March 1, 1944. Wade document 10/20.

Kelly, Father Herbert. Father Herbert Kelly to Dorothy L. Sayers, October 1, 1937. Wade document 261/90. Part of this letter is included in Barbara Reynolds, ed., *The Letters of Dorothy L. Sayers*, vol. 2 (Cambridge: Dorothy L. Sayers Society, 1997), 42.

———. Father Herbert Kelly to Dorothy L. Sayers, October 14, 1937. Wade document 261/66.

Marsden, Iris. Iris Marsden to Dorothy L. Sayers, September 11, 1947. Wade document 235/28.

McCarthy, Doris. Doris McCarthy to Dorothy L. Sayers, November 24, 1947. Wade document 21/101.

Palmer, S. L. S. L. Palmer to Dorothy L. Sayers, May 26, 1942. Wade document 183/32.

Parkander, Dorothy. Dorothy Parkander to Dorothy L. Sayers, March 1957. Wade document 25/11.

Pratt, C. J. L. C. J. L. Pratt to Dorothy L. Sayers, June 23, 1941. Wade document 13/133.

Radcliffe, Major R. A. C. Major R. A. C. Radcliffe to Dr. J. H. Oldham, April 3, 1942. Wade document 341/16.

Reynolds, George F. George F. Reynolds to Dorothy L. Sayers, July 2 (year not given; it may be 1953). Wade document 1/73.

Russell, Ralph. Ralph Russell to Dorothy L. Sayers, November 8, 1941. Wade document 406/75–76.

Sayers, Dorothy L. Address delivered at St. Martin's in the Fields, February 6, 1942. Wade document 486/131.

———. Address delivered at "Sword of the Spirit" meeting, May 11, 1941. Wade MS-243.

———. Address delivered to a group of clergy, date/specific audience unknown. Wade document 486/77.

———. "'Cat O' Mary': Unpublished Semi-autobiographical Manuscript Written under the Pseudonym 'Joanna Leigh,'" ca. 1934. Wade MS-81. This is now available in published form in Barbara Reynolds, ed., *Dorothy L. Sayers: Child and Woman of Her Time*. Vol. 5, *A Supplement to the Letters of Dorothy L. Sayers*. Cambridge: Dorothy L. Sayers Society, 2002.

———. "The Christian Faith and the Theatre." Wade MS-43.

———. "The Church as Teacher." Address delivered to a group of clergy, date unknown. Wade document 486/59–96.

———. "Church Publicity in the Church of England." Wade document 486/8.

———. Constantine research notebook with timeline. Wade MS-80.

———. Correspondence with Dorothy Milner Brown, September–October 1941. Wade document 13/87–107.

———. Correspondence with G. F. Littleboy, February 15–March 31, 1951. Wade document 21/40–21/49. One of these letters is published in Barbara Reynolds, ed., *The Letters of Dorothy L. Sayers*, vol. 4 (Cambridge: Dorothy L. Sayers Society, 2000), 2–3.

———. Correspondence with W. T. Williams, October–November 1941. Wade document 13/175–79.

———. "Creed or Chaos?" Unpublished BBC radio addresses delivered in 1940. Lot 292, iii of the Sotheby's collection, Wade Center.

———. "The Dictatorship of Words." Address delivered to the Modern Language Association, January 1939. Wade MS-67.

———. Dorothy L. Sayers to A. E. Phelps, March 12, 1941. Wade document 139/3.

———. Dorothy L. Sayers to Alec Craig, February 1, 1951. Wade document 2/12.

———. Dorothy L. Sayers to Alec Robertson, February 28, 1947. Wade document 509/188.

———. Dorothy L. Sayers to Alfred Wright Jr., October 29, 1946. Wade document 28/29.

———. Dorothy L. Sayers to Amy Davies, November 26, 1941. Wade document 135/14–17.

———. Dorothy L. Sayers to Arnold Ehrhardt, September 21, 1945. Wade document 9/7.

———. Dorothy L. Sayers to Barbara Barclay Carter, November 14, 1947. Wade document 228/43.

———. Dorothy L. Sayers to Charles M. Bruch, July 4, 1956. Wade document 526/34.

———. Dorothy L. Sayers to Colin Hardie, date unknown. Wade document 25/50.

———. Dorothy L. Sayers to Colin Hardie, December 2, 1957. Wade document 370/5.

———. Dorothy L. Sayers to Colin Hardie, June 12, 1957. Wade document 370/13.

———. Dorothy L. Sayers to Count Michael de la Bedoyere, October 7, 1941. Wade document 210/44.

———. Dorothy L. Sayers to C. S. Lewis, August 1, 1946. Wade document 96/19.

———. Dorothy L. Sayers to C. S. Lewis, July 19, 1948. Wade document 95/74–75. Part of this letter was published in Barbara Reynolds, ed., *The Letters of Dorothy L. Sayers*, vol. 3 (Cambridge: Dorothy L. Sayers Society, 1999), 387 88.

———. Dorothy L. Sayers to David Higham, March 24, 1948. Wade document 122/63.

———. Dorothy L. Sayers to David Higham, June 3, 1949. Wade document 124/59.

———. Dorothy L. Sayers to D. Burton of Cornwall, February 24, 1942. Wade document 520/93–94.

———. Dorothy L. Sayers to Dorothy Rowe, April 25, 1937. Wade document 427/74.

———. Dorothy L. Sayers to Dr. Helmut Kuhn, May 23, 1944. Wade document 251/6.

———. Dorothy L. Sayers to Dr. J. H. Oldham, June 16, 1941. Wade document 341/27.

———. Dorothy L. Sayers to Dr. J. H. Oldham, March 4, 1942. Wade document 341/22.

———. Dorothy L. Sayers to Dr. S. J. Curtis, February 14, 1949. Wade document 367/45ff.

———. Dorothy L. Sayers to Dr. S. J. Curtis, January 31, 1949. Wade document 367/69.

———. Dorothy L. Sayers to E. M. Royds Jones, October 3, 1945. Wade document 151/47.

———. Dorothy L. Sayers to Eric Fenn, date unknown (March or April 1946). Wade document 28/45–46.

———. Dorothy L. Sayers to Eric Fenn, January 21, 1941. Wade document 442/23.

———. Dorothy L. Sayers to Eric Fenn, March 26, 1941. Wade document 443/46.

———. Dorothy L. Sayers to Eric Fenn, October 28, 1946. Wade document 194/26.

———. Dorothy L. Sayers to E. V. Rieu, April 4, 1941. Wade document 19/56.

———. Dorothy L. Sayers to E. V. Rieu, April 6, 1941. Wade document 19/59.

———. Dorothy L. Sayers to E. V. Rieu, August 19, 1941. Wade document 19/41.

———. Dorothy L. Sayers to E. V. Rieu, August 26, 1941. Wade document 19/38.

———. Dorothy L. Sayers to E. V. Rieu, January 28, 1942. Wade document 19/31.

———. Dorothy L. Sayers to E. V. Rieu, March 25, 1946. Wade document 18/295.

———. Dorothy L. Sayers to Father Herbert Kelly, May 7, 1941. Wade document 260/71.

———. Dorothy L. Sayers to Father Herbert Kelly, October 10, 1937. Wade document 261/54–55.

———. Dorothy L. Sayers to Father Kenelm Foster, January 27, 1956. Wade document 177/34.

———. Dorothy L. Sayers to Fr. Alec Vidler, undated. Wade document 398/43.

———. Dorothy L. Sayers to Freeman Wills Croft, December 20, 1937. Wade document 43/3.

———. Dorothy L. Sayers to Fr. J. P. Valentin, June 11, 1943. Wade document 510/138.

———. Dorothy L. Sayers to General Sir Kenneth Wigram, March 12, 1948. Wade document 504/60.

———. Dorothy L. Sayers to G. Glave Saunders, January 13, 1942. Wade document 346/19.

———. Dorothy L. Sayers to G. L Bickersteth, June 12, 1957. Wade document 227/14.

———. Dorothy L. Sayers to G. R. Collings, March 1955. Wade document 19/131.

———. Dorothy L. Sayers to Harriet Felkin, 1949. Wade document 5/51 (typed version in folder 158).

———. Dorothy L. Sayers to H. E. B. Rye, February 18, 1955. Wade document 25/49.

———. Dorothy L. Sayers to Henry and Mary Sayers, July 18, 1916. Wade document 67/53.

———. Dorothy L. Sayers to Henry and Mary Sayers, late May or early June 1909. Wade document 71/25.

———. Dorothy L. Sayers to H. J. Massingham, September 26, 1941. Wade document 151/78.

———. Dorothy L. Sayers to J. B. Upcott, September 1, 1941. Wade document 347/13.

———. Dorothy L. Sayers to John Anthony Fleming, June 17, 1952. Wade document 335/42.

———. Dorothy L. Sayers to John Anthony Fleming, October 20, 1937. Wade document 337/58.

———. Dorothy L. Sayers to John Wren-Lewis, June 18, 1954. Wade document 387/6–8.

———. Dorothy L. Sayers to John Wren-Lewis, undated (Barbara Reynolds says it is March 1954). Wade document 387/20–36.

———. Dorothy L. Sayers to J. W. Welch, August 1, 1941. Wade document 433/37.

———. Dorothy L. Sayers to J. W. Welch, June 9, 1942. Wade document 434/63.

———. Dorothy L. Sayers to J. W. Welch, October 30, 1942. Wade document 434/28.

———. Dorothy L. Sayers to K. C. H. Warner, November 26, 1941. Wade document 151/87.

———. Dorothy L. Sayers to Lady Boileau, November 22, 1940. Wade document 239/10.

———. Dorothy L. Sayers to Marjorie Barber, October 25, 1942. Wade document 422/34–35.

――――. Dorothy L. Sayers to Mary Hodges, May 5, 1952. Wade document 1/106.

――――. Dorothy L. Sayers to Maurice Reckitt, May 8, 1941. Wade document 409/24.

――――. Dorothy L. Sayers to Maurice Reckitt, May 14, 1941. Wade document 409/29.

――――. Dorothy L. Sayers to Maurice Robins, November 20, 1939. Wade document 522/184.

――――. Dorothy L. Sayers to Messrs. A. R. Mowbray & Co., January 4, 1951. Wade document 173/5.

――――. Dorothy L. Sayers to Miss Alice Curtayne, March 30, 1955. Wade document 25/53.

――――. Dorothy L. Sayers to Miss Cicely Hood, December 18, 1950. Wade document 3/15.

――――. Dorothy L. Sayers to Miss Dorothy Parkander, March 27, 1957. Wade document 25/10.

――――. Dorothy L. Sayers to Miss Hella Georgiadis, February 26, 1951. Wade document 525/46.

――――. Dorothy L. Sayers to Miss Mary Parsons, May 14, 1952. Wade document 321/46.

――――. Dorothy L. Sayers to Miss P. M. Potter, October 19, 1951. Wade document 191/95.

――――. Dorothy L. Sayers to M. le Pasteur Pierre Maury, November 21, 1946. Wade document 194/10.

――――. Dorothy L. Sayers to Mlle. Michele Gautray, September 21, 1948. Wade document 323/81.

――――. Dorothy L. Sayers to Mme. D. R. Vallender, October 20, 1952. Wade document 21/26.

――――. Dorothy L. Sayers to Monsignor Ronald Knox, August 26, 1941. Wade document 249/27.

――――. Dorothy L. Sayers to Monsignor Ronald Knox, February 14, 1951. Wade documents 2/8 (handwritten fragment) and 249/11 (typed version).

――――. Dorothy L. Sayers to Mr. Graham, undated. Wade document 338/6.

――――. Dorothy L. Sayers to Mr. Hill of Winchester, March 24, 1941. Wade document 13/75.

――――. Dorothy L. Sayers to Mr. Kendon, undated. Wade document 343/15.

――――. Dorothy L. Sayers to Mrs. E. C. F. Bickersteth, December 9, 1947. Wade document 227/116.

――――. Dorothy L. Sayers to Mrs. G. K. Chesterton, June 15, 1936. Wade document 41/3.

――――. Dorothy L. Sayers to Mrs. R. E. Large, April 6, 1948. Lot 291, v, Wade Center.

――――. Dorothy L. Sayers to Muriel Jaeger, December 12, 1918. Wade document 22/93.

――――. Dorothy L. Sayers to Muriel Jaeger, January 11, 1919. Wade document 22/108.

――――. Dorothy L. Sayers to Muriel Jaeger, September 21, 1914. Wade document 22/12.

――――. Dorothy L. Sayers to Noel Davey, October 18, 1945. Wade document 28/105.

――――. Dorothy L. Sayers to Patrick McLaughlin, April 4, 1941. Wade document 284/23.

――――. Dorothy L. Sayers to Patrick McLaughlin, September 25, 1940. Wade document 284/51.

――――. Dorothy L. Sayers to Professor Paolo Milano, June 24, 1955. Wade document 21/5.

――――. Dorothy L. Sayers to R. C. Bretislav Hodek, April 19, 1949. Wade document 324/69.

————. Dorothy L. Sayers to Rev. A. R. James, March 10, 1939. Wade document 326/31.

————. Dorothy L. Sayers to Rev. B. E. Payne, February 11, 1942. Wade document 520/104.

————. Dorothy L. Sayers to Rev. Canon J. W. Poole, April 29, 1940. Wade document 487/58.

————. Dorothy L. Sayers to Rev. Canon Roger Lloyd, March 2, 1943. Wade document 11/66–67.

————. Dorothy L. Sayers to Rev. Canon S. M. Winter, February 2, 1943. Wade document 235/39.

————. Dorothy L. Sayers to Rev. D. A. McKinnon, August 27, 1940. Wade document 369/42.

————. Dorothy L. Sayers to Rev. D'Arcy, March 17, 1950. Wade document 373/2.

————. Dorothy L. Sayers to Rev. Eric Fenn, June 11, 1940. Wade document 444/17.

————. Dorothy L. Sayers to Rev. Father Lattey, August 19, 1943. Wade document 263/4.

————. Dorothy L. Sayers to Rev. Father M. C. D'Arcy, July 19, 1941. Wade document 205/15ff.

————. Dorothy L. Sayers to Rev. Geoffrey Treglown, October 9, 1941. Wade document 181/72.

————. Dorothy L. Sayers to Rev. George Every, July 18, 1947. Wade document 372/12.

————. Dorothy L. Sayers to Rev. G. E. Wigram, January 14, 1943. Wade document 235/50.

————. Dorothy L. Sayers to Rev. Gilbert Shaw, November 15, 1946. Wade document 256/15.

————. Dorothy L. Sayers to Rev. Harold Riley, June 27, 1947. Wade document 509/205.

————. Dorothy L. Sayers to Rev. J. C. Heenan, August 31, 1940. Wade document 212/24.

————. Dorothy L. Sayers to Rev. John Shirley, December 28, 1939. Wade document 254/68.

————. Dorothy L. Sayers to Rev. J. Phillips, March 20, 1947. Wade document 509/209.

————. Dorothy L. Sayers to Rev. J. W. Welch, February 18, 1940. Wade document 433/121–22.

————. Dorothy L. Sayers to Rev. P. A. Micklem, March 10, 1940. Wade document 184/17.

————. Dorothy L. Sayers to Rev. Patrick McLaughlin, April 15, 1940. Wade document 297/39.

————. Dorothy L. Sayers to Rev. Ralph Russell, December 1, 1948. Wade document 406/44.

————. Dorothy L. Sayers to Rev. Ralph Russell, July 30, 1951. Wade document 406/36.

————. Dorothy L. Sayers to Rev. Ralph Russell, June 18, 1952. Wade document 406/29.

————. Dorothy L. Sayers to Rev. R. D. Oakes, September 30, 1949. Wade document 152/12.

————. Dorothy L. Sayers to Rev. R. E. G. Williams, April 8, 1947. Wade document 7/96.

————. Dorothy L. Sayers to Rev. S. L. Palmer, May 28, 1942. Wade document 183/30.

————. Dorothy L. Sayers to Rev. V. A. Demant, October 2, 1941. Wade document 44/39.

————. Dorothy L. Sayers to Rev. V. James, April 21, 1952. Wade document 403/17.

————. Dorothy L. Sayers to Rev. V. James, March 19, 1952. Wade document 403/34.

———. Dorothy L. Sayers to Rev. W. H. J. Mercer, September 14, 1948. Wade document 235/14.

———. Dorothy L. Sayers to R. S. Price, November 25, 1942. Wade document 235/62.

———. Dorothy L. Sayers to R. W. Wordley, April 29, 1941. Wade document 504/101.

———. Dorothy L. Sayers to Sayers family, "First Sunday in Advent," possibly 1914. Wade document 81/22.

———. Dorothy L. Sayers to Sayers family, March 28, 1910. Wade document 73/53.

———. Dorothy L. Sayers to S. F. A. Coles, March 5, 1952. Wade document 310/3.

———. Dorothy L. Sayers to Sir Francis Fremantle, February 10, 1942. Wade document 510/155.

———. Dorothy L. Sayers to Stephen Talmadge, April 5, 1954. Wade document 189/120.

———. Dorothy L. Sayers to Stephen Talmadge, April 12, 1954. Wade document 189/115.

———. Dorothy L. Sayers to the Archbishop of Canterbury, February 9, 1948. Wade document 198/60.

———. Dorothy L. Sayers to the Archbishop of York, December 7, 1953. Wade document 189/91.

———. Dorothy L. Sayers to the bishop of Bristol, February 18, 1942. Wade document 181/148.

———. Dorothy L. Sayers to the bishop of Derby, February 25, 1942. Wade document 112/4.

———. Dorothy L. Sayers to the bishop of Dover, February 17, 1948. Wade document 198/57.

———. Dorothy L. Sayers to the bishop of Pretoria, June 21, 1943. Wade document 410/33.

———. Dorothy L. Sayers to unknown correspondent, date unknown. Wade document 42/13.

———. Dorothy L. Sayers to unknown correspondent, date unknown, maybe 1949. Wade document 5/49.

———. Dorothy L. Sayers to V. A. Demant, June 27, 1947. Wade document 44/15.

———. Dorothy L. Sayers to Victor Gollancz, April 23, 1951. Wade document 473/30.

———. Dorothy L. Sayers to William Paton, date unknown, probably early September 1941. Wade document 140/9.

———. Dorothy L. Sayers to William Paton, November 17, 1941. Wade document 140/5.

———. Dorothy L. Sayers to William Paton, September 17, 1941. Wade document 140/8.

———. Dorothy L. Sayers to Wilson Midgeley, February 14, 1951. Wade document 21/51.

———. Dorothy L. Sayers to W. R. Twitterton, undated but probably early to mid February 1943. Wade document 28/131.

———. "God the Son." Unpublished BBC addresses delivered in June and July 1941. Listed in Colleen Gilbert, *A Bibliography of the Works of Dorothy L. Sayers*, #E21, 210 (Hamden, CT: Archon Books, 1978). Lot 292, iii of the Sotheby's collection, Wade Center.

———. Manchester presentation, July 16, 1942. Wade document 17/209–34.

———. Materials related to the "Oecumenical Penguin." Unaccessioned lot 292, i, Wade Center.

———. "The Sacrament of Matter." BBC radio addresses delivered in 1940. Lot 292, iii of the Sotheby's collection, Wade Center.

———. Stage directions for *The Emperor Constantine*. Wade MS-83.

————. "Vitae" of sorts, dated by Reynolds as 1928. Wade document 21/9ff.

————. Vita, undated, maybe 1928. Wade document 21/9–10.

Smith, A. Handel. A. Handel Smith to Dorothy L. Sayers, July 6, 1949. Wade document 151/18.

Smith, George. George Smith to J. P. Valentin, June 3, 1943. Wade document 510/140.

Speaight, Robert. Robert Speaight to Dorothy L. Sayers, July 28, 1943. Lot 290, ivc, folder 3/3, Wade Center.

Taylor, Charles. Charles Taylor to Dorothy L. Sayers, Christmas 1953. Wade document 1/78.

Trueman, Henry G. Henry G. Trueman to Rev. J. W. Welch, May 11, 1942. Wade document 434/67–69.

Twitterton, W. R. W. R. Twitterton to Dorothy L. Sayers, February 8, 1943. Wade document 28/133.

Valentin, J. P. J. P. Valentin to Canon George Smith, late May 1943. Wade document 510/141.

————. J. P. Valentin to Dorothy L. Sayers, August 28, 1941. Wade document 13/163–64.

Wallich, Elinor. Elinor Wallich to Dorothy L. Sayers, October 5, 1941. Wade document 13/169–70.

Welch, James W. James W. Welch to Dorothy L. Sayers, December 24, 1941. Wade document 434/145.

————. James W. Welch to Dorothy L. Sayers, September 15, 1941. Wade document 433/33.

Secondary Sources

Anonymous. Article on The Emperor Constantine. Church Times, August 24, 1951, page unknown. Wade document 525/25.

————. "Dorothy L. Sayers." British Weekly, August 30, 1951, 9. Wade document 342/40.

————. Review of "The Importance of Being Vulgar," by Dorothy L. Sayers. Daily Telegraph (London), February 13, 1936, page unknown. Dorothy L. Sayers Society archive document 10.78.

————. Review of The Man Born to Be King, by Dorothy L. Sayers. Listener, May 20, 1943.

Aristotle. "The Poetics." In Criticism: Twenty Major Statements, edited by Charles Kaplan, 20–51. Scranton, PA: Chandler Publishing, n.d.

Arndt, William F., and F. Wilbur Gingrich, eds. A Greek-English Lexicon of the New Testament and Other Early Christian Literature. Chicago: University of Chicago Press, 1967.

Ashcroft, Mary Ellen. "Exorcising the Angel by Craft: Writing as Incantation/Incarnation in the Work of Dorothy L. Sayers." Ph.D. diss., University of Minnesota, 1992.

Banks, Robert. Redeeming the Routines. Wheaton: BridgePoint, 1993.

Basney, Lionel. "The Refiner's Fire: Detective Stories." Christianity Today 18, no. 23, August 30, 1974, 16–17.

————. "Sayers and the 'Bonny Outlaw': Her Work as a Lay Apologist." Paper presented at the Modern Language Association conference, Chicago, IL, December 1977.

Battenhouse, Roy W. "The Relation of Theology to Literary Criticism." In Religion and Modern Literature, edited by G. B. Tennyson and Edward J. Ericson Jr., 85–94. Grand Rapids: Eerdmans, 1975.

Beaumont, Lord. "Dorothy L. Sayers as a Lay Theologian." Unpublished paper, June 3, 1978, Wade Center.

Boyd, Ian. "The Legendary Chesterton." In *G. K. Chesterton and C. S. Lewis: The Riddle of Joy*, edited by Michael H. MacDonald and Andrew A. Tadie, 53–68. Grand Rapids: Eerdmans, 1989.

Brabazon, James. *Dorothy L. Sayers*. New York: Charles Scribner's Sons, 1981.

Bray, Suzanne. "Making the Church Attractive in the Novels of Dorothy L. Sayers." In *Proceedings of the 1997 Convention*, 38–45. Hurstpierpoint, W. Sussex: Dorothy L. Sayers Society, 1998.

Brown, Colin. "Charles Gore." In *Creative Minds in Contemporary Theology*, edited by Philip Edgcumbe Hughes, 341–74. Grand Rapids: Eerdmans, 1966.

Brown, Janice. *The Seven Deadly Sins in the Work of Dorothy L. Sayers*. Kent, OH: Kent State University Press, 1998.

Brown, Robert McAfee. "The Need for a New Theology of Work." Nyvall Lectures, Northpark College, 1986.

Brunsdale, Mitzi. *Dorothy L. Sayers: Solving the Mystery of Wickedness*. New York: Berg, 1990.

Burleson, James. "A Study of the Novels of Dorothy L. Sayers." Ph.D. diss., University of Texas at Austin, 1965.

Cairns, Earle E. *Christianity through the Centuries: A History of the Christian Church*. Grand Rapids: Zondervan, 1981.

Carpenter, Humphrey. *The Inklings: C. S. Lewis, J. R. R. Tolkien, Charles Williams, and Their Friends*. Boston: Houghton Mifflin, 1979.

Chadwick, Owen. *The Secularization of the European Mind in the Nineteenth Century*. Cambridge: Cambridge University Press, 1975.

Chesterton, G. K. *The Autobiography of G. K. Chesterton*. New York: Sheed & Ward, 1936.

———. *Tremendous Trifles*. Beaconsfield, Eng.: Darwen Finlayson.

Clines, D. A. "The Image of God in Man." *Tyndale Bulletin* 19 (1968): 53–103.

Connolly, Francis X. Review of *The Mind of the Maker*, by Dorothy L. Sayers. *America* 67, May 9, 1942. Wade document 133–34.

Coomes, David. *Dorothy L. Sayers: A Careless Rage for Life*. Batavia, IL: Lion Publishing, 1992.

Dale, Alzina Stone. "Caveat Christian." *Christianity Today* 22, no. 21, September 8, 1978, 36, 38, 40.

———. "L'Engle and Sayers: The Artist as Model." *Episcopalian* 148, no. 5 (May 1983): 12.

———. *Maker and Craftsman: The Story of Dorothy L. Sayers*. Wheaton: Harold Shaw, 1992.

———. "*The Man Born to Be King*: Dorothy Sayers's Best Play." Paper presented to the Modern Language Association, 1976.

———. *The Outline of Sanity: A Biography of G. K. Chesterton*. Grand Rapids: Eerdmans, 1982.

———. "Some Ideas on a Christian Core Curriculum from the Writings of G. K. Chesterton, T. S. Eliot, and Dorothy L. Sayers." In *Permanent Things*, edited by Andrew A. Tadie and Michael H. Macdonald, 253–69. Grand Rapids: Eerdmans, 1995.

———, ed. *Dorothy L. Sayers: The Centenary Celebration*. New York: Walker & Co., 1993.

Derrick, Christopher. "Some Personal Angles on Chesterton and Lewis." In *G. K. Chesterton and C. S. Lewis: The Riddle of Joy*, edited by Michael H. MacDonald and Andrew Tadie, 3–19. Grand Rapids: Eerdmans, 1989.

de Voil, Paul. "The Theology of Dorothy L. Sayers." Address delivered at the 1978 seminar of the Dorothy L. Sayers Literary and Historical Society, Witham, Essex, England.

Disney, Jennifer H. "Being Human: Dorothy Sayers on Vocation and the Feminine." *Mars Hill Review* 13 (Winter/Spring 1999): 53–61.

Donahoe, Mary A. "The Sacramental Aesthetic in the Plays of Dorothy L. Sayers." Ph.D. diss., University of Oregon, 1992.

Doyle, Paul A. *Evelyn Waugh: A Critical Essay.* Grand Rapids, Eerdmans, 1969.

Duran, Leopoldo. *Graham Greene.* San Francisco: HarperSanFrancisco, 1994.

Durkin, Mary Brian. *Dorothy L. Sayers.* Boston: Twayne, 1980.

———. "Dorothy L. Sayers: A Christian Humanist for Today." *Christian Century* 96, November 14, 1979, 1114–19.

Edwards, David L. *Religion and Change.* London: Hodder & Stoughton, 1969.

Eliot, T. S. *The Idea of a Christian Society.* London: Faber & Faber, 1939.

Ellul, Jacques. *The Ethics of Freedom.* Grand Rapids: Eerdmans, 1976.

———. "Work and Calling." *Katallagete* 4, nos. 2–3 (Fall–Winter 1972): 8–16.

Fasching, Darrell. *The Thought of Jacques Ellul: A Systematic Exposition.* Toronto: Edwin Mellen, 1942.

Gaillard, Dawson. *Dorothy L. Sayers.* New York: F. Ungar, 1981.

Gardner, Howard. "Good Work, Well Done: A Psychological Study." *Chronicle of Higher Education* 48, no. 24, February 22, 2002, B7.

———, Mihaly Csikszentmihalyi, and William Damon. *Good Work: When Excellence and Ethics Meet.* New York: Basic Books, 2002.

Gilbert, Colleen. *A Bibliography of the Works of Dorothy L. Sayers.* Hamden, CT: Archon Books, 1978.

Glyer, Diana Pavlac. "A Reader's Guide to Books about C. S. Lewis, and Other Resources." In *The Pilgrim's Guide: C. S. Lewis and the Art of Witness,* edited by David Mills, 257–73. Grand Rapids: Eerdmans, 1998.

———, and Laura K. Simmons. "Dorothy L. Sayers and C. S. Lewis: Two Approaches to Creativity and Calling." *VII: An Anglo-American Literary Review* (forthcoming).

Goldingay, John. "On Being Human." *Theology, News, and Notes* 45, no. 4 (December 1998): 6.

Green, Roger Lancelyn, and Walter Hooper. *C. S. Lewis: A Biography.* New York: Harcourt Brace Jovanovich, 1974.

Gunn, Giles B., ed. *Literature and Religion.* New York: Harper & Row, 1971.

Hadfield, Alice Mary. *Charles Williams: An Exploration of His Life and Work.* New York: Oxford University Press, 1983.

Hale, Edward Everett, Jr. *Dramatists of To-Day.* New York: Henry Holt, 1905, 1911.

Hannay, Margaret P. *As Her Whimsey Took Her: Critical Essays on the Work of Dorothy L. Sayers.* Kent, OH: Kent State University Press, 1979.

Harmon, Robert B., and Margaret A. Burger. *An Annotated Guide to the Works of Dorothy L. Sayers.* New York: Garland Publishing, 1977.

Hastings, Adrian. *A History of English Christianity, 1920–1990.* Philadelphia: Trinity Press International, 1991.

Heilbrun, Carolyn. "Dorothy L. Sayers: Biography between the Lines." In *Dorothy L. Sayers: The Centenary Celebration,* edited by Alzina Stone Dale, 1–14. New York: Walker & Co., 1993.

———. *Writing a Woman's Life.* New York: Ballantine Books, 1988.

Hesla, David H. "Religion and Literature: The Second Stage." *Journal of the American Academy of Religion* 46, no. 2 (June 1978): 181–92.

Hill, Kent R. "The Sweet Grace of Reason: The Apologetics of G. K. Chesterton." In *G. K. Chesterton and C. S. Lewis: The Riddle of Joy*, edited by Michael H. MacDonald and Andrew A. Tadie, 226–48. Grand Rapids: Eerdmans, 1989.

Hitchman, Janet. *Such a Strange Lady*. New York: Harper & Row, 1975.

Hone, Ralph E. *Dorothy L. Sayers: A Literary Biography*. Kent, OH: Kent State University Press, 1979.

Johnston, Araminta Stone. "The Christian Aesthetic of Dorothy L. Sayers." M.A. thesis, Wake Forest University, 1986.

Kenney, Catherine. "The Comedy of Dorothy L. Sayers." In *Dorothy L. Sayers: The Centenary Celebration*, edited by Alzina Stone Dale, 139–50. New York: Walker & Co., 1993.

———. *The Remarkable Case of Dorothy L. Sayers*. Kent, OH: Kent State University Press, 1990.

Klein, Kathleen Gregory. "Dorothy Sayers." In *Ten Women of Mystery*, edited by Earl F. Bargainner, 10–39. Bowling Green, OH: Bowling Green State University Popular Press, 1981.

———, ed. *Women Times Three: Writers, Detectives, Readers*. Bowling Green, OH: Bowling Green State University Popular Press, 1995.

Knepper, Marty. "Sexual Equality in Dorothy L. Sayers's Essays and in Her Peter Wimsey-Harriet Vane Novels and Stories." In *Women and Equality: Selected Proceedings of the University of South Dakota's Fifth Annual Women's Research Conference*, edited by Susan J. Wolfe, Jane D. Bromert, and Catherine A. Flum, 58–72. Vermillion, SD: University of South Dakota Press, 1989.

Kronke, David. "Leading Man." *Southwest Airlines Spirit*, December 1998, 52–55, 102, 105–6, 108, 115, 118.

Kungl, Carla Therese. *Women Writers and Detectives: Creating Authority in British Women's Detective Fiction 1890–1940*. Ph.D. diss., Case Western Reserve University, 2000.

Langford, Thomas A. *In Search of Foundations: English Theology 1900–1920*. Nashville: Abingdon, 1969.

Lewis, C. S. "Christianity and Literature." In *Religion and Modern Literature*, edited by G. B. Tennyson and Edward J. Ericson Jr., 46–54. Grand Rapids: Eerdmans, 1975.

———. "The Funeral of a Great Myth." In *Christian Reflections*. Grand Rapids: Eerdmans, 1978.

———. *The Great Divorce*. New York: Macmillan, 1946.

———. "Modern Theology and Biblical Criticism." In *Christian Reflections*. Grand Rapids: Eerdmans, 1978.

———, ed. *Essays Presented to Charles Williams*. Grand Rapids: Eerdmans, 1981.

Loades, Ann. "Creativity, Embodiment, and Mutuality: Dorothy L. Sayers on Dante, Love, and Freedom." In *God and Freedom: Essays in Historical and Systematic Theology*, edited by Colin Gunton, 103–18. Edinburgh: T & T Clark, 1995.

Lubot, Donna. "Good Work Well Done: A Study of Dorothy L. Sayers's Detective Novels." M.A. thesis, University of Tennessee, 1981.

Maio, Kathleen L. *Unnatural Woman: A Feminist Study of Dorothy L. Sayers*. Goddard/Cambridge Graduate Center, October 1975.

Mann, Jessica. *Deadlier than the Male: An Investigation into Feminine Crime Writing*. London: David & Charles, 1981.

Mascall, E. L. *The Secularisation of Christianity*. London: Darton, Longman, & Todd, 1965.

———. "What Happened to Dorothy L. Sayers That Good Friday?" *VII: An Anglo-American Literary Review* 3 (1982): 9–18.

McInerny, Ralph. "Unsoothing Sayers." In *Dorothy L. Sayers: The Centenary Celebration*, edited by Alzina Stone Dale, 123–28. New York: Walker & Co., 1993.

Miller, J. Hillis. "Literature and Religion." In *Religion and Modern Literature*, edited by G. B. Tennyson and Edward J. Ericson Jr., 31–45. Grand Rapids: Eerdmans, 1975.

Mouw, Richard. *Called to Holy Worldliness*. Minneapolis: Fortress, 1980.

O'Connor, Flannery. "Novelist and Believer." In *Religion and Modern Literature*, edited by G. B. Tennyson and Edward J. Ericson Jr., 68–75. Grand Rapids: Eerdmans, 1975.

Packer, J. I. "Tecs, Thrillers, and Westerns." *Christianity Today* 29, no. 16, November 8, 1955, 12.

Paul, Robert S. "Theology and Detective Fiction." *Hartford Quarterly* 6, no. 3 (Spring 1966): 21–29.

Pavlac, Diana Lynne. "The Company They Keep: Assessing the Mutual Influence of C. S. Lewis, J. R. R. Tolkien, and Charles Williams." Ph.D. diss., Graduate College, University of Illinois at Chicago, 1993.

Pottle, Frederick. "The Moral Evaluation of Literature." In *Religion and Modern Literature*, edited by G. B. Tennyson and Edward J. Ericson Jr., 95–107. Grand Rapids: Eerdmans, 1975.

Ramsey, Arthur Michael. *From Gore to Temple: The Development of Anglican Theology between* Lux Mundi *and the Second World War, 1889–1939*. London: Longmans, 1960.

Reynolds, Barbara. *Dorothy L. Sayers: Her Life and Soul*. New York: St. Martin's Press, 1993.

———. *The Passionate Intellect*. Kent, OH: Kent State University Press, 1989.

Roberts, Michael. *The Recovery of the West*. London: Faber & Faber, 1941.

Rockwell, Rhonda Jean. "All's Fair: Gender, Imagination, and World War." Ph.D. diss., University of California at Berkeley, 1993.

Ross-Bryant, Lynn. *Imagination and the Life of the Spirit*. Chico, CA: Scholar's Press, 1981.

Russell, Dom Ralph. Review of *The Mind of the Maker*. Wade document 406/87.

Sansbury, Kenneth. *Truth, Unity, and Concord: Anglican Faith in an Ecumenical Setting*. London: A. R. Mowbray, 1967.

Say, Elizabeth. *Evidence on Her Own Behalf: Women's Narrative as Theological Voice*. Savage, MD: Rowman & Littlefield, 1990.

Schwartzbaum, Lisa. "Offensive Play." *Entertainment Weekly*, July 23, 2004, www.ew.com/ew/article/latest/0,11892,7451,00.html (accessed July 30, 2004).

Selbie, W. B, to the editor. *Spectator*, July 12, 1940. Wade document 348/64.

Sencourt, Robert. *T. S. Eliot: A Memoir*. London: Garnstone Press, 1971.

Sidney, Sir Philip. "An Apology for Poetry." In *Criticism: Twenty Major Statements*, edited by Charles Kaplan, 104–42. Scranton, PA: Chandler Publishing, n.d.

Siebald, Manfred. *Dorothy L. Sayers*. Wuppertal, Ger.: R. Brockhaus, 1989.

Simcox, Carroll R. Review of *Creed or Chaos?* July 17, 1949. Wade document 152/21.

Simmons, Laura K. *Theology Made Interesting: Dorothy L. Sayers as a Lay Theologian*. Ph.D. diss., Fuller Theological Seminary, 1999.

———, and Diana Pavlav Glyer. "Dorothy L. Sayers and C. S. Lewis: Two Approaches to Creativity and Calling." *VII: An Anglo-American Literary Review* 21 (2004): 31–46.

Simpson, Shona Elizabeth. "Making Scenes: Modernism and the Romance in 1930s Fiction by British Women Writers." Ph.D. diss., Duke University, 1996.

Smedes, Lewis B. *The Incarnation: Trends in Modern Anglican Thought*. Kampen: J. H. Kok, 1953.

Soloway, Sara Lee. "Dorothy Sayers, Novelist." Ph.D. diss., University of Kentucky, 1971.

Southwark, Richard. Review of "The Greatest Drama Ever Staged." *Diocesan Gazette*, ca. July 7, 1938. Wade document 525/126.

Spencer, William David. *Mysterium and Mystery: The Clerical Crime Novel.* Ann Arbor: UMI Research Press, 1989.

Sprague, Rosamond Kent, ed. *A Matter of Eternity: Selections from the Writings of Dorothy L. Sayers.* Grand Rapids: Eerdmans, 1973.

Tadie, Andrew A., and Michael H. Macdonald, eds. *Permanent Things: Toward the Recovery of a More Human Scale at the End of the Twentieth Century.* Grand Rapids: Eerdmans, 1995.

Tennyson, G. B., and Edward J. Ericson Jr. eds. *Religion and Modern Literature.* Grand Rapids: Eerdmans, 1975.

Thiede, Carsten Peter. *Rekindling the Word: In Search of Gospel Truth.* Valley Forge, PA: Trinity Press, 1995.

Thurbon, W. T., to the editor. *Daily Telegraph* (London), December 31, 1941, page unknown.

Thurmer, John. "The Analogy of the Trinity." *Scottish Journal of Theology* 34 (1981): 509–15.

———. *A Detection of the Trinity.* Devon, U.K.: Paternoster, 1984.

———. "Judas in *The Man Born to Be King.*" In *Proceedings of the 1997 Seminar,* edited by Christine R. Simpson, 46–52. W. Sussex: Dorothy L. Sayers Society, 1998.

———. *Reluctant Evangelist: Papers on the Christian Thought of Dorothy L. Sayers.* W. Sussex: Dorothy L. Sayers Society, 1996.

———. "Re-Review: *The Mind of the Maker.*" *Modern Churchman* 30, no. 3 (1941): 38.

———. "Response to Dorothy L. Sayers's 'Worship in the Anglican Church.'" *VII: An Anglo-American Literary Review* 14 (1997): 53–58.

———. "The Theology of Dorothy L. Sayers." *Church Quarterly Review* 168 (1967): 452–62.

Tischler, Nancy M. *Dorothy L. Sayers: A Pilgrim Soul.* Atlanta: John Knox, 1979.

Trembley, Elizabeth A. "Collaring the Other Fellow's Property': Feminism Reads Dorothy Sayers." In *Women Times Three: Writers, Detectives, Readers,* edited by Kathleen Gregory Klein, 81–99. Bowling Green, OH: Bowling Green State University Popular Press, 1995.

Urang, Gunnar. *Shadows of Heaven: Religion and Fantasy in the Writings of C. S. Lewis, Charles Williams, and J. R. R. Tolkien.* Philadelphia: Pilgrim Press, 1971.

Walsh, Andrew. "Church, Lies, and Polling Data." *Religion in the News* 1, no. 2 (Fall 1998): 9–11.

Watson, Giles. "Dorothy L. Sayers and the Oecumenical Penguin." *VII: An Anglo-American Literary Review* 14 (1997): 17–32.

Webster, Deborah. "Reinterpreter: Dorothy L. Sayers." *Catholic World,* May 1949, 330–35.

Welch, Claude. *In This Name: The Doctrine of the Trinity in Contemporary Theology.* New York: Charles Scribner's Sons, 1952.

Whyte, James B., to the editor. *Evening Dispatch* (Edinburgh, Scot.), January 12, 1942, 4b. Wade document 346/56.

Williams, Charles. *Outlines of Romantic Theology.* Grand Rapids: Eerdmans, 1990.

Wilson, John. "An Appraisal of C. S. Lewis and His Influence on Modern Evangelicalism." *Scottish Bulletin of Evangelical Theology* 1 (Spring 1991): 22–39.

World Council of Churches. *Baptism, Eucharist, and Ministry.* Geneva: World Council of Churches, 1982.

Young, Morris I. "Strong Meat: A Wholesome Corrective." *Methodist,* September 2, 1939. Wade document 488/33.

Youngberg, Ruth Tanis. *Dorothy L. Sayers: A Reference Guide.* Boston: G. K. Hall, 1982.

Index